WITHDRAWN FROM
THE LIBRARY

UNIVERSITY OF

KT-520-406

)02

.)04

KA 0192947 X

Marlowe and the Politics of Elizabethan Theatre

By the same author

Amazons and Warrior Women (St. Martin's Press, 1981)
The Women's Sharp Revenge (St. Martin's Press, 1985)

Marlowe and the Politics of Elizabethan Theatre

Simon Shepherd
Lecturer in English Drama,
University of Nottingham

St. Martin's Press   New York

© Simon Shepherd, 1986

All rights reserved. For information, write:
St. Martin's Press, Inc., 175 Fifth Avenue, New York, NY 10010
Printed in Great Britain by Anchor Brendon Ltd, Tiptree, Essex

First published in the United States of America in 1986

ISBN 0–312–51546–4

Library of Congress Cataloging-in-Publication Data

Shepherd, Simon
 Marlowe and the politics of Elizabethan theatre.

 Bibliography: p.
 Includes index.
1. Marlowe, Christopher, 1564–1593—Criticism and
interpretation.   2. English drama—Early modern and
Elizabethan, 1500–1600—History and criticism.
3. Theater and state—England.   4. Politics in
literature.   I. Title.
PR2674.S54   1985   822'.3   85–19598
ISBN 0–312–51546–4

KING ALFRED'S COLLEGE
WINCHESTER

822.3 MAR 019294 7X
SHE

To the memory of Chris Ruscombe-King,
with my love and my great respect

Contents

Foreword

Once I found myself accidentally reading a learned book-review, in which the reviewer censured the author for saying things that had been said before in other places by other people, whom he clearly didn't know about—and he should have done if he was a proper author (it was by the way a he, and the reviewer was a she). I found this terribly frightening, because there are lots of books I haven't read and lots of my ideas have probably been thought often before (which is to give them a perhaps unwarranted dignity). So if you value this commodity for its novelty, sorry.

Two works I know of adopt positions similar to mine, but they express their ideas with a good bit more learning and panache. Stephen Greenblatt's essay 'Marlowe and Renaissance Self-Fashioning' in *Two Renaissance Mythmakers* and Jonathan Dollimore's *Radical Tragedy* both examine the relationship of drama and ideology in a way that produces a properly political understanding of the artworks. All students should therefore read these two texts.

My practice in quotation from Elizabethan sources is silently to modernise spelling and punctuation. Often I have re-used or re-interpreted Elizabethan quotations from secondary sources, which seems a worthwhile practice especially for students who cannot get to see originals in far-off libraries. From what I know of many English Departments, some of my terminology will seem obscure, so students should demand from their teachers more serious education in critical theory; this demand, however, will assist neither in raising the level of my thought nor in unravelling its tortuousness of expression, for which I apologise, but it will enable you to read some very useful books.

Occasionally, I have been what I've been accused of being before, cantankerous. As far as I can see one isn't meant to show anger. But as I write, the National Union of Mineworkers has been heroically pursuing its just struggle for six months; and while I worked on the book it seemed that the age of the first Elizabeth in all its brutalities was all too like the age of the second: and I think I have been insufficiently cantankerous. There's no undoing history, but I hate to see it repeated. May the miners, therefore, win – however long it takes.

The only debt of which I am aware is to Mick Wallis, of course, as ever.

Simon Shepherd, September 1984.

A Beginning

The problem about the title of this book is the 'and'. The relationship between Marlowe and Elizabethan theatre is concealed from focus for the greater part of the book. There are general arguments about Elizabethan theatre and specific studies of plays of Marlowe, but the connection is not explicitly theorised.

The problem is to know what is being connected with what. For a start, the name 'Marlowe' may be taken in several different senses. There is the Christopher Marlowe/Morley who was living and working in London in the late 1580s. Biographies have been written about him but we still know all too little to make a satisfactory approach to his writing through a study of his associations and contacts. A new insight has been gained into the work of later dramatists such as Massinger, Middleton and Shirley in this way, but for Marlowe there is just guesswork. For example, we could guess that his links with Ralegh, who spoke up in defence of hounded sectaries such as the Brownists, and with Harriot, whose attitude to the inhabitants of the New World was more enlightened than most, might imply an antipathy to the extreme forms of racism in London and thus make for a different reading of *The Jew of Malta* (1589/1633)—a play about racism, not a racist play. And Kyd's remark that before his death Marlowe was intending to go to James's court in Scotland may imply that like Essex, Bacon, Cecil—and many puritans—he looked for new hope in grim times to the new man; and that this may explain the stress on the naturalness of kinship that characterises Edward III's continuity from his murdered father. Or he may just have been wanting to get out of London. Not only can we not know what views he shared, but sufficient biographical work of this sort has already been done without making anything more certain. It's there for us to use if we want to.

The biographical work is bedevilled, however, by another 'Marlowe'. This one used to be called Kit Marlowe and he is something of a mythical figure. He is called Kit by those who present him as the 'enfant terrible' of a bawdy, sinister Elizabethan London, in which usage 'Elizabethanism' denotes a 'spirit of the age' rather than a chronological specificity. The suspicious death and the 'atheism' play a large part in this myth, but so too does the apparent homosexuality. Perhaps I should invent a further 'Marlowe' here—the homosexual writer. This homosexuality has nothing to do either with Elizabethan ideas of sexuality or with theories of a gendered subject, but is seen instead as a sort of pathological condition. Most people who write about Marlowe don't like homosexuality in writers, if at all, for it seems to lead to a failure in artistic discipline in that Marlowe feels compelled to drag it into his works (why heterosexuality, stamp collecting or wine tasting don't have similar effects I'm not sure). Kocher (1962), liberally, urges us 'not to waste too much twentieth century disgust' (p.58) on Marlowe's reflections on St John's relationship with Christ, though he thinks the treatment of homosexuality 'betokens some degree of personal passion'(p.209). It's this last point that matters, for Marlowe the homosexual is always eventually to be understood as a flawed writer because of this obsession which he could not control. Sanders invents this into a whole reading of Marlowe, who chose the reign of Edward II for a play because it offered him an opportunity to 'treat a forbidden sexual deviation', but not to treat it critically because of his 'compulsively driven' imagination, 'delivered up to deep internal drives'; so 'the most disturbing thing that bubbles up in the dark pool of the playwright's consciousness [Sanders likes a bit of metaphor] is an ecstatic impulse to "do dirt on humanity"'; Sanders says 'I am making no revolutionary proposal if I suggest that there is a strange congruency in the fates of Edward, the dabbler in sodomy, and of Faustus, the religious sceptic, which might be accounted for as a neurotic desire for symbolic punishment and expiation' (Sanders, 1968, pp.123, 125, 140). No dear, not at all revolutionary, in fact hideously repressive (and, of course, we have to pass over in silence Sanders's strange worry about dirt and deep drives, and his clearly more than botanical distress about pools).

Marlowe the homosexual partly explains the status of another 'Marlowe', the Marlowe of A level and degree courses, the Marlowe of Eng. Lit.. This is Marlowe-who-isn't-Shakespeare, the leading playwright in what is always called 'pre-Shakespearean' drama but who, in comparison with Shakespeare, is found to be immature. The characterisation is not as subtle and the construction of the plays neither as ordered nor as consistent as those of Shakespeare. This opinion depends on the notion that the Marlowe texts have the same sort of dramatic project as Shakespeare's, that they are trying for 'realism' of character or an assumed coherence of style. This notion is allowable for as long as Elizabethan dramatic practice is not seen as a specific product of particular conditions of production at a particular historical juncture: Elizabethan drama is what filled in between Moralities and Shakespeare (Harbage calls the structures of *The Jew* and *Doctor Faustus* (c.1592/1604) 'primitive', derived from—but not exploring?—Tudor interludes), and it was practised by many who didn't know what the art of the theatre was. Of *The Jew*, F. P. Wilson cautions (hilariously): 'To suppose that the same man who wrote the first two acts was wholly responsible for the last three is revolting to sense and sensibility, for these belong to a different world of art, if indeed they can be said to belong to the world of art at all' (Wilson, 1953, p.65)—'art' is used here with definite values, but it clearly can't cope with what Marlowe made. As will become clear, I hope, I think the Marlowe plays have specific and subtle strategies of their own, and were very far from what Shakespeare seemed to be attempting. Indeed, if anyone asked me, I would suggest that had he lived Marlowe might well have produced a set of texts of an artistic quality that would rival if not excel Shakespeare's—but this fantasy turns into nightmare when I realise that it would have given us a Royal Marlowe Company and a Marlowe Memorial Theatre, and I wouldn't want to wish that on the already long-suffering inhabitants of Deptford. Such a fantasy plays precisely the degree-course game of evaluation: Marlowe-who-isn't-Shakespeare obscures discussion of Marlowe-who-is-Marlowe (or of Shakespeare-who-isn't-Marlowe).

Which returns me to the problem of the meaning of 'Marlowe', which I have tried to solve by limiting my use of it to the name that appears appended to certain playtexts. I am not writing about Christopher Marlowe nor Kit Marlowe because that would duplicate biographical and historical work already done, and because it is always easy to slip into an analysis whose terms of reference are supplied by assumptions about the author—so you read the work to confirm what you know about the author. Nor have I written about Marlowe the homosexual, for similar reasons, but I have discussed texts that treat sodomy and sexual relations more generally. I have, however, I'm afraid, written of Shakespeare-who-isn't-Marlowe, and generally pushed Shakespeare to the edges of the book; the reason for this is that our thinking about Renaissance drama is so Shakespeare-dominated that he becomes a principle, an absolute, not a set of rhetorical structures, and positive discrimination is needed to move out of the intellectual trap. A study of the critical construction of Marlowe-who-isn't-Shakespeare is needed, as is similar work on the institution of Literature for all authors, but my main objective has led to a concentration on Elizabethan theatre.

'Elizabethan theatre' here designates the theatrical institution and its texts contemporary with Christopher Marlowe's working life, so there is a cut-off point after 1593/4. For most readers the contentious word in this part of the title must be 'politics', so let me suggest what the 'politics of Elizabethan theatre' could be said to involve, and in doing so define further my own area of interest. First, there could be a stress on 'theatre'—the politics of a social institution, which is to say the material and ideological relationship between the institution and the rest of society. Elizabethan theatres were seen by London authorities as centres of potential social unrest and as dens of iniquity which made people restive. Many documents survive and have often been analysed, but it is harder to know what the audiences thought of the theatres—why they went, what they thought they were watching, how they perceived the theatre's relationship with the rest of their lives; most work here is guesswork, and it is worth the reader remembering that when I (or anyone else) assert that a particular text is radical or whatever, there are very few grounds for knowing if any or all of the audience saw it that way (which doesn't mean they didn't, either). I have, however, tried to discuss how the plays address their audience, how they ideologically place the viewer, so that something might be inferred about the position from which audiences make judgements of a playtext. It will, indeed, be my argument that the plays take their place alongside other texts and rhetoric (such as pageants, preaching or proclamations) addressed to the people who comprise the audience; and that the playtexts acting upon some of those rhetorical addresses construct an awareness of the values they embody, if not a resistance to them.

Another way of looking at the theatrical institution in its society is to explore the links between its personnel and those of other institutions. This is where the work on Christopher Marlowe and the Ralegh circle comes in, although little here is conclusive. It is difficult to know the status of a connection that is made: for example, Robert Wilson was in the company that Leicester took with him to the Netherlands, so in view of the connection is it possible to argue that the corrupt merchant and virtuous Turk in *The Three Ladies of London* (1581/1584) reflect Leicester's interests in opening up trade with Turkey and his antipathy to the power of the ruling merchant oligarchies in the Netherlands? This would assume that Wilson understood Leicester's views as we might read them now, and that he single-mindedly trotted out the views of a patron; whereas the theatres offered a source of income which was not conditional upon the obedience of patronage. The dangers in this approach are a concentration on the named author rather than on other members of the institution, and the assumption that the named author was totally responsible for the text which comes down to us. It is just as likely that texts were shaped partly in rehearsal (quite apart from the modifications produced by censorship) and that the important members of the company, the leading actors, had an influence on the text in its construction and performance (we cannot know how much the reputation of his personal success contributed to the meaning of the parts Alleyn acted).

A more widely researched area of the 'politics of Elizabethan theatre' is the playtext as bearer of political ideas and theories, leading among other work to studies of Machiavelli and Marlowe and to analysis of the portrayed relationships of rulers, counsellors and people. Slightly less thoroughly examined is the detailed correspondence between the playtexts and political events, though work has been done on the issues around Mary of Scots and succession debates, for example. There is a tendency, however, to discuss the political ideas or events presented in texts without focusing too closely on the means of presentation, the rhetorical strategies specific to the artwork, so that what is discussed are general correspondences of ideas and not (semi-)autonomous artworks, politics but not politics of or in *theatre*. I have, therefore, tried to stress the specific rhetorical practices of the playtexts, in general and in particular examples, in order to argue that the politics lies in a combination of form with ideas, that it is the means of presenting those ideas which shapes them and which draws them to the attention of the audience. To see the text as something simply to be quarried for correspondence or reflections of reality is to ignore the fact that the text works actively on its audience, bringing ideas to their notice, situating them ideologically, making problems of concepts that might usually have been taken for natural or commonsensical. The language and form of a professional theatre play would, I think, affect an audience very differently from the way a pageant addressed that same audience: it is reasonable to argue that the differences between the description of obedient watchers of pageants and riotous watchers of plays lies not simply in the authorities' efforts to indict theatres and approve pageants, but in the fact that the audiences were differently 'constructed' by the differing artworks. The referential language of the profession-al theatre text is different from that of the pageant or most court plays. The selected language and forms partly make their meanings because of the sort of language and forms they are; they are indeed part of the political content of the professional plays (see the arguments of della Volpe, 1978).

When this specific artistic practice 'works on' its audience politically it uses theatrical pleasure in an exploration of the dominant ideas and assumptions that the audience might hold. Those ideas would have been built, for example, by the discourses of monarchy and the church and contain whole sets of moral and social values which were approved by a dominant class. The artwork can lead to questioning of dominant ideologies and it can also affirm them, by working specifically as a piece of theatre. The questioning or revealing power seems to be acknowledged by Elizabethans. Attacking the reign of Mary Tudor, Goodman speaks of 'The nobles also, which . . . have in like manner, as men disguised upon a stage, turned their nobility to open shame amongst all nations, which now behold their folly' (Goodman, 1558, p.35). The nobles may have disguised their feelings, but being on the stage exposes them. Thus Elizabeth told the House of Commons: 'we Princes, I tell you, are set on stages. . . . The eyes of many behold our actions; a spot is soon spied in our garments, a blemish quickly noted in our doings' (Neale, 1969, II, p.119); and Walsingham's private anxiety about the handling of Mary of Scots is expressed in the theatre metaphor: 'I hold them happiest in this government that may be rather lookers-on than actors' (Read, 1925, p.57)—as if performance brings judgement, encourages critical inspection. At the same time the theatre can affirm certain values: for example, the legendary obstinacy of the English in defence of their rights, a national characteristic which emerges, disguised, in 'the stubborn Jews' whom Oseas preaches to or the Saxons who wilfully resist Canutus; in one play it is disapproved of, in the other celebrated, but in neither questioned as a characterisation. And connected with the affirmation is a placing, as in siege scenes (two good examples being in *Edmund Ironside*, ?1590s, and *The Troublesome Reign of John King of England*, 1587–91/1591) where anonymous 'citizens' are caught up in campaigns between enemy monarchs: the citizens appear on the walls (the balcony), raised up above the contesting monarchs on stage, anonymous and peripheral to most of the narrative but temporarily talking out from beyond and above competing rulers, represented as a group not as individuals; this could be taken as a political placing of those who would mainly comprise the audience.

It is the relationship between dominant ideologies and the

questioning/affirming strategies of the individual text that I am taking to be the politics of Elizabethan theatre. To this end I have shaped the book to spend three chapters looking at certain formal characteristics which I believe may partly construct a specific audience response, and then three chapters looking at some typical figures represented in the autonomous fictional worlds. Within this structure the Marlowe texts are distributed. I want to get away from traditional author-centred approaches, with their not always useful ideas of intention and biography, etc. So the earlier sections of the book try to lose Marlowe's works within a wider context. I hope, however, that it is clear that modes of analysis used and conclusions reached in looking at non-Marlowe plays may be applied, by extension where appropriate, to Marlowe. As the book progresses I gradually concentrate the focus on Marlowe as a central figure, with the chapter on sexual politics devoted almost entirely to his works, for there his analysis seems singular.

My principal reason for splitting up analyses of the Marlowe texts is that I don't wish to suggest I have a complete and coherent reading of any one text, because this tends to imply that I am offering some sort of fixed and true interpretation. Each text, or bit of it, is instead interpreted within the dominant interests of a chapter or section; on the basis of specific, named criteria and interests, a reading can be made, but that reading is always provisional. This seems to me the case with any act of interpretation, though a lot of people don't admit it. I should say, however, that there are limits to the readings I would countenance and, as with everybody else, these limits are set by my own political values and commitments—in my case I work from a position which is socialist and anti-patriarchal.

The importance of stating the values from which the critic works has bearing on the final meaning of 'politics of the Elizabethan theatre', and that is the politics involved in studying Elizabethan theatre. As I implied when looking at the Marlowes, the critical text comes bearing all sorts of its own assumptions about the way the world is and should be (for example, that homosexuality is disgusting). So, too, the concentration on authors, the arrangement of authors into hierarchies, the privileging of the activity of editing above criticism and both above theorising, all these as many people now realise are part of the politics of that institution known as Eng. Lit.. Editing in particular, especially editing Shakespeare (because he's the national dramatist) is worth political analysis because it affirms all sorts of values even while it claims to be dispassionate, almost a science. Thus, for instance, the editor of the Penguin *2 Henry VI* (c.1590/1623) talks in his introduction (p.35) of 'the Swiftian extreme' of 'the stinking mouth of Cade himself' (stinking!?), and prefers the Folio stage direction which makes Cade confront the landowner Iden alone as opposed to a Quarto direction which has Iden enter with 'his men' (thus marking his social power) and Cade lying down and eating herbs (starving), for the editor notes (p.265) that the scene indicates Cade's death on the 'property of the ideal English country gentleman', so presumably Iden has to be sympathetically seen. There are no thoughts here of how the Folio directions may have been influenced by the political status of the late Shakespeare nor the Folio's status as book, a class object. The edition is made to inflect certain assumptions, which may well come from the editor rather than the text as originally performed. Similarly, my students have made short work of the annotations and added stage directions of male editors of such texts as *The Taming of the Shrew*. But all of this remains to be written up elsewhere, and perhaps the politics of the study of Elizabethan theatre is best examined where solutions to problems can be found, in practice within educational institutions.

My answer to the problem of the 'and' with which I began will perhaps become clearer as I go along, and is provisionally stated at the end.

CHAPTER 1

Language and Power

(i) Overview

The flourishing of Elizabethan theatre began in the years of state repression. In particular the government was aiming to crush the well-organised puritan movement, and in 1583, to administer the operation, Elizabeth appointed to the see of Canterbury Archbishop Whitgift, a sort of sixteenth-century Norman Tebbitt. The campaign escalated in the late 1580s, helped by the death of John Field, the great puritan organiser, in March 1588, and by that of Leicester, the powerful protector of puritans who lent increasingly to the radical wing, in September 1588. Other doyens of Elizabethan government died in quick succession leaving power with the new men. The threat from puritanism was that of a more or less democratic movement organised on a structure of local congregations and regional conferences. It promoted debate over religion and questions about government. The state sought to silence it by toughening controls over printing through a Star Chamber decree of 1586 and policing by the Stationers' Company, by searching out 'unauthorised' books in the counties, by enforcing uniform use of the Prayer Book (the rituals of which allowed little space for independent preaching) and by interrogating and imprisoning those who resisted. Useful publicity attached to the hunt for the press and printers of the Marprelate tracts, the imprisonment of leading MPs, the showtrials of Udall and Cartwright in 1590/91. Some said it was worse than the repression under Catholic Mary.

One of the Parliamentary radicals, Job Throckmorton, called the church a 'dumb ministry'. Not only did ministers have to swear the oath to Whitgift's articles of faith and keep silent to survive, but preaching was under attack. The imposition of the Prayer Book, which kept what Wentworth described as a 'deep silence' on the subject of preaching, was but the latest toughest step in a sustained campaign: back in 1571 the *Admonition to the Parliament* had complained: 'By the word of God, it is an office of Preaching; they make it an office of reading' (p.9), and noted that preachers had to be licensed. At the same time, in the House of Commons radical members persistently argued for freedom of speech, particularly the freedom to debate those issues which the queen disallowed. In 1576 Peter Wentworth made a much reported oration in defence of free speech and was afterwards interrogated by Privy Councillors, as were, at other times, Bell and Morrice. Such positions and punishments made a focus for the testing of the power of the Commons gentry against the power of royal officials and their monarch's pretensions to absolutism. In these debates MPs asserted traditional freedom of conscience, puritans claimed they spoke the word of God, royal officers talked of licence and sedition. This is the ideological language of the power contests, and the emotional force of that ideology is apparent in one like Wentworth whose conscience, he said, motivated him to speak out even against his monarch, or in those puritan ministers whose belief in religious truth required them to refuse the oath in full knowledge of the penalties.

This chapter seeks to connect these campaigns and debates with the plays in that it describes tensions within the plot situations between speech, writing and silence. Its method is to isolate recurrent scenes and phrases from a group of plays, thus 'revealing' in them a structure of oppositions beyond their individual textual projects or authorial intentions. This particular element of the group of plays may be said to be homologous with the relationship of official repression and free speech, as perceived by those under threat. The values at stake are akin to those of liberal and puritan gentry, the class whose economic situation, apart from their ideological commitments, made them wary of central government's attempts to exert authority in the counties, particularly in the form of taxation.

In general this chapter argues that Elizabethan playtexts often show scenes or stories in which, for instance, individual speech is repressed or in which official speech-making is viewed critically. Language is not here used as a transparent medium for expressing the inner person; instead its operations are defamiliarised and connected with the functions of political power. Several drama historians have examined the links between rhetoric and drama: Doran (1954) has attempted to show how rhetorical concepts have influenced dramatic form and Hawkes (1973) writes of the speech/writing opposition in Shakespeare's work. My interest is in the politics of rhetoric, its social function. I have sought briefly to outline Elizabethan ·assumptions about language use, particularly with regard to ideas of social order. Then I shall suggest that plays examine and problematise these dominant assumptions in order to present not only a different picture of language in society, but the connections between language and power. Drama was specifically capable of thus challenging dominant ideas, given the nature of its pre-written oral medium, for a mass audience, produced by those who were equated with vagabonds.

The players were not, however, vagabonds, and I suggested above that their texts tended to inflect gentry values. This point stands, as we shall see, in apparent contradiction to what I said about the questioning of rhetoric. That contradiction derives from the historical situation of the texts, which speak, within the ideology of free speech and censorship, of the tension of the 1580s between an aggressive administration and its gentry class.

(ii) Rhetoric

Students are regularly encouraged to admire Shakespearean speeches for the accuracy and subtlety of feeling they manage to convey. Language, it is assumed, simply expresses or tries to express the inner person. The Elizabethan theorist, however, tended to see language as an institution with its own rules existing independently of individual speakers. Ascham suggests that 'good understanding must first be bred in the child, which, being nourished with skill and use of writing . . . is the only way to bring him [sic] to judgement and readiness in speaking' (Ascham, 1570, p.18). Proper speaking is not spontaneous expression, writing precedes speaking, the individual intellect is shaped by education—by writing; this writing is the product of a social class; the child is trained to speak as a class member. Individual expressivity is not possible without the learnt rules and conventions. 'Speech is not natural to man saving for his only ability to speak'; he naturally utters 'with sounds and voices diversified many manner of ways': only when 'a speech is fully fashioned to the common understanding' does it become an agreed language (Puttenham, 1589, pp.143, 144).

When a child learnt how to speak properly it studied an 'art to set forth, by utterance of words, matter at large' (Wilson, 1560, p.1). Many rhetoricians drew up notorious lists of such verbal devices as might be useful, labelled with crazy and ever-changing names. But what remains consistent in rhetoric is the study of how to say the right thing to a particular audience to achieve the required aim. It is an art concerned directly with the business of social interaction, with negotiation, diplomacy, persuasion: 'An orator must be able to speak fully of all those questions which by law and man's ordinance are enacted and appointed for the use and profit of man, such as are thought apt for the tongue to set forward' (*ibid.*, p.1). There is nothing here of individual expression: the orator tackled public issues. The objective is to change other people's minds, if not their behaviour. As de Mornay puts it: 'Grammar teacheth us to bring the divers parts of speech into one congruity, and the end thereof is to speak; and the end of speaking is society. Rhetoric teacheth to draw men's minds to one selfsame opinion.' (de Mornay, 1587, p.222) Speech has to be learnt: the grammar which facilitates individual speech thus constructs the person into a part of a unified whole. Correct speech has the ideological function of subsuming the individual subject within a social unit.

Poetry was frequently defended on the grounds that it had a civilising effect: 'men were first withdrawn from a wild and savage kind of life to civility and gentleness, and the right knowledge of humanity, by the force of this measurable or tunable speaking' (Webbe, 1586, p.22). Sidney says that poetry—with all its carefully placed words—charms people

into listening to philosophical or moral topics, or, as Webbe
has it, 'instruction of manners and precepts of good life'
(*ibid.*, p.24). Poetry does not so much teach manners to but
change the nature of the hearer, aiming 'to soften and polish
the hard and rough dispositions of men' and, crucially, 'make
them capable of virtue and good discipline' (Harington, 1591,
p.2). There is that in the ordered language of poetry that
teaches social order: Orpheus 'brought the rude and savage
people to a more civil and orderly life' (Puttenham, 1589,
p.6). Language can construct the person; poetry is a form of
social control which operates through a pleasure produced by
ordered language in turn creating a desire for ordered living.
Those who are savage are those to whom poetry has to be
brought, that is to say, the non-literate, as perceived by those
who write about poetry, who all belong to a dominant literate
class: Harington a knight, Sidney a gentleman, Ascham
placing himself (in *The Schoolmaster*'s preface) among
aristocrats dining in Cecil's chamber at Windsor.

To illustrate the social usefulness of fine speaking Sidney
tells the famous story of how Menenius Agrippa talked to and
calmed a riot of Roman people. That the material demands of
the oppressed can be forgotten in the magic of oratory is a
belief that suits the interests of a dominant class—it's also
cheap. *Coriolanus* will later show the need to back up
Menenius with military force, but the Elizabethan state tried
to avoid any such crisis. The opinion of Thomas Smith was
that the people should be 'sooner looked unto that they
should not offend, than punished when they have offended'
(Smith, 1583 p.89), and to that end worked processions and
pageants, proclamations and preaching. When the aldermen
of London wanted people to be in church rather than at plays
they wanted them where they would hear approved texts
about morality and obedience. The homilies available for the
use of Anglican preachers were written by central government and dealt with most topics: after the 1569 Northern
Rising a new one on rebellion was added. It was a belief in the
power of words that led puritans to demand the space for
their preaching against the attempt to impose on them the
Prayer Book with its prescribed rituals. Field said that 'the
quantity of the things appointed to be read, said, sung, or

gone over . . . is so great that through the tediousness thereof
it maketh the minister unable to speak and the people unapt
to hear' (Collinson, 1967, p.359). Curiously, Hatton, for the
government side, admitted this silencing effect, although of
course it suited him, when he claimed that the virtue of set
prayers was that illiterate people could learn them by hearing
them often and then 'comfort' themselves even when they
were out of church. Both sides seemed to see the Prayer Book
as an attempt to use the forms of language to shape people's
understanding.

    Hatton and his associates regarded puritan preaching as
disorderly speech in two senses: it questioned rule of state
and broke rules of form. Often the appraisal of decorum of
language contains (unmentioned) within it political strictures,
as when Elizabeth answered a petition for freedom of speech
for the Commons: 'She knoweth that speech fit for the state,
well placed and used in matters convenient, is very necessary:
which she granteth unto you. But there is a difference
between staring and stark blind' and she goes on to attack
'Trifling digressions from matters proposed' (Neale, 1969, I,
p.245). Speech that is 'fit' observes the proprieties of rank as
well as rhetoric. Thus the theorist of poetry writes a book so
that 'the right practice and orderly course of true poetry' may
be distinguished from the 'uncountable rabble of rhyming
ballad-makers and compilers of senseless sonnets' (Webbe,
1586, pp.17, 36)—where what is 'true' is what is 'orderly'.
The literate culture distances itself from the oral one by
speaking the language of a hierarchically divided society, so
that Chapman (1595) says 'in my opinion, that which being
with a little endeavour searched adds a kind of majesty to
poesy—is better than that which every cobbler may sing to
his patch' (Jones, 1953, p.169). The language assumes distaste
for cobblers and such, and indicates that levels of understanding reinforce hierarchy, add majesty. The image projected by
the Tudors of the relationship between crown and people
informs Harvey's discussion of metrical experiment: he draws
the line where 'we are licensed and authorised by the ordinary
use, and custom, and propriety, and idiom, and as it were
majesty of our speech: which I account the only infallible and
sovereign rule of all rules' (Harvey, 1580, I, p.103). The

blend of majesty, ordinariness and custom finds its dramatic equivalent in scenes where monarch and worthy commoners chat familiarly together (like Princess Margaret on *The Archers*).

The language that Puttenham advises the poet to use is

> that which is spoken in the king's court, or in the good towns and cities within the land, than in the marches and frontiers, or in port towns where strangers haunt for traffic sake, or yet in universities where scholars use much peevish affectation of words out of the primitive languages, or finally in any uplandish village or corner of a realm, where is no resort but of poor, rustical or uncivil people: neither shall he follow the speech of a craftsman or carter, or other of the inferior sort, though he be inhabitant or bred in the best town and city in this realm, for such persons do abuse good speeches by strange accents or ill-shapen sounds and false orthography. But he shall follow generally the better brought up sort, such as the Greeks call . . . men civil and graciously behavioured and bred.
> (Puttenham, 1589, p.144)

No such abstract criteria as purity of language or tradition: correct speech is socially correct, the language of the court and oligarchy. Thus what is spoken north of the Trent may be 'purer English Saxon . . . yet it is not so courtly nor so current as our Southern English is'. Correct speech can be geographically defined: 'the usual speech of the court, and that of London and the shires lying about London within 60 miles and not much above' (*ibid.*, p.145); it is found in that area of Britain which was most wealthy, anything beyond inclining to savagery (as the BBC still seems to observe). The connection of civility and wealth is not only Puttenham's: 'it is much better to be born in Paris than in Picardy, in London than in Lincoln. For that both the air is better, the people more civil, and the wealth much greater and the men for the most part more wise.' (Wilson, 1560, p.13). We often hear that poetry is written for profit and delight: Wilson reminds us that the word 'profit' means both 'the getting of gain and the eschewing of harm' (*ibid.*, p.29). (I have not, by the way, continued to put [sic] after 'men'; we are reading about a male education only [sick?].)

The rules of rhetoric require that the distinctions of hierarchy be written into the individual's act of uttering. Charles Gibbon points to the difference between a 'pleasant story (which we may handle according to our humour) and a grave discourse (which must be penned according to the platform)' (Jones, 1953, p.172); the author inherits a style from the hierarchy of which s/he is a part, and the choice of it is not individual. Similarly a hierarchic perception is written into the reader's experience of the text, in that the doings of princes may be described in 'high' style while the 'low' is appropriate for 'the doings of the common artificer, serving-man, yeoman, groom, husbandman, day-labourer, sailor, shepherd, swineherd' (Puttenham, 1589, p.152). Style defines for the reader the hierarchic importance, the 'high or base nature', of what she reads. The reader is not free to assess the importance for herself in that the matter is presented already ranked: the style makes the reader complicit in its own hierarchies. The poet does not speak 'words as they chanceably fall from the mouth, but peising each syllable of each word by just proportion according to the dignity of the subject' (Sidney, 1595, p.28). The poet's writing expresses the already established order of society and ideology (where subjects have their proper dignity) and constructs the reader into that order.

Appropriately, Puttenham places poets alongside 'legisla-tors, politicians and counsellors of estate' (p.19). His rhetorical theory has its eye on the centre of power ('*our* Southern speech', like Harvey's majesty of '*our* language'); the outward drive of that power is mirrored in the assumed need to civilise savages both in England and overseas:

> And who in time knows whither we may vent
> The treasure of our tongue; to what strange shores
> This gain of our best glory shall be sent
> T'enrich unknowing nations with our stores?
> What worlds in the yet unformed occident
> May come refin'd with th'accents that are ours?
> (Daniel, 1599, 'Musophilus', ll.957–62)

Just as Puttenham's praise of civilised Home Counties

language ignored the real economic direction, of wealth into the centre, so Daniel's imperialist fantasy suppresses the rip-off of natives which accompanied the extension to them of the glories of English, with its refined words like 'slave', 'sword', 'rack'. Written into the poetic theory of English imperialism is a history of what it was trying to silence culturally. There is the contempt for cobblers' ballads, and more seriously for the Irish poets who, according to Thomas Smyth (1561), 'chiefly maintain the rebels; and further they do cause them that would be true to be rebellious thieves, extortioners, murderers, raveners, yea and worse if it were possible' (Edwards, 1979, p.11). It is not, clearly, poetry itself that is admired, but its political affiliations. Standing against the dominant ideology, the radical 'atheist' Harriot learnt the language of the Indians he found in America. More pressingly important, because more large-scale, was the evidence in the cultural centre itself that the theory about poetry and order did not necessarily work: theatre audiences shouted back at the stage. They were seen as 'seditious', not as ripe for civilising but as deliberate opponents to order. In saying this, however, I am not suggesting they were all conscious opponents of the ideological position held by most poetic theorists. But the practice of drama, with its specific relationship between form and audience, the social composition of its audience, and maybe too the radicalism of some of its authors, created a new site for the interrogation of ideas about language and power.

(iii) Parody and plainness

Some Elizabethan dramatists took up the rhetorical prescription that people from differing classes should speak in appropriate styles: 'to frame each person so,/That by his common talk you may his nature rightly know' (Edwards, 1565/1571, p.11). Thus there occur those texts which contribute to the notion that Elizabethan theatre is immature, for instead of the reader being able to discover for herself the inner qualities of characters, the styles of writing do it for her, heavy-handedly 'getting in the way' to make the points. Such a reaction does, I think, not only misread the projects of many plays (though those are difficult to establish), but assumes a fixed correspondence between styles. It is my contention, in this section, that the rhetorical hierarchy of style becomes upset in drama, mainly through the use of the active responses of that element in the artistic production relations that rhetoric assumes to be passive or tameable: the audience.

Jack Straw (?1591/1594) is an example of a play that very nearly succeeds in using stylistic decorum to draw the audience into its (dominant) ideological view. The play tells of Jack Straw's failed rebellion; the king and officials speak in iambic blank verse, the rebels in lines of varying lengths with occasional couplets. Blank verse was by this time much the most frequent form in drama and hence seems 'normal' against the rebels' jingles. The playtext then makes political sense of this juxtaposition:

> These people are not to be talked withal,
> Much less with reason to be ordered:
> That so unorderly with shrieks and cries
> Make show as though they would invade us all.
>
> (ll. 539–42)

The rebels' verse which deviates from the norm is presented as disorder and unreason. Indeed, throughout the text the rebels are said to be 'unnatural'; the impression of this 'unnaturalness' is constructed by stylistic contrast with the 'natural', because more commonly used, blank verse.

This linguistic/political opposition in the play is nearly wrecked by clowning parody when Tom Miller pleads for money from the Queen Mother. He adopts what he thinks is the appropriate official language: 'Now sir, understanding your worship is the King's Mother, lamentably in the behalf before spoken, to stand between me and the gallows, or to beg my pardon. . .' (ll.823–6). Part of the pleasure in the joke confirms the hierarchy, in that the clown can't properly speak officials' language; but partly there is delight in hearing the authoritative speech turned into nonsense play, which is added to by the inability to acknowledge the convention that the Queen Mother role is not played by a boy. By foregrounding the decision to try out official language the clown scene potentially indicates that such language is not natural to its users but is learnt, that its status is constructed. In other plays the parody is more explicit, as can be illustrated by two examples.

The clown Bullithrumble addresses the audience: 'Then come on and follow me—we will have a hog's cheek and a dish of tripes and a society of puddings—and to field!—A society of puddings! Did you mark that well used metaphor? Another would have said a company of puddings' (*Selimus*, ?1591/1594, ll.1981–4). When the user stops to inspect his language he de-naturalises it, although this part of the joke plays on his lack of taste in metaphor, his clownish inability. On the other hand, the concern with figurative utterance highlights the way the main plot talks—and what I shall never know is whether the clown actor mimics tragic delivery when he refers to 'Another'. The lines have in them a good opportunity for double-take: I would *guess* that while Bullithrumble delights naively in language the Bullithrumble-actor gives a display of agile physical skill. (A parallel case would be Ralph the Cobbler's statement to his superior companions who

> think these words for me unfit
> And guess I speak for lack of wit—
> Stand aside, stand aside, for I am disposed to spit.
> (*The Cobbler's Prophecy*, 1594, ll.343–5)

At the point where he recalls the idea that linguistic decorum labels the person, words are replaced by slapstick: suddenly the superior companions look silly, the social hierarchy marked by language loses its order.)

Acknowledging the connection between social status and language, Bullithrumble promises the audience: 'if you dwell with me long, sirs, I shall make you as eloquent as our parson himself' (ll.1984–6). The remark is funny, I think, precisely in that it promises deviation from scholarly training. This is the repeated joke of my second example, Strumbo, who presents himself as scholar and lover. He tells Dorothy: 'the fecundity of my ingenie is not so great that may declare unto you the sorrowful sobs and broken sleeps that I suffered for your sake'; exiting, he tells the audience: 'If any of you be in love, provide ye a capcase full of new-coined words' (*Locrine*, 1591/1595, ll.384–7, 408–9). It is comic because it is how not to do it. The joke against 'new-coined words' is part of a larger language debate and the laughter is at Strumbo. But another feature of his delivery is pronounced alliteration and here a much more unsettling joke is made through contrast with the main plot, for to start the next scene Locrine tells the princes of 'brave Britanny' of the entombment of his father 'As best beseemed so brave a prince as he' (ll.415, 417). He then announces his marriage, which now parallels Strumbo in narrative as well as alliteration. Strumbo's linguistic deviations call into question the dignity of the main plot by foregrounding style.

About the clowns thus far I have talked ahistorically of pleasure and play in the belief that these are analysable functions of human psychology (though I haven't engaged in any such close analysis). The problem here is not knowing how physical comedy or tone of voice were used. The clowning can also be looked at in historical context, and here, for example, Strumbo's comedy relates to the broad movement towards a plain style of language. Strumbo is unnecessarily overelaborate, Dorothy asks him to be plain. Rhetoric was consigned to ornamental status by the educational programme of Peter Ramus, which influenced much scholarly theory. Ramus wrote in the vernacular and attacked medieval logic because 'ordinary people don't talk like that' (Ong, 1958, p.54). Many translators thought like Ramus in seeing translation as a democratic movement: Ramus talks of 'the envious, that thinketh it not decent to write any liberal art in the vulgar tongue, but would have all things kept close either in the Hebrew, Greek or Latin tongues' (Ramus, 1574, p.15). It was noted that the invading ruler William the Conqueror 'sought to suppress and extinguish our English speech' (Merbury, 1581, p.33). The dominant culture spoke in foreign tongues, scholars in Latin, the laws in Norman French; Burghley liked controversial papers to be in Latin (Read, 1961, p.41). A Catholic (quoted in 1567) accused Protestant translators of prostituting the scriptures to 'prentices, light persons and the riff-raff of the people' (Jones, 1953, p.63), but the puritan Leicester patronised writings in the vernacular.

In a sermon in 1578, John Stockwood said that 'the word of the Lord simply and plainly handled is able, without the help of the persuading speech of man's wisdom, to pierce even to the heart' (Jones, 1953, p.104). Such a sentiment seems to indicate the democracy of plainness, in that truth can speak to those outside the learned culture of the upper orders, that it does not require their learnt skills. Within ideology, plainness becomes a sign of truth. Thus the language of plainness can in turn be appropriated by any authority that presents itself as truth-telling, so it is not therefore a guarantee of democracy. At the close of the 1576 Parliament Elizabeth spoke to a Commons that had raised difficulties over freedom of speech: 'If any look for eloquence, I shall deceive their hope. . . . If I should say the sweetest speech with the eloquentest tongue that ever was in man, I were not able to express that restless care which I have ever bent to govern for the greatest wealth' (Neale, 1969, I, p.364). The image of the really caring monarch is constructed by the rejection of eloquence, yet the speech is an attempt to resist democratic demands upon her. As with most of Elizabeth's speeches it was a carefully written piece, and she sent a copy to her godson for his instruction.

The queen's claim to plainness is clearly a strategy to inhibit the critical speeches of the Commons. In 1571 she sent a message to say they 'should leave to talk *rhetorice* and speak *logice*' (*ibid.*, p. 190); continually the debates about prohibited issues are called frivolous, with the implication that plainness and truth are associated only with what the queen allows. In the rhetoric of official debate plainness was much claimed and contested by each side, but in practice that very plainness was what the authorities disallowed. The career of Peter Wentworth is testimony to this: in his written account of his interrogation after his plea for free speech he is asked why he did not utter it in 'better terms', and he questioned the value of uttering a 'weighty matter in such terms as she should not have understood to have made a fault. Then it would have done her Majesty no good' (*ibid.*, p.328).

Frequently 'authorities' censure writing or speech because it is 'disordered' or not 'fit', which is to say it is not written in 'terms' which will curtail its impact or restrict it to a social group. Indeed, Martin Marprelate argues: 'The most part of men could not be gotten to read anything written [of Christ's government or against bishops' dealings]. I bethought me, therefore, of a way whereby men might be drawn to do both; perceiving the humours of men in these times . . . to be given to mirth. I took that course. I might lawfully do it. Aye, for jesting is lawful by circumstances, even in the greatest matters. . . .. I never profaned the Word in any jest. Other mirth I used as a covert, wherein I would bring the truth into light.' (Marprelate, 1588–9, p.239).

The ideological values of 'plainness' form part of the comedy of clowns when they parody the utterances of main plots. But clown scenes are frequently outside the main narrative so that it is difficult to relate the implications of their comedy (indeed, one of the notable features of *Doctor Faustus* is that the detailed parallelism of the clown action forces an audience to notice its bearing on the main plot and makes its estranging effect). For examples of a more focused analysis of the relationship between class and speech style I would instance *The True Tragedy of Richard III* (c.1590/1594) and two plays by Marlowe. The first play contrasts three men's reactions to Jane Shore's appeals for help. She is the mistress of the dead Edward IV and there is a ban on aiding her, yet she assisted each of the men in the past. Lodowick, a former servant but now land-owner, says that since there is a proclamation against helping her 'I will shun her company and get me to my chamber, and there set down in heroical verse the shameful end of a king's concubine' (ll.1076–8). A citizen accuses her of being 'the shame of her husband, the discredit to the city. Here you, lay your fingers to work and get thereby somewhat to maintain you' (ll.1122–4). A servant wants to help her but dare not because he is being watched, and therefore has to lie. He is the only sympathetic one, the other two using language appropriate to their rank—heroical poetry, city moralising—to legitimate their denials of assistance.

In *The Massacre at Paris* (1593/?1602) Ramus is killed by

aristocrats who scorn his low birth. He is alone, poor, simple speaking; sympathetically contrasted with the villainous Guise who shows off his learning to. accuse Ramus:

> Excepting against doctors' actions
> And *ipse dixit* with this quiddity:
> *Argumentum testimonii est inartificiale*
>
> (ix.32–4)

The aristocrat uses technicalities and Latin. His repression combines obscure speech with physical violence whereas the scholar is vulnerable and plain. The scene could be said to contest the propaganda about princely plainness.

More complex for an audience is my third example, from *1 Tamburlaine* (1587/1590). Mycetes is a comic king in that he is inept. When his commander Meander outlines battle plans, Mycetes interrupts to ask about one of the poetical allusions Meander has made: 'tis a pretty toy to be a poet', he concludes,

> Well, well, Meander, thou art deeply read;
> And having thee, I have a jewel sure.
> Go on, my lord, and give your charge I say,
>
> (II.ii.54–7)

Like the clown, Mycetes foregrounds figurative language and thus renders its persuasive potential useless. His fascination with verbal ornament is comical, but the staging of the scene can work to show that laughter here is misplaced, for Mycetes remains powerful and brutal. He owns Meander like a 'jewel', he has Meander give orders for a massacre. As Meander speaks an audience sees Mycetes standing silent, the ruler with an effective spokesman; when Mycetes speaks he shows a silly interest in poetry but Meander stands there ready to give orders for slaughter. Clowning about language, jokes about plainness, are placed within a structure of power. Rhetoric suggested that a person's standing and dignity might be revealed by language. The plainness campaign attributed moral or truth value to speech style, which sustained the view that speech revealed. Marlowe's scene here, as elsewhere, directs its audience to a notion of a power that operates apart from language, that cannot be placed or revealed: a linguistic contrast of Mycetes and Meander here would misrepresent their relationship.

(iv) Language expressing truth

In an effort to describe the contrast of styles, I moved rather fast over an idea which is central to plainness and apparently counter to rhetorical decorum. This is the idea that language always expresses the inner person: 'We have also framed unto ourselves a language whereby we do express by voice or writing all devices that we conceive in our mind; and do by this means let men look into our hearts and see what we think' (Ralph Lever, 1573, in Jones, 1953, p.125). Rhetoric talks of selecting appropriate style, even of the person being constructed by education. Expressivity implies that the heart and mind precede speech, that there is an essence to be put into words. Speech thus could be seen as a transparent medium through which the inner feelings are revealed to the listener. Feelings so revealed are therefore presented as 'true'. Debate about plainness tended to imply the selection of plain words; expressivity suggests that the sincere utterance simply obeys the pressure from inside without concern for selecting words. As Speaker Puckering put it: 'you and I may speak that which both the truth of the things and the duty of our hearts do draw out of our mouth' (Neale, 1969, II, p.248).

The importance of this idea is that words construct a sense of something that is beyond words, a presence awaiting expression. Hence truth is not debatable, not something rival sides may claim, but a unitary presence that exists before speech. When one of Elizabeth's speeches claims not to be eloquent, it is establishing a distinction between mere speechifying and the (superior) reality of her own feelings. Thus, later in the speech, she can seem to 'explain' her decision not to marry: 'all those means of leagues, alliances, and foreign strengths I quite forsook, and gave myself to seek for truth, without respect, reposing my assured stay in God's most mighty grace' (*ibid.*, I, p.365). The constructed discourse of 'truth' makes this seem like a rational answer, truth and grace having a material status. Ten years later, under heavy pressure to take action against Mary of Scots, she tells the Commons of 'our weakness, who cannot sufficiently set forth His wonderful works and graces, which to me have been so many, so diversely folded and embroidered one upon another, as in no sort am I able to express them' (*ibid.*, II, pp.116–17). The carefully arranged words create a sense of the presence of God behind her speech, more real than that speech ('folded and embroidered'), which gives her the authority, indeed the aura, to get away with her 'answer-answerless'.

The 'truth' which the royal speeches construct seems to be defined in the Introduction to a play written for performance in front of her in 1588, *The Misfortunes of Arthur*. The main plot has been taken to reflect on Elizabeth's problems with Mary of Scots (Waller, 1925; Armstrong, 1955), but in the Introduction three muses accuse Astraea, goddess of justice, of holding poetry in disdain. One of their captive law-students defends her: 'The language she first chose, and still retains,/Exhibits naked truth in aptest terms' (ll.85–6), which is a fusion of rhetorical decorum with expressivity. More importantly, he has already defined this truth:

> No eloquence, disguising reason's shape,
> Nor Poetry, each vain affection's nurse;
> No various history that doth lead the mind
> Abroad to ancient tales from instant use;
> Nor these, nor other moe, too long to note,
> Can win Astraea's servants to remove
> Their service
>
> (ll.68–74)

This is a fascinating political statement. It values reason and use against deceptive eloquence (a view Ramus would have shared) and against history that is distracting and unreliable. I would push it further to see an inflection of Elizabeth's handling of the Commons, for she told them to speak logically not rhetorically and censured their 'frivolous' speeches (the ones about prohibited topics); against her, they found historical precedents to support their cases. These

servants of Astraea, as Inns of Court students, may have
expected to go on to serve the real Astraea-substitute,
Elizabeth (indeed one of the authors, Francis Bacon, did).
For the truth acknowledged by the text is that Elizabeth sits
in the audience as the focal point of the show, where the text
makes its full meaning. The claimed nakedness of the text
expresses her as her speeches express God's grace. The
law-students do not show to the muses the homage of
'subjects' allegiance', for they are loyal to Astraea/Elizabeth,
the source of truth.

The discourse of the essential unitary truth was not
confined to the monarch and her officers but was spoken, in
opposition to them, by puritans who followed their conscien-
ces in expressing the truth of God's word, the word that
precedes all other speech. It is not the opposing sides but the
discourse itself which concerns me, for I want to argue that
some playtexts show this 'truth' to be not an absolute
expressed by transparent language but a value constructed in
language by speakers for certain ends. My argument will rest
almost exclusively on *1 Tamburlaine* since this reading can
present it as a particularly radical text. At points in the
argument there are clear parallels with other plays, working
in the same direction, especially with Lodge's *The Wounds of
Civil War* (1586–9/1594) (which some people date before
Tamburlaine, performed 1587).

The early sections of the play contrast Tamburlaine with
rulers whose ineptitude is marked by their linguistic disability
(Shakespeare uses a similar marking for Henry VI). Mycetes
finds himself 'insufficient' to express his sense of grievance,
he has to have other people speak for him, and his own
attempts at oratory lose themselves in mixed metaphors and
bland couplets. His seemingly more capable brother Cosroe
breaks out into alliteration whenever he talks of unseating
Mycetes: 'our powers in points of swords . . . clos'd in
compass of the killing bullet' (II.i.40,41 and elsewhere).
Language that is revealed to be so arranged loses its persuasive
power; it is seen as stylistically opaque as contrasted with the
transparency of those more capable. Even Bajazeth's first
appearance teaches an audience to be sceptical of his rhetoric,
for his last speech of the scene (III.i) is a break in manner, an

implied efficiency which makes the earlier speeches look like bluster. Tamburlaine's encounters with other rulers are constructed to privilege him where there is little distinction morally. Mycetes has comic crown-hiding business and is physically pathetic while Tamburlaine speaks wittily. Cosroe, in his death scene, grovels wounded, the fallen braggart of the previous scene; his wound makes it difficult to speak while Tamburlaine is imperturbable and lucid; Cosroe's speech looks inward towards his dying self, Tamburlaine talks of ambition and natural order. This is the scene of the 'earthly crown' speech, where Tamburlaine apparently reveals the baseness of his ambition, but I want to suggest that it is difficult to ignore the contextualising of that speech in the visual and verbal contrasts of the scene, that there is a discourse of capability constructed apart from that of the morality of ambition. In moral and political terms, indeed, Cosroe is an emblem of fallen pride while Tamburlaine is the monarch loyally supported by his captains.

The first confrontation with Bajazeth influenced a number of other confrontation scenes in which there is no clear contrast between good ruler and bad. Where a monarch deals with rebels or a nation deals with its enemy, rhetoric is seen to persuade the recalcitrant: in *Gorboduc* (1561–2/1565) rebellion is to be put down by persuading 'by gentle speech'; Hieronimo advises that 'a politic speech beguiles the ears of foes' (*1 Hieronimo*, ?/1605, i. 49). An audience of these scenes is assumed to recognise who the enemy is, but it is difficult to fix the moral superiority of Tamburlaine or Bajazeth where one is a cruel usurper and the other is a braggart Turk. Rhetorical theory often implies the virtue of the fine speaker, a virtue apparent perhaps in the ability to be rhetorical, but where one 'politic speech' is answered by another the sense of a pre-spoken virtue or 'truth' vanishes. Marlowe's scene is constructed as a series of speech units where each topic of Bajazeth's brag is matched by Tamburlaine: the language expresses no essential truth, it reveals no eternal moral hierarchy. Such a scene is often used to show the constructed rather than expressive speech of rulers.

Yet there is a difference between Tamburlaine and Bajazeth

in that Tamburlaine refers to 'every common soldier' in his
camp and refers to his army as '*Our* conquering swords'
while Bajazeth says '*I* have of Turks, Arabians,' etc.
Tamburlaine's language has sufficient about it to recall the
plain-spoken monarch, at one with his men. Some of this
contrast is carried through into the first scene of Bajazeth's
captivity where much of the Turk's imagery invokes hellish
brutalities while Tamburlaine speaks of the 'frame of heaven',
'the triple region of the air': no longer plain, Tamburlaine is
eloquent where the Turk curses on his knees, ineffectually.
As set up in these contrasts, Tamburlaine's speech is not
redundant rhetoric; it seems rational, it seems to express what
will happen.

   Placed against the dominant eloquence are silences. Zenocrate speaks most when Tamburlaine is absent, and in the
scene with Agydas silence falls when he enters; he then greets
her and takes her away wordlessly. Zenocrate becomes
increasingly silent, except where slaughter forces speech.
Bajazeth loses control of the grammar of his own speech in
that his syntax becomes dislocated, he can't say what he
wants to say: 'Accursed Bajazeth, whose words of wrath,/
That would with pity cheer Zabina's heart' (V.ii.206–7) —
trapped in a world without a language of love. His
penultimate speech describes alienation from his own organs
of perception: his eyes continue to see horrors, his words
won't allow expressions of love; his language has ceased to be
able to cope with 'our expressless banned [cursed] inflictions'
(l.218). When Zabina sees his corpse all her rational discourse
collapses into mad talk.

   The stage images of the play measure expressive eloquence
against silence and suffering. Cosroe silenced by wounds
when Tamburlaine talks of crowns, Bajazeth caged while
Tamburlaine feasts. Within this imagery an audience can be
led to be sceptical of the most inward emotion. The stage
direction for Tamburlaine's entry to the Damascus virgins
specifies that he is 'very melancholy' and his speech seems to
show pity: 'Alas, poor fools, must you be first shall feel/The
sworn destruction. . .' (V.ii.2–3); he rationalises about his
honour and custom. All this sincerity is, nevertheless,
murderous although, importantly, the audience is not to see

the killing. He tells the virgins that death sits on the point of his sword: 'But I am pleas'd you shall not see him there;/He now is seated on my horsemen's spears,' (ll.50–1)—the dirty work happens elsewhere, the moment of mercy is a moment of deferral. So far it is easy to be sceptical about Tamburlaine's personal emotion since it is viewed in the narrative, but now the playtext turns out to address its audience, for Tamburlaine is given a beautiful solo speech which claims to be expressing the nobility of his love for Zenocrate. The speaker calls attention to his own efforts to select appropriate language: 'Fair is too foul an epithet for thee' (l.73). He acknowledges the text written by Beauty who 'comments volumes with her ivory pen,/Taking instructions from thy flowing eyes' (ll.82–3), and so successful is the creation of a sense of poetical performance that it is possible to forget why Zenocrate's eyes are 'flowing'. The speech progresses to discuss poetry, which is seen as transparently expressive of human thoughts: 'Wherein, as in a mirror, we perceive/The highest reaches of a human wit' (ll.104–5) (note the 'we' that speaks for the audience). He observes that there are grace and wonder 'Which into words no virtue can digest' (l.110). The speech claims expressivity for poetry but constructs a wonder beyond words.

Tamburlaine asks if such reflections are 'unseemly . . . for my sex,/My discipline of arms and chivalry' (ll.111–12), but concludes that 'beauty's just applause' is appropriate to the warrior. He ends by presenting his own manly 'virtue'. The speech discusses decorum and poetry, and conspicuously *is* poetry. It is spoken by the man with an appreciation of proper manhood and devoted to a beautiful woman who is absent. Yet the audience is drawn into a misrecognition, or at least forgetfulness, of the narrative events, for the absent Zenocrate is weeping over Tamburlaine's cruelty and the virgins are being killed, on his orders, even while he speaks. The speech claims to be a fullness of expression of Tamburlaine's inner emotion; like its 'mirror' image it claims to show everything. But in fact it suppresses consciousness of the real violence against the conquered town and the real relations of man and woman—it is difficult to notice that a speech which begins addressed to a woman ends up being addressed to its male speaker. The speech is a display of decorous and courtly rhetoric; it seems to express inner feelings and to acknowledge the grace that cannot be spoken. Yet the discourses of decorum and truth conceal the violence that is the real basis of the speaker's power, as an audience discovers when the speech finishes.

The importance of the speech is that the audience is suddenly subject to persuasion, for it is easy enough in an objective narrative to see rhetoric as dissimulation (as Ramus said it was) and to see the rhetorical device of amplificatio as a redundance (it had vanished from Ramist arts of discourse), but the address that includes the audience makes such viewing more difficult. The text stages the appeal that a ruler's expressivity makes even while it shows that expressivity to be a deceptive construction. Concealed by Tamburlaine's speech, as by Elizabeth's, is the violence of rule. (But 'Truth' was always eventually to be defined only by material power, which Puckering admitted at the trial of the puritan Udall when he said that Udall's claim to truth had to be disproved to prevent it being buzzed in the people's ears (Collinson, 1967, p.407).)

Lodge's *The Wounds of Civil War* interrogates expressivity by avoiding the person of a central speaker. The two major roles are the rival leaders Marius and Scilla, both unattractive. The play opens with the Roman senate in debate, with rival supporters urging the merits of their heroes, constructing their characters. Neither here nor in the confrontation of the leaders is the audience able to judge on 'real' grounds which might verify or falsify the words. The playtext foregrounds a concern with actions and words that *beseem* or *befit* a heroic mind, and characters invite an audience to approve a speech or victory that is 'fitting', yet the minds plan slaughter and the victories are based on battle-action that appears random or unpredictable. Much attention is paid to language but it does not transparently reveal a moral hierarchy; a concern with its proprieties is distracting.

When Young Marius kills himself in defence of Praeneste he offers his suicide as exemplary of his courage and honour: 'To let thee see a constant Roman die' (V.iii.82). His example is followed by citizens who plead before they die for the lives of their wives and children. The suicides take place on the walls, watched below by Lucretius and his men—a stage picture, the decorum of which Lucretius admires: 'A wondrous and bewitched constancy,/Beseeming Marius' pride and haughty mind' (ll.94–5). The example is fitting and expressive. But it has no impact: 'Come, let us charge the breach. The town is ours./Both male and female, put them to the sword' (ll.96–7). The scene is less testing on its audience than Tamburlaine's love-speech, since Lodge provides an onstage spectator, yet the questioning of the exemplary and expressive is there. It is part of the unsettling effect of Lodge's play that what Marius calls noble, Lucretius calls haughty: everything can be questioned. Moments of apparent sincerity become linguistically opaque:

> magnanimity can never fear,
> And fortitude so conquer silly fate,
> As Scilla, when he hopes to have my head,
> May hap, ere long, on sudden lose his own.
>
> (II.ii.27–30)

The thoughts 'beseem' Marius's heroism, apparently expressing it; yet the alliteration and the clichéd play on hope/hap call attention to the constructed verbal surface. There is little sense of an extra-linguistic presence, of 'truth' or 'grace', waiting to be expressed. All is simply linguistic construction, assertion and denial, endless discourse which is punctuated only by slaughter.

Before I leave verbal 'truth' I should like to point to a visual analogy to the procedures I have described. Both *Wounds* and *Tamburlaine* use a similar transformation effect. In the first, at the end of the opening senate debate the stage direction has: 'Here let the Senate rise and cast away their gowns, having their swords by their sides'. Suddenly violence is shown underneath 'civil' debate. At the end of the second, Tamburlaine crowns Zenocrate and tells his captains: 'Cast off your armour, put on scarlet robes' (V.ii.460). The clothing of peace is, however, ambiguous, because the red robes visually connect with the bleeding corpses at the foot of the tableau. Tamburlaine's promise of truce to the world is made against a blood-red stage, the image saying what the words suppress. Both transformations take what is apparently fixed and subvert its meaning. The stage uses its technical resources to unsettle the visual truths that are promised by pageants.

(v) Writing

In terms of the structure of ideas, writing is opposed to speech. It is an antithesis that makes the oral seem sincere or spontaneous, although as we have seen that notion can itself be deconstructed. It is worth recalling that this thematic opposition does not reflect a social reality in that the printing press was used by those against authority as well as for it, the scripture was important to those who defied the Prayer Book. But it could be argued that the opposition is of a piece with a particular ideology of the individual versus the state. Let me first sketch the structure.

A short exchange in *The Cobbler's Prophecy* assumes a connection between class and writing, for when the muse Thalia asks for a pen to write down a 'pageant', Ralph the Cobbler says 'I use no such tool' (l.474). Puttenham, addressing a more select audience, writes that inferior persons receive their praise 'not in written lauds so much as in ordinary reward and commendation to be given them by the mouth of the superior magistrate. For histories were not intended to so general and base a purpose, albeit many a mean soldier and other obscure persons were spoken of and made famous in stories' (Puttenham, 1589, p.43). The history recorded by the muse Clio was 'The works of famous kings and sacred priests. . ... The lives of ancient sages and their saws,/Their memorable works, their worthy laws' (ll.560, 564–5). The register of memorable acts is also a source-book of moral sayings and law, and the fact that Clio has nothing to write of the present is an indictment of current rulers. When Edward I's queen hopes to make the chronicles 'crack' (=boast/brag) with record of her liberality, or Lluellen tells his soldiers with their swords to 'write in the book of time' (*Edward I*, 1590–1/1593, l.611), they acknowledge the moral pressure of the book of history. The text of the royal advice play, *Misfortunes of Arthur*, attempts to make its royal audience locate itself within, and hence obey the obligations of, the written continuity: Conan addresses a future audience:

> They'll think they hear some sounds of future facts,
> And not the ruins old of pomp long past.
> 'Twill move their minds to ruth and frame afresh
> New hopes and fears and vows and many a wish,
> And Arthur's cause shall still be favour'd most.
>
> (IV.iii.31–5)

Elizabeth is positioned between Arthur's cause and the future of Britain, the old text is still being written by its modern audience (and thus, Elizabeth must fix the succession).

Fictional rulers worry constantly about the recording of their acts, for the written outlasts, and judges, the personal. The images of the Chronicle, the book of time, God's register posit a world of fixed moral values. Similarly the motto on the shield of the chivalric knight is the written ideal that the person aspires to, and the Three Lords of London are thus labelled. The pageant text will indicate the meaning of a person by writing on her, by fixing her as type or allegory. In the trial scene at the end of *The Three Ladies of London* (1581/1584) the judge asks: 'What letter is that in thy bosom, Conscience?' (p.366). Despite her oral attempts to cover up, it is the written text which declares her real guilt. The authority of the written over the personal is used by Elizabeth when she attacks the independence of puritan preachers and urges they be compelled to 'preach all one truth; and that such as be found not worthy to preach, be compelled to read homilies' (Neale, 1969, II, p.70). The written ensures uniformity, confirms that truth is unitary.

The imposition of homilies was a practical act of a different order from a belief in the Chronicle of history, although it may have received justification from the ideological status of the written. As an act it related to the here-and-now legislation of human beings, which playtexts tend to treat separately from the eternal moral metatext (whose standing is very rarely dislodged). The ruler can be seen as the source of written legislation which in the conservative *Jack Straw* is healthy: 'Your pardons and your letters patents/ Shall be forthwith sent down in every shire' (ll.742–3). In the more oppositional *Thomas of Woodstock* (c.1592), however, Richard II's corrupt legal adviser Tresilian has a nefarious scheme for raising money by forcing the richer sort to sign blank charters on which the sums will later be written by royal officials. Tresilian's comic servant Nimble anticipates how they will 'domineer over the vulgar' (l.1268), and indeed the exercise is not seen to be confined to the rich. He and the Bailiff of Dunstable, who has already been intimidated by 'the high shrieve's warrant' (l.1496), also investigate seditious libels, secretly writing down speeches, while they go about collecting signatures. The action neatly fuses anxieties about royal demands for subsidy with the enforced swearing to Whitgift's articles for religious uniformity, which Burghley himself saw as a sort of Spanish inquisition. Eventually, someone is arrested for whistling.

Woodstock employs a politically overt image for the action of the written on the personal, whereas such action is more usually looked at in letter scenes (I shall also consider these by looking at Messengers later). The arrival of the letter disrupts the spoken text: Ragan reads in dumb-show, Mustaffa in silence while Bajazeth speaks the contents of the letter. It cannot be proved, but reading aloud may have been marked by performance style for in printed texts such moments can appear titled: 'The letter'. In *Friar Bacon and Friar Bungay* (c.1589/1594) the intrusion is signalled by a clash of styles when Margaret reads out an ornately written letter from her lover Lacy giving her the push (though it's really just testing her, as we later discover—he he [sic]). The usurpation of her own spontaneous speech by the calculatedly written male text acts out her threatened destruction by her lover's ambition. Margaret's belief in what she reads is symptomatic of her sex: in *Edmund Ironside* the hero, Edmund, sees through a treacherous letter, he 'is not lunatic,/So like a woman to be won with words' (ll.1302–3). Both scenes work, eventually, to show that the written text of the letter must be treated with scepticism, a reaction built by exposing the audience to the sound of their scripted authority before they are shown to be fake. But the scenes contrast in siting the woman in relation to text: it is maleness, especially aristocratic maleness, which is able to sort out the true written.

Reception of the letter shows text's effect on person, but the writing-of-the-letter scene deals with class and power. *Edmund* shows the villain Edricus writing a treacherous letter: he bids his clown-servant Stitch fetch him implements, and Stitch misunderstands, which is the occasion for jokes which foreground the class status of writing. Edricus has trouble selecting a style: 'Pluck Cyllen's feathers and make pens with them;/Borrow the Muses' aid' (ll.1173–4). He says it would have been easy to 'have filled my pen and raised my speech' to the flattery of a mistress or monarch (l.1180). Now, however, he decides to write

> in the plainest sort,
> For that is cousin german unto truth.
> 'Truth needs no colours.' Though I mean to lie
> My simple writing shall deceive his eye.
>
> (ll.1195–8)

The treacherous educated man can construct plainness and its truth-effect; the scene shows 'transparent' language to be opaque, but the text curtails its own scepticism by showing that Edricus' plainness does not deceive (by contrast, for example, Thomas of Woodstock's plainness of language and dress is seen in that play to be politically ineffectual, though sincerely meant).

A second letter scene, from *1 Hieronimo*, through its staging invites more detailed scrutiny of the frequently uninspected relationship of power and writing. Hieronimo dictates a letter to warn Andrea that Lorenzo plans to murder him. The main activity highlights what is silently assumed when rulers, particularly bad rulers such as Richard II and Richard III, use proclamations or messages to deal with their enemies, namely that the ruling class not only knows how to write, but has the power to compel others to do the writing or to carry the messages. Here Hieronimo has his son do the writing because he is educating him to be a proper gentleman, that class education being located by the narrative in close proximity to the internal power struggles of that class. The physical status of the letter is stressed, as Hieronimo instructs how to fold the paper and how to shape words, while the son, Horatio, is an instrument, repeating as he writes. Horatio quibbles over calling Lorenzo an 'honest lord', because he wants to state his feeling that Lorenzo is villainous, naively not understanding that true writing is less useful than a decorously deceitful text. Hieronimo threatens him: 'Take up thy pen, or I'll take up thee' (vi.28); he silences the next question with sarcasm asking if the scholar 'canst not aim at figurative speech?' (l.38). Threat and sarcasm combine to discipline Horatio to be an echo of his father, who meanwhile, says the stage direction, is 'trussing of his points', tying the ornamental tags on rich clothing. The stage action makes a metaphor for the preparation of the decorously dressed text, which is produced by bullying and expresses neither the truth of personal feeling nor the terms of its class position. (By contrast, when Edward III has Lodowick write in praise of the Countess of Salisbury (*Edward III*, ?1590/ 1596, l.408ff.), the written text cannot do justice to the emotion he feels: that his passion unhealthily exceeds and disrupts the discipline of the written is a moral pointer, but it is also a sentimentalising of the relationship of emotion and text when compared with the scene in *1 Hieronimo*.) After the letter is read out Hieronimo claims it has a moral, 'as much as to say, knavery in the court and honesty in a cheesehouse' (l.76), a conventional anti-court jibe the ordinariness of which conceals Hieronimo's own status as gentleman and the class-power exemplified in the production of the letter. The genteel text suppresses the terms of its own production.

Kyd's scene shows how concealment is part of the production of the text, an observation about rulers which is repeated: Scilla and Richard III temporarily remain silent about the contents of letters received, Tresilian's charters are ominously blank. The sender of the letter is absent, hidden, when the letter is received. A ruler may command murder without needing to speak, or even to write it directly, as Marlowe demonstrates in Mortimer's letter which remains perfectly ambiguous for as long as it remains unspoken. This secrecy is staged most often as a denial of a full communicating text to the audience. When characters whisper it is a sign of secret dealings. As a *sign*, however, this could be said to be satisfyingly communicative, although narrative information is suppressed. More deliberately dissatisfying is the construction of simultaneous off-stage action, unknown, unseen, which has bearing on what can be seen, as for example when Marius gives a secret instruction to Lectorius while he deals with Scilla's kinswomen—the women's speeches of courage are decentred because of the mystery of what is going on off-stage.

It is a text of Marlowe's, again, that could be said to reveal for its audience, to give them knowledge of, the modes of state utterance. It is my argument throughout that Marlowe's texts successfully question and reveal through a process of estrangement, so that as well as viewing objective signs of repression, etc. in the diegesis the privileged viewing relationship is so shaped that the repression, etc. is subjectively experienced, as, for example, uncertainty or discontinuity. In scene ii of *The Jew of Malta* Ferneze requests 'aid' from the Jews to pay the Turkish tribute. He silences Barabas's argument by having the articles of the new decrees read, thereby demonstrating that all oral debate was redundant since the legislating text was already written, its writing pre-dating speech. Barabas apparently demurs until Ferneze threatens 'half is the penalty of our decree;/Either pay that, or we will seize on all.' (I.ii.89–90) But the choice is not a choice, for when Barabas offers half, he is told he has denied the articles. Something unseen is going on, an impression confirmed when officers depart on a sign from Ferneze. In their absence the conversation becomes moralistic on the traditional topics of wealth, Jews and usury and only returns to the material matters of the present, with a threat to Barabas's home, when the officers are about to re-enter. It emerges that they have been seizing the goods and wares of Barabas, on an order presumably issued before the conventional moralising about Jews and wealth which would supposedly have offered its rationale. That moralising, which seems so appropriate and expected in a text with a Jew Vice figure, is redundant; the intellectual satisfaction promised by serious moralising is thwarted when the 'real' narrative of the off-stage action is established; the apparent fullness of the Morality play confrontation is later experienced as fiction and cheat. The practices of the Christians are signalled by writing and silence and felt as uncertainty, so that the audience experiences a set of power relations within which 'Barabas as Vice' is a deliberate red herring.

(vi) Silence and dismemberment

Authorities are shown to produce ordered texts, whether written or spoken, and in showing this plays frequently dispute the ideological value that rhetoricians place on such texts. Of as great, perhaps more pressing, political import-ance was the representation of those addressed, for these in their riotous numbers were those who the documents of control claimed attended the theatres. The plays potentially represented the commons to themselves, but there is little about the playtexts that makes consciousness of that social place. Only clowns claim community with their audience, and these were the most nonrepresentational performers, often more important as stars in their own right than as characters in a plot. The common people are otherwise mainly referred to as other, as distant offstage presences, on the margins of the text that performers share with audience.

Representing the people within the dominant speech/ writing opposition, plays locate them as *murmurers*. 'Mur-muring' is discontent figured as disordered speech: it is sound that cannot be written down and that is authorless, circulating between speakers, sometimes seen as a non-human being— Rumour or Report; in Averell's *Mervailous Combat* (1588) the tongue is a trouble-maker, associated with lying papists (see Hale, 1971, p.95). Such attributions are consistent with the authorities' terminology, the 'nature of the multitude', said the MP Digges, 'being prone to credit rumours' (Neale, 1969, I, p.279). Two points should be made about 'murmur-ing'. The first is that within the discourse of order it aligns with what Elizabeth designates as frivolous or self-indulgent speech, which deviates from the serious topics which she allocates to the Commons. Spoken words are supposedly insubstantial whereas official business or law-making have permanence, spoken words are the product of ungoverned temperaments as opposed to the discipline of the written. Thus Burghley warned Elizabeth in 1586 that unless she gave the Commons some proof of her readiness to act on their urgings about Mary of Scots the realm might 'nickname it a Parliament of Words' (Neale, 1969, II, p.132). The second point is that 'murmuring' represented a practical political threat. The Commons constantly worried that its debates were discussed outside the House, where no check could be placed on them. Similarly, when James Morrice was released from imprisonment for attacking the *ex officio* oath he was told that 'if aught were amiss in the Church or Commonwealth, I should not straightway make it known to the common sort, but declare it to her Majesty' (Neale, 1969, II, p.276); again, it is to be kept behind closed doors. On the other hand, the puritan leader Field was prepared to mobilise the people in campaigns against Parliament. The ideological devaluing of such 'murmurings' is clearly part of the state's efforts to maintain its secrecy. (There is a long history to the state secrecy which so forcefully operates today.)

The designation 'murmuring' seems specifically to counter those political theorists who give the people a role in government, for example Thomas Smith, who noted that John's abdication was partly illegal because the people had not approved it, conceded that the 'popular or rascal and viler sort' can seize power because 'they be moe in number' (Smith, 1583, p.11). Long was the tradition that the English people were more jealous of their rights than were the people of other nations. And those who knew their Machiavelli would have found him affirming that 'the populace is more prudent, more stable, and of sounder judgement than the prince. Not without good reason is the voice of the populace likened to that of God' (Machiavelli, 1531, I, p.343). It was the banned theorist Christopher Goodman who specified how the 'murmuring' discourse operated politically: 'And because their doings are counted tumults and rebellion (except they be agreeable to the commandments, decrees and proceedings of their superior powers and magistrates, and

shall in doing the contrary be as rebels punished) therefore of
all others (say they) we have least to do, yea nothing at all
with the doings of our rulers.' (Goodman, 1558, pp.145–6)

Few dramatists follow Goodman in stepping beyond the
muttering discourse (although in *Edward II*(1592/1594) the
people, in whose name much is done, are shown to be absent
from the doings of their rulers): what we can find is
revaluation of it in *The True Tragedy* and *Woodstock*. In the
first the villainous Richard is told that, at news of his
protectorship, 'Some murmur, but, my lord, they be of the
baser sort' and on becoming king, 'The commons murmur at
it greatly that the young king and his brother should be
imprisoned' (ll.455, 1043–5). The murmurings are correct in
their forebodings and, I think, in line with audience
sympathies. In *Woodstock* royal agents seek to discover the
source of 'strange songs and libels cast about the market
place' (l.1518); Nimble describes the Grasier's complaints as
murmuring, and writes him and his friends down as
'whisperers'; then he arrests the man for whistling, telling
him that it's the same as speaking (a system of arrest not,
perhaps, confined only to the first Elizabethans). Nimble is a
funny man, but he is also the corrupt servant of a corrupt
Chief Justice. The assault on rural middle England is grim as
well as comic.

The murmurers here are victims of bad kings. More
difficult politically is the portrayal of organised people, for in
the language of 'murmuring' they can hardly exist. Whitgift's
language struggles with itself not to recognise the efficacy of
puritan organisation: 'it imported a conspiracy and had the
show of a tumult or unlawful assembly. This disordered
flocking together of them from divers places and gadding
from one to another argueth a conspiracy amongst them. . .'
(Collinson, 1967, p.254). There appear to be numerous
examples of a people prepared to support oppositional causes.
The radical MP, Job Throckmorton, was elected for Warwick
against the wishes of the town's aldermen; in his campaign
against the monopoly of the Stationers' Company in 1583 the
printer Wolfe and his confederates 'incensed the meaner sort
of people throughout the city as they went, that it became a
common talk in alehouses, taverns and such like places,

whereupon ensued dangerous and undutiful speeches of her Majesty's most gracious government.' (Gerber, 1907, p.132). On the stage we have Jack Cade the rebel who has the Clerk of Chartham hanged 'with his pen and inkhorn about his neck' because he admits to an education that has taught him to write his name (*2 Henry VI*, IV.ii. 101–2). Cade is opposed to education, indicting Lord Say for corrupting 'the youth of the realm in erecting a grammar school' and introducing printing (IV.vii.30). In this confrontation Say is the sympathetic party: he defends himself to Cade in a display of educated civility:

> Kent, in the *Commentaries* Caesar writ,
> Is termed the civilest place of all this isle;
> Sweet is the country, because full of riches,
> To people liberal, valiant, active, wealthy;
>
> (ll.55–8)

Even Cade is eventually moved, signalling the virtue of Say's combination of book-learning and civil patience with the myths of nation and obedient people. Jack Straw's follower Tom Miller has a 'bonfire here of a great many of bonds and indentures and obligations' (*Jack Straw*, ll.780–1) for law and its misuse were common targets. Alice Arden, a sexual 'rebel' against her husband, is moved by her adulterous passion for Mosby to tear up a prayer book (*Arden of Faversham*, 1588–91/1592, viii. 116–20). Cade assaults English tradition itself: 'Burn all the records of the realm; my mouth shall be the parliament of England' (IV.vii.11–13). The rebel's demagogic orality is unsympathetically opposed to the democratic written; here as elsewhere Shakespeare's early texts reinvest the written with an aura that his contemporaries often demolished (no wonder academics love his work!), and also attack the common people (no wonder academics, etc. . .).

Lord Say's concept of a worthy populace (in their place) together with his desire to argue seriously with Cade inflect the Tudor myth of an accessible, benevolent ruler. This myth, it could be said, informs the dramatic presentation of popular utterance in that bad rulers are seen to silence it.

Lucre, in *The Three Ladies of London*, wants to live among
the poorest 'Because they dare not speak against our sports
and sweet delight' (p.337); Richard III's murderer Terrill tells
the Lieutenant of the Tower not to ask questions about what
goes on between him and the king. In a theatre where the
audience apparently shouted back at the stage these lines are
provocations precisely to speak out about the ways of bad
rulers. Such shouting (if it happened) is a form of illegal
utterance in that it is not always specifically recognised by the
diegesis of the play (and therefore is defined as intrusion) and
it also corresponded presumably with what the authorities
would designate as the riotous behaviour of theatre audiences. Thus I am not certain how much of the Tudor myth is
inflected, for it did envisage the common person speaking
only when spoken to, and other official conceptions of
rulership recommended obedient silence at all times. So the
fifth (most toadying) act of *Gorboduc* has:

        In act nor speech, no not in secret thought
        The subject may rebel against his lord,
        Or judge of him that sits in Caesar's seat,
        With grudging mind to damn those he mislikes.
        Though kings forget to govern as they ought,
        Yet subjects must obey as they are bound.

                                              (V.i.46–51)

Elizabeth spoke against the 'newfangledness' that encouraged
people to make judgements of their princes. Against this idea
we could read as more radical the point in *The True Tragedy*
when a poor man decides to help Jane Shore, whom there is a
ban on helping. His attempt to share what he has with her is
prevented by the entrance of the king's page, and he is
compelled to lie about his feelings. The class is specifically
indicated by the playtext, in an opposition of poor truth
against official silencing, and audience sympathy is motivated
against both silence and the officials who keep it. Charles
Merbury noted that 'The good king taketh pleasure to be
freely advertised, and wisely reprehended when he doth
amiss; the Tyrant can abide nothing worse than a grave, free
spoken and a virtuous man' (Merbury, 1581, p.13)—which is

rather more a warning to Elizabeth than a reflection of her. That the good king should listen to counsel was a political truism. The worthy counsellor Eubulus says early in *Gorboduc* that he feels able to speak what he thinks although the king will dislike it, which is effectively an announcement of the whole text's project. So bad kings are those who refuse to listen to, impose silence upon, their advisers. Leir, Locrine, Scilla threaten; Richard II murders plain-spoken Woodstock. The sympathy for silenced counsellors could be taken to draw its political force from early debates about royal succession, when oppositional arguments portrayed the counsellors as the guardians of the true continuity of England and the crown (much as in *Woodstock*)—where the body politic is permanent though the natural bodies of monarchs may come and go (see Axton, 1977). Yet in certain of the plays counsellors contribute to the imposition of silence. When Ralph the Cobbler wants to warn the king of popular unrest, the Scholar claims he raves and should not be allowed near; Lorenzo prevents Hieronimo's suits for justice in *The Spanish Tragedy* (1585–7/1592), on the grounds that his passions 'ill beseem'd the presence of a king' (III.xiv.80)—decorum represses. Against Lorenzo, seen very much as a politic new man, the play constructs an association between the silenced old magistrate Hieronimo and the 'common love' for him, those whom Lorenzo calls 'the vulgar, liberal of their tongues' (l.74). Note the detail selected: Hieronimo's sincere passions, later to be mad, and the common speech are excluded on grounds of decorum. In *Woodstock* Lancaster wants to organise the common people in opposition to Richard and he survives while the patient Woodstock dies. A division in the counsellors is presented in both cases, between those who associate with the commons and those around the king. The silencing is produced by new men in power. The point of view is like that of Knollys who, after the sacking of the puritan Archbishop Grindal, said 'King Richard the Second's men will flock into Court apace' (Collinson, 1967, p.200).

I have tended to lose the playtexts within other texts amid speculations on the structure of political oppositions. Let me return more fully to plays with my final point in this chapter:

the violence that marks state silencing. After he gets his revenge and before stabbing himself, Hieronimo bites out his tongue so he can't be forced to talk under torture. The principal tragedy has, however, happened because his earlier pleas for justice were not heard; biting out the tongue thus becomes an appropriate gesture for one whose communication has been repressed. Violence is often directed to organs of perception or communication: Acomat dislikes the message Aga brings so he pulls out his eyes and cuts off his hands; Marius has the orator Antony beheaded. Elizabethan theatre is notorious for its bloodiness, and academics have tried to rationalise this in various ways, often by arguing that it is iconographic. I think this is really an attempt to explain away violence which is felt to be too crude or extravagant, a feeling that derives ultimately from the unspoken modern academic commitment to a theatre of psychological realism. Instead I want to argue that stage violence as violence can make a statement about a political regime (as, for example, in plays and films about police states: the independent videos made of the 1984 Miners' Strike needed specifically to focus on the vicious police violence against miners' pickets simply because this was precisely the activity not shown on television news). The problem is with the meaning made by the violence, and I would suggest that, read within a discourse of speech/writing/silence, some Elizabethan violence means more than sensationalism.

Tyrants, I have noted, produce injury and death; in turn that violence intimidates others. Scilla has Granius executed for opposing him, and later he has the head brought on stage. In its presence he asks his followers if they approve him General and they agree, the juxtaposition implying that the 'free' oral consent is compelled by fear (I diverge here from Fleischer's suggestion (1974, p.196) that the severed head shows, iconographically, the removal of tyranny). Similarly, when Tamburlaine demands 'Who think you now is king of Persia' (II.vii.56), the corpse of Cosroe is at his feet. His crown, he says, is securer 'Than if the gods had held a parliament' (l.66), a reference which clarifies the type of rule—absolutist, non-parliamentary — which he is after. Scilla and Tamburlaine compel consent to their rule, and in doing so make a picture that cynically counters the more rosy idea of Elizabethan civil government Hooker was to express in his theory that, to remove troubles, the people 'gave their common consent all to be ordered by some whom they should agree upon' (Hooker, 1593, I, p.190). Such cynicism about the politics of consent may well have grown from the experience of Elizabeth's orders to imprison those MPs who demanded free speech and so terrify the others; or from an attitude to execution such as Burghley's towards the Babington conspirators (1586): 'if the fashion of the execution shall be duly and orderly executed, by protracting of the same both to the extremity of the pains in the action, and to the sight of the people to behold it, the manner of the death would be as terrible as any other new device could be' (Brooks, 1946, p.290); or the deliberate publication of accounts of the executions of rebels and plotters (Lowers, 1953).

The sight of violence on stage is seen to distort or suppress speech: Bajazeth claims to be speechless in the presence of the mutilated Aga, Zabina speaks madly when she sees her Bajazeth dead. In *Wounds* two common soldiers try to speak about the dead orator Antony: as they look at his head their speeches acquire what was his poetic eloquence, speaking of the 'honey on his temper'd tongue', 'The crystal dew of fair Castalian springs' (IV.ii.156, 157). The Captain who ordered the execution shuts them up: 'Leave these presumptuous praises' (l.162)—'presumptuous' because the soldiers speak out of turn; in front of the evidence of what the state does to unwanted orators, common soldiers themselves become disobediently eloquent, moved by a sympathy which the authorities disallow.

The prolonged attention to Antony's head forces an audience to look at it, as does the insistence on the length of time that the bodies remain on stage at the end of *1 Tamburlaine*. The violence was possibly especially noticeable on the Elizabethan stage since, while much of the representation was emblematic and sketchy, the blood effects were real in that a sheep's bladder full of animal blood might be used. The theatre, it can be said, experimented technically with illusionism specifically in the effort to represent the bloodiness of blood. Thus when contrasted with speech the violence

is exciting and, indeed, very real, and that contrast is
constructed to signify the redundance of the spoken—for the
soldiers' eloquence is impermissible (and can't resurrect
Antony) and Zenocrate's rhetorically formal display of the
corpses can happen only in Tamburlaine's absence. At the
end of that play Tamburlaine's speeches mainly ignore the
corpses; it is a rhetoric of power that suppresses mention of
what everyone can see. An audience can learn how the
discourse of order functions, and it may be interesting to
relate this to Bodin's attack (1576) on the misreporting of
history: he says 'the first men that bare rule had no greater
honour and virtue than to kill, massacre and rob men' but
some classical historians mistakenly claim that 'the first kings
were chosen for their justice and virtue; and have hereof
feigned unto us I wot not what heroical and golden worlds'
(quoted in Bawcutt, 1970, p.41). Certain texts of the
Elizabethan stage could be said always to refuse the myth of
attainable golden worlds, and through their intertextuality
always show rulers speaking the discourse of order with its
concomitant repression and violence.

The ideological oppositions of speech/writing/order/si-
lence fade out of later drama, a change announced by that
very new play *Titus Andronicus* (c.1593/1594). Lavinia, raped
by the Empress's sons, with her tongue and hands mutilated,
is the image of tyrannically repressed communication. But
she learns to communicate through books, finding a parallel
with her case in the Ovidian tale of Philomel. Her kin have to
learn to interpret and read her 'signs', she has to learn to
write, which she does with a staff in her mouth:

> here display at last
> What God will have discovered for revenge.
> Heaven guide thy pen to print thy sorrows plain
>   (IV.i.72–4)

Writing is heaven-directed and will reveal truth. Lavinia
writes in Latin and Titus will make the text permanent by
writing it 'on a leaf of brass'; he in turn will write more on his
quest for revenge. Here are all the features of the written
culture—classical books, scholars' language, permanent

truth-telling text. This writing is not oppressive but sympathetically central. So too poetic eloquence is revalued: when Marcus first sees Lavinia he speaks for nearly fifty lines (cut in Brook's famous production). The oral text ornaments and enlarges what can be seen: 'a crimson river of warm blood,/Like to a bubbling fountain stirred with wind' (II.iv.22–3); the real, seen injuries are simultaneously figuratively transformed in words. This differs from the soldiers talking to Antony's head: instead of a words/image opposition there is a fit; the soldiers were disallowed but Marcus has plenty of talking space. He wants to know the culprit so he 'might rail at him to ease my mind' (l.35)—the speech has an emotionally expressive function. When Zenocrate spoke of corpses her speech was noticeably patterned and addressed directly to the audience, but Marcus the character expresses Lavinia's injuries to himself. The fit of words and image does not induce the critical awareness produced, say, by the split between Tamburlaine's speech and his victims' bodies. The tension of written against oral fades, the ideological status of books and poetry is shifted, in the exploration of a newer expressivity.

When language is used simply to express the 'inner' person its operations are no longer foregrounded, no longer critically inspected. Thus with the development of a new sort of dramatic writing, a more 'psychologically expressive' drama, an exploration of the political operations of language was lost. Thus also was lost a particular knowledge of power relations within society.

THEATRE BAD.

CHAPTER 2

Form and Disorder

(i) Overview

As a social institution the Elizabethan professional theatre was regarded by the authorities as harmful. It was said to encourage its audiences to be lewd, unchaste, seditious or riotous: the language of disapproval blends together political and moral threat. Most of the opposition to the players came from the governing authorities of London, the Lord Mayor and Common Council, for whom gatherings of the 'meaner sort' meant a possible danger to the good order of the city. The class basis of the worry was given a moral colouring through the sustained propaganda, the public sermons and pamphlets, of puritans against the theatre (see the documents reprinted chronologically in Chambers, 1923, IV). The players were initially supported, against the City, by the Privy Council who claimed that they had to perform in order to rehearse the productions they were eventually to show to the queen. Walsingham wrote thus to the Lord Mayor in 1583, but by 1586 the Privy Council was recommending the inhibiting of playing (they use the excuse of plague-threat but anxiety about disorder also appears). This change in the Privy Council attitude may be connected with the ascendancy of the Whitgift faction during Leicester's absence in the Netherlands, 1585–6, for Leicester not only personally patronised players and writers but may well have influenced a policy of opposition to the City in the same way as he sought in the Netherlands to circumvent the power of the ruling merchants by allying with the popular radical party. Leicester very much defended his old-style aristocratic power.

Some inconsistencies in the opposition to players need exploring. The immorality charge was ironically scrutinised by Nashe, who noted that there were already in existence plenty of brothels and places to gamble and booze (Nashe,

40

1592, p.114). The City authorities persistently connected the activities of the professional theatres with sports such as bear-baiting, effectively differentiating them from the theatrics they themselves sponsored, namely the Mayor's and guild shows. A crucial distinction between civic pageantry and playhouses was that the former was controlled by the very structure on which the government of London rested, the trades guilds (Foster, 1977); the players, on the other hand, were associated with vagabonds and masterless men, those who were outside guild control and hierarchy. Yet, although they were 'outside', the players clearly made money and audiences were conspicuously prepared to watch them, despite the dominant ideology of the worthy citizen dedicated to proper work. To strengthen their independence from the City authorities the players appealed for protection to their nominal aristocratic patrons, but effectively their receipts made them also independent of the need for patronage. Thus the 'ungovernable' characteristics of the playhouses may partly be explained by their unusual economic status, which depended on neither of the accepted governing authorities.

The aldermen of the City claimed that the playhouses attracted people away from church worship, and the puritan organiser John Field said that the flags and trumpets that announced performances 'will sooner prevail to fill those places than the preaching of the holy word of God' (Field, 1583, sig.B4v). This mainly puritan opposition to theatres is notorious, but puritan propagandists were not averse to using a dramatic mode of writing to teach. Field himself wrote dramatic dialogues between puritan martyrs and episcopal persecutors (Neale, 1969, II, p.230), Wentworth wrote an account in dialogue of his interrogation, Knox and the Scottish presbyterians taught religion in dramatic representation (Watson, 1939, p.356) and, of course, Thomas Norton was co-author of *Gorboduc*, in which he incorporated arguments from the work of the Marian exile Christopher Goodman. The differences between didactic dialogues and playhouses are, firstly, that the former can exert a certain amount of control over their audience in that the audience have to be the sort of people who are literate, or 'perform-

ance' may be attended by the presence of a minister;
secondly, the puritan dialogue is invested with the authority
of what it communicates, God's word. The pageant, too,
spoke a true message in that it celebrated occasions of known
importance in the government of state or city; it was part of
the ritual of government and among its performers were the
real-life governors, in the case of royal pageants Elizabeth
being both chief spectator and chief performer to whom the
whole allegoric structure pointed. The splendours of the
Mayor's show were financed by the real wealth of the guild
and displayed it; the importance of various guild members
was marked by their roles in the pageant. By contrast, in
playhouses those like masterless men acted kings in a text
which served rather than controlled its performers: the
anecdote of Tarlton suddenly playing both clown and judge
in *The Famous Victories of Henry V* (>1588/1598) (Bullough,
1962, IV, p.289) shows both improvisation on the written
and the direct communication with the audience by performer as well as role (Hattaway, 1982, suggests audiences went
to *Tamburlaine* specifically to see the star Alleyn). While
pageants and processions indicated their real social importance by conspicuous redundancy of performers and expendi-
ture (compare shows at the Teatro Olimpico, see Nagler
(1959), pp.81–6), the players doubled up parts and used
obvious stage props. The performance conditions of pageants
and puritan didactic pieces strengthened their claim to speak a
truth; at the centre of Elizabeth's coronation pageant was a
'true' text, the English Bible given to her by the figure of
Truth, whereas in 1574 the Common Council of London was
worried about the 'uttering of popular, busy and seditious
matters' among other crimes at play performances (Chambers, 1923, IV, p.274).

Alongside the problems of social control raised by the
existence of playhouses there was also a challenge to the
authority of 'truth', whether it be the 'truth' spoken by the
state or the 'truth' of God's word spoken by oppositional
puritans. In the second half of this chapter I shall be arguing
that what contributed to the 'sedition' of playhouses, besides
the sense of social indiscipline, was the artistic form of texts,
which unsettled the authority of truth. Before looking at

formal structure, however, it might be as well to discuss those watching that structure.

(ii) Addressing an audience

Describing the Queen's coronation pageant Mulcaster (1559) says: 'the city of London' was 'a stage wherein was showed the wonderful spectacle of a noble-hearted princess toward her most loving people, and the people's exceeding comfort in beholding so worthy a sovereign' (Bergeron, 1971, p.15). Mulcaster writes in the people's response as something that completes the pageant. There is no sense of a distanced spectator, the whole of London is itself the stage. So too in church the congregation is not an audience: in Anglican ritual it supplies the responses, its spiritual life is under the scrutiny of the minister and, in radical sectarian gatherings, all scrutinise each other. A power relationship is established by the structure of watcher and watched. In the theatre, too, the performer addressed the audience but this time not with the authority of truth, for in fact it was the representation which addressed the audience. That audience had also paid to finance what they were seeing, thus privileging their status as watchers. The comparison of playhouses with bear-gardens assumes a spectacle where the performer does not look, or looks less powerfully (being an animal), back at the audience that watches it. Contemporaries speak of an audience shouting back at the stage: Gosson tells how a piece of trickery may be met with approving cheers (Gosson, ?1590, sig. C8v). The relationship of watched to watcher was, however, unsettled precisely by the development of 'realistic' character that speaks sincerely to the audience.

It is not proper to imply, as I have done, that the audience is free to respond objectively, since the artwork addresses its audience and in addressing them it constructs for them positions from which to view or read the artwork. The text may be said to function ideologically insofar as it tells its audience, for example, what is right or good (although this may form a critique of a dominant ideology). Of primary importance here is how the playtext addresses its audience, what picture of themselves it encourages them to recognise, and where it tells them they are situated in the social order. It may be useful, though perhaps improper, to borrow Therborn's description 'subjection-qualification' for the way ideology forms human subjects: 'The amorphous libido and manifold potentialities of human infants are subjected to a particular order that allows or favours certain drives and capacities, and prohibits or disfavours others. At the same time, through the same process, new members become qualified to take up and perform (a particular part of) the repertoire of roles given in the society into which they are born, including the role of possible agents of social change.' (Therborn, 1980, p.17)

Mulcaster assumed that people were 'comforted' by recognising the authority to which they were subject; the Prologue to *Three Lords and Three Ladies of London* (c.1589/1590) constructs a community based on that subjection and recognition: London speaks of 'the love wherewith God loves our Queen,/In whom, for whom we do possess/ More grace, more good, than London can express' (p.373). In failing to 'express', the persona admits (constructs) the greater reality 'we' all share. In court plays the claiming of community between performer and audience encourages the audience to recognise their positions as rulers; for example when the Messenger in *The Misfortunes of Arthur* describes Arthur's discovery that his own son has fortified Britain against him: 'Where erst we sought abroad for foes to foil,/ Behold, our Fates had sent us foes unsought' (II.i.63–4), the pronouns establish the relevance of the Arthurian fiction on the basis of a shared problem with internal security (specifically with Catholic plots and Mary of Scots). The sense of community was reinforced by the social status of the directors and authors of this play, who as Inns of Court students would be expected themselves to become governors of the realm (Axton, 1977, pp.152–3; Ramel, 1967). Early in *Misfortunes* the ghost of Gorlois asks Cassiopeia not to prevent his revenge, hailing her as 'This climate's joy, plac'd in imperial throne' (I.i.56); similarly in Wilmot's *Tancred and Gismunda* (?1566/1591) there is a reference to a 'virgin' 'without compare' (p.49). Both references operate metadramatically to acknowledge the presence of Elizabeth as chief spectator and thereby construct relations of subjection to her as the prime Subject, of both state and drama. It is only the reality of her presence that completes the communication from the fiction, or so it is claimed.

In the playhouse there was no such authorising presence to which the fiction deferred, no metadramatic social relations that sited the performance within the structures of rule. It was most frequently the clown who acknowledged the audience: Simplicity, played by Tarlton in *Three Ladies*, bends to let Conscience use him as a writing-desk: 'Here is the right picture of that fellow that sits in the corner,' he says, and refuses to bend again because 'I am afraid yonder boy will mock me' (pp.288, 289). In *Locrine* the clown Strumbo provocatively 'recognises' the assumed sinfulness of the audience: 'How do you, masters, how do you? How have you 'scaped hanging this long time?' (ll.1598–9). Simplicity and Strumbo both encourage noisy responses through horseplay that is seemingly not acknowledged by the main plots. An audience may laugh at Strumbo's attempts to use ornate courtly-love language but in the following scene Locrine, announcing his marriage, is told 'your subjects every one/Must needs obey your highness at command' (ll.421–2); Miles, a clown in *Friar Bacon*, has comic business based on his ineptitude at serving at table to the 'great lords'. The clown looks at the audience, calls them 'my masters' and does comic business which marks his stupidity or inferiority; the characters of a main plot tend to address each other or their own inner selves rather than recognise the audience. The split in performance modes would appear to subject the audience to the elevated plot while giving them authority over the clown. This subject position can be complicated by developments in characterisation: for example, in *The True Tragedy* an old ostler realises he has to betray the good Earl Rivers who is to be imprisoned in his inn: 'Ah, masters, masters, what a troublesome vocation am I crept into: you think we that be inn-keepers get all the world, but I think I shall get a fair halter to my neck' (ll.581–3)—the metadramatic joke about inn-keepers is almost refused, certainly tempered, by the sympathy diegetically acquired by the inn-keeper, producing a problem of response that explores the subject position constructed by clowns versus main plots.

The clown's address also sets up response to other characters: when Fraud gives himself gentleman's airs, Simplicity says: 'A goodly gentleman ostler! I think none of all you will believe him' (*Three Ladies*, p.256). The lines call for the classic pantomime yell: when Simplicity has to serve Lucre he asks: 'How say ye, sirrah, can I not? I'll be judg'd by you' (p.323). Yet the judging need not be restricted to clowning scenes, as when Richard's page in *The True Tragedy* notes that 'my Lord is fully resolved to climb, but how he climbs—I'll leave that to your judgements; but what his fall will be—that's hard to say' (ll.475–7). The audience that is invited to watch *how* events take shape is one that consciously watches political and social interaction; an audience interested only in *what* will happen is an audience that is mainly kept in ignorance (this is the distinction that informs Brecht's theory of political theatre). Many Elizabethan plots are constructed to give the audience a knowledge greater than that recognised by characters, thus for example Queen Elinor is known to lie when she denies killing the Mayoress and likewise when Lucre denies her deeds; the use of an overlapping time-scheme, as in *The True Tragedy*, creates an interest in how characters will respond to the news that an audience knows awaits them. The famous example of signalling such privileged knowledge is when the Vice figure is given a line that claims no one hears his plans.

The judging position of the audience is frequently associated with the chronicles of history. Thus when Richard II says: 'Not all our chronicles shall point a king/To match our bounty, state and royalty' (*Woodstock*, ll.1197–8), he is known to be incorrect for his main claim to fame is as a deposed monarch who wasted money on favourites; the ambivalence of 'our' establishes the subject position, for the chronicles do not record what Richard (in the regal plural) wants them to say, but what 'we' the present audience know them to say. There are numerous references to chronicles in which the real chronicle record fits with the audience assessment of the character, despite her/his assertions: Queen Elinor wants the chronicles to 'crake with record' of her liberality but she is known for her pride; King Leir is told his 'care' deserves 'To be enrolled in chronicles of fame' (*King Leir*, received 1594/1605, l.73), but he is famous for irrational affection. The audience's judgement is named in the texts as the true chronicle record. This naming marks their qualification to judge against the claims of fictional rulers. When Canutus asks how to erase a crime 'Out of the brass-leaved book of living fame' (*Edmund*, 1.749) the line places the audience as the posterity that always judges.

What the chronicle image suppresses, in all its associations with literacy and non-humanity, is the picture of common people judging a monarch. Despite all the hostile assessment of Richard II, the Duchess of Gloucester can assure the queen that 'England's not mutinous:/'Tis peopled all with subjects, not with outlaws' (*Woodstock*, ll.1036–7). There is no common person in the drama who speaks with the judgement of the chronicles, the commons are shown to be 'subjects' to the ruler even while the rhetorical strategies of the text may qualify the audience to be more active 'subjects' of history in their critique of rulers. The 'meaner sort' is not generally encouraged to recognise its qualification, as the meaner sort, to judge. Its assessments of dramatic events are split from any talk of 'murmuring' commons within the diegesis. But this split, as I noted in Chapter 1, is sometimes joined: the opinions of those called murmurers coincide with audience judgement. Thus, in *Woodstock*, the corrupt favourite Greene says how the commons have been murmuring and should have their mouths stopped with food, but the playtext encourages its audience to desire change of rule and, hence, to be cynical about traditional charity. The dissociation from passive subject reactions is encouraged elsewhere. For example, when the tyrannous Scilla says 'men of baser mettle and conceit/Cannot conceive the beauty of my thought' (*Wounds*, II.i.14–15), the awareness of his material cruelty precedes an appreciation of his intellectual beauty; when the villainous Richard says 'A mighty arm will sway the baser sort, authority doth terrify' (*The True Tragedy*, 1.456) the audience is likely to refuse its identification as 'baser sort' by the known villain, and refuse the passive terror. The classic line of the Machiavel or the Vice assumes the acquiescence of cowed commons; Locrine arrogantly opines that 'Kings need not fear the vulgar sentences' (*Locrine*, l.1520). These lines, as much as those of clowns, *presumably* (I don't know) produced vocal counter-reaction, a dramatic pleasure that simultaneously refuses the silent subject position and acts out the riot that was 'recognised' by authorities in theatre audiences.

Indecorous as it might have been, the shouting of the audience could still be seen to speak from a position very much encouraged by Elizabethan propaganda. For the shouting at a bad monarch who thinks to disregard 'vulgar sentences' implies recognition of the good monarch who listens to people, which was the claim made by Tudor royal myth. Against this, some in the audience may have had knowledge of the real censorship and repression. It is possible that some may have seen playtexts as ironic critiques of the charge of sedition. The senators in *Wounds* who oppose the tyrant Scilla are said to have 'seditious brains'; when Richard's troops go over to the virtuous Richmond he charges that 'our subjects seeks the subversion of the state, the fall of their prince, and sack of their country' (*The True Tragedy*, ii.1631-3). In both cases those on the side of the sedition or subversion are known to be unjustly accused by someone who supports a tyranny. This, for a modern reader, makes a fine ironic rebuff to the Common Council of London, but it remains impossible to state that members of an audience connected the way they were daily addressed with a fictional Roman senate or medieval England. Interpretations would eventually also depend on the commitments and ideas of individuals interacting with the subject position constructed for a whole audience.

(iii) Problems of form

It is as well to be cautious about interpretation since much modern criticism assumes an ideal viewer who will always acknowledge the justness, the 'common sense', of the observations made by the critic. Unless I am careful, my analysis of the structuring of scenes and plots will imply that the meanings that can be found by me now can be found always, irrespective of material or historical situation. I should say that I am not seeking to validate my readings by claiming them to be intended by authors, but that the text can generate meanings despite its proclaimed project, especially given the 'loose' mode of construction typical of the episodic dramas of the Elizabethan stage. We are ourselves not free viewers of the drama since we are regularly taught by and read critical commentaries which tell us, ideologically, that incoherence is bad and coherence is good, and, further, that Elizabethan writers were, as a fact, seeking for unity of style and structure. An example of the problems of looking and interpreting may be the episode of *Coronation Street* for 30 July 1984 (randomly chosen): we were shown two telephone calls (there were others, unseen) which separately involved the characters Sally Waterman and Derek Wilton. These two characters are, in different ways, self-promoting. The activity of telephoning visually links them. So, too, do newspapers: the clearly displayed *Daily Telegraph* being read, typically, by the pompous Wilton in the Rovers pub was ironically related to the conceited Waterman's attempts to turn the local advertising sheet into a scandal paper. Each's personal attempt to impose her/himself on (and disrupt) the community bore metaphoric relation to the function of daily news media. But someone engaged with the story as narrative, particularly as realistic narrative, or someone with a different political viewpoint might challenge that I am reading something into nothing. But the text, whatever even its authors might say, permits in its structure my reading.

When modern commentators write of the incoherence of Elizabethan playtexts they are repeating the discourse of control spoken by City authorities whose censure of the playhouses' 'unfit and uncomely matter' combines artistic and moral disapproval. Their documents lump together 'plays, interludes, comedies, tragedies or shows' (Chambers, 1923, IV, p.276), linking plays with bear-baiting and fencers. A similar use of standards of decorum in order to devalue what is politically threatening can be found in those descriptions of unfit, frivolous or superfluous speech in the House of Commons—usually applied to attempts to debate issues forbidden by the queen (see Chapter 1); or again in the view that sectarian worship was disordered because the ministers departed from the pre-written text of the Prayer Book or even improvised prayers. Martin Marprelate thus explained the reason for puritan attacks on him: 'Those whom foolishly men call puritans like (of) the matter I have handled, but the form they cannot brook' (Marprelate, 1588–9, p.304). The influential puritan Cartwright told Burghley that he disapproved of the 'disordered proceeding' of Martin (Collinson, 1967, p.393): it was presumably the popular appeal of the Marprelate tracts that disturbed those whose radicalism was limited by their class position. Visions of social disorder are never far from discussions of artistic form and rhetorical decorum, as may be noted in Sidney's judgement of players: 'all their plays be neither right tragedies nor right comedies, mingling kings and clowns, not because the matter so carrieth it, but thrust in the clown by head and shoulders to play part in majestical matters with neither decency nor discretion' (Sidney, 1595, p.67). His description of professional plays echoes the City authorities in its refusal to recognise the shapes of the plays as intellectually or artistically planned: 'having indeed no right comedy, in that comical part of our tragedy we have nothing but scurrility, unworthy of any chaste ears, or some extreme show of doltishness, indeed fit to lift up a loud laughter and nothing else' (*ibid.*, p.67). The words of Gosson appeal to the familiar discourse of truth: 'How is it possible that our playmakers' heads, running through genus and species and every difference of lies, cosenages, bawdries, whoredoms, should present us any schoolmistress of life, looking glass of manners, or image of truth? (Doran, 1954, p.96). Truth is the opposite of plays' form in that it is unitary and fixed; the disorder cannot be allowed to be a mirror, for artworks were only mirrors insofar as they reflected an ideal order, the what-should-be rather than what-is. Disorder in plays, mingling kings and clowns, could not be seen as truth or reflection.

Bacon attacked Marprelate's 'immodest and deformed manner of writing . . . whereby matter of religion is handled in the style of the stage' (Collinson, 1967, p.393). Implicitly, Marprelate and the players do not do what decorous writers do, that is, create a sense of order and truth. Behind Sidney's worry about form lie Castelvetro's theories (1576) about observation of unities as a way of creating verisimilitude; verisimilitude was important since, while history and science sought truth of fact, poetry imitated the 'truth of the accidents of humanity's lot' so that verisimilitude was necessary to confirm the possibility of things that could happen (Charlton, 1913, p.41). Castelvetro's poet creates the truth-appearance by arranging coherence and unity in the material; this 'truth' then gives authority to the example or moral. In the same way Barclay and Blundeville saw that history provided its readers with moral examples, and that a continuous historical narrative shaped by the historian was more useful for teaching purposes than an episodic chronicle (see Campbell, 1947, p.43; Rosenberg, 1955, p.64). Again there is the connection between ordered arrangement and moral authority: 'an orderly register of notable things said, done, or happened in time past, to maintain the continual remembrance of them, and to serve for the instruction of them to come' (Amiot in North, 1570, p.xiv). In his attack on his rival historian Stow, Grafton (1570) said that to tell history wrongly was to encourage disobedience: in Stow's works 'the gates are rather opened for crooked subjects to enter into the field of rebellion than the hedges or gaps of the same stopped'— what stops a gap is an example that teaches obedience to the prince (Rosenberg, 1955, p.75).

This list of quotations may indicate, I think, that the urgency behind strictures on form derived from a political fear that the disordered work played to a large audience might open the gaps for 'crooked subjects', and fail to create the truth-effect which would give authority to examples of necessary obedience. I shall move on to survey different sorts of formal disorder in playtexts and comment on their deviations, but I shall not necessarily discriminate between 'intended' and accidental disorder: to sustain the picture of a single author for these texts is to obscure their conditions of production, for they might be written by one or more writers, contributed to by other actors, contributed to again by audiences reacting to actors or scenes, shaped for printing by a printer operating with a whole different set of criteria about artworks (and then reshaped over the centuries by editors with their own sets of criteria).

The first sorts of disorder to list are those which affect the interpretation of a whole play. One way of fixing the meaning of a dramatic text was to frame the 'human' action with scenes of allegorical dumbshow or supernatural choric commentary. Thus the first act of *Gorboduc* is prefaced by a show of a bundle of sticks being broken one by one and ended by a chorus which recalls the image to explain how the human action illustrates the idea that disunity leads to weakness. *The Rare Triumphs of Love and Fortune*, in which the action confirms alternately the strengths of love or fortune, can only be ended when the framing goddesses introduce the new idea of wisdom to settle human affairs. The frame shows direct their comments to Elizabeth (in court plays), whose presence and policies constitute the standpoint from which to interpret. In playhouses, without a chief spectator, the frame itself loses the authority of its overview. For example, in *The Spanish Tragedy* the watching figure of Revenge falls asleep (which gives a comical twist to the Senecan cliché, 'Awake, Revenge'); and the ghost of Andrea, looking to be revenged, has so single-minded an interest that he ignores any political analysis of the court and misunderstands Hieronimo's plan to await opportunity for action. Similarly *The Scottish History of James IV* (1591/1598) uses a sleeping commentator and a misinterpreting commentary: when Bohan promises 'we'll see/The pride of folly, as it ought to be' (I.Chorus, 14–15) there follows a highly formal tableau of two virtuous women, sewing, seriously discussing wealth and honesty; likewise the Chorus's interest in the king and marginalising of the clowns misses much of the conspicuous social commentary of the play. The framing figures can lose their authority: notoriously Marlowe opens *Dido, Queen of Carthage* (>1593/1594) with a frivolous and sodomitical Jupiter. This contributes to a shift in dramatic priorities so that the human action is altogether more complex (and more moving) than the frame can state: I shall examine this in *Dido* later, but in *Faustus*, for example, the Chorus's presentation of Faustus in moralised biography describes neither his emotive complexity nor the status of those around him.

The frame, in particular the Chorus, relates to the figure of the Presenter, who as narrator shows the audience mimetic scenes selected for their bearing on the overall narrative. It is thought that the Presenter originally would have been the poet or author, and this gives him greater importance than other figures in the show in that he could be said literally to own the work as his and to speak the narrative truthfully. The language of the Presenter is, however, often given to villain figures who invite the audience to behold their handiwork: Selimus, for example, announces that the next pageant will be that of his brother Corcut—clearly he means murder, and it is a mark of his power that he can thus announce it, but that power is certainly not morally neutral. *The Jew of Malta* makes a fine ambiguity when Machevil appears 'to present the tragedy of a Jew' (Prologue, l.30) for this identity and reputation should cause scepticism about the reliability and truthfulness traditionally associated with the Presenter: metadramatic knowledge enters and disrupts the performance at the precise point at which it lays claim to be able to speak truthfully.

A third way of fixing the overall meaning is to make a clear message from the ending. This is the place where gods re-enter or worthy counsellors say 'I told you so'. But at the end of *King Leir* the wicked daughters are merely defeated, not dead and at the end of *Edmund Ironside* (which may be a Part 1, though we don't have Part II) the villain has the last speech promising vengeance. Peele's *Edward I* ends with a tableau in which Gloucester mourns for his dead wife Joan while Mortimer stands silently holding the head of the defeated rebel Lluellen; the king has gone off to repeal the Scottish invasion. Gloucester speaks of the impermanence of 'pomp' and the uselessness of his own tears; Mortimer stands as the image of a victor, but the king has to be absent, funerals have been ordered and Gloucester weeps. There is no feeling of confident full security in kingship and virtue; the emphasised image is death. This ending illustrates the difficulty of dealing with the form of Elizabethan plays, because many would argue that the text of *Edward I* is very corrupt and that Peele could not have written an ending like this because he has the reputation for being a patriotic writer. That reputation is open to reconsideration, of course, and Marlowe has an ambiguous head scene at the end of *Edward*

II; but nothing can be argued on the basis of a corrupt text. A further problem is that the extent of the text's corruption may relate not only to its physical characteristics but to an assumed sense of the dramatic unity and decorum that the author was striving for; in other words, although there might be bits missing, this is where the play always ended. I raise these difficulties because they can turn open-endedness (perhaps rightly) into an accident: suffice it to say that the incomplete end is not uncommon, in texts both corrupt and virtuous.

The undercutting of the authority of the frame makes the message of the text rather more complex and opaque than the single, and normative, lessons that Nashe lists: 'the ill success of treason, the fall of hasty climbers' etc. (Nashe, 1592, p.114). Further complexity is created by what Stanley calls 'mingling kings and clowns': in *Locrine* the death of Brutus leads to a funeral procession and, presumably while it exits, the clown Strumbo enters 'above in a gown'—not only does clown follow funeral but his black scholar's gown, so inappropriately worn, makes a connection with funeral robes. In *Faustus*, notoriously, a main plot which deals with a man's soul gives way to scenes of clowning. Some scholars argue that the *Faustus* funny scenes should be regarded as interpolations and disregarded: it is an argument which frequently contains uninspected ideas about dramatic decorum and unity. But contrasts of tone and breaches of 'mood' are a common feature of Elizabethan playtexts and rather than regard them as accidents and faulty workmanship it might be better to privilege them by employing a theory of montage. Thus the distinctive features of Elizabethan drama could be seen as a specific and positive practice, although one that was untheorised except by those whose ideological position prevented them from recognising the meanings that could be made by such a practice.

The most famous theorist and practitioner of montage, Eisenstein, explains its operation thus: 'take a grave, juxtaposed with a woman in mourning weeping beside it, and scarcely anybody will fail to jump to the conclusion: a widow' (Eisenstein, 1968, p.14). The two visual elements combine to form an idea that is more than the sum of its

parts—'widow' specifying social place, if not type, in a way
that 'weeping woman by grave' does not. There is no
narrative explaining or commenting on the images; the work
of connection in order to interpret is undertaken by the
audience. Such a method of construction requires a more
actively interpreting audience than does narrative delivery.
Furthermore, each meaning is made provisionally and is
always redefined; no fixed or unitary truth is transparently
expressed, especially since some of the elements of the
montage may oppose or contradict one another. A reading
can be made in consciousness of its opposite. This mode of
viewing and understanding may not have been theorised in
relation to stage practice but it was not alien to the sceptical
Renaissance thinkers who were interrogating the notions of
law and custom. Montaigne speaks of a world of continual
enquiry: 'Thus can nothing be certainly established, nor of
the one nor of the other; both the judging and the judged
being in continual alteration and motion. . . .. Thus, seeing all
things are subject to pass from one change to another, reason,
which therein seeketh a real subsistence, finds herself
deceived as unable to apprehend anything subsistent and
permanent' (Montaigne, 1603, p.364). Similarly Agrippa
(1569) speaks of the mutability of manners and custom: 'that
which at one time was vice, another time is accounted virtue
. . . that which to us just, to other is unjust, according to the
opinion or laws of time, of place, of estate, and of men'
(Haydn, 1950, p.141). I am quoting here to illustrate the
existence and shape of contemporary sceptical thought (see
Dollimore, 1984), but I am not trying to suggest some sort of
suppressed Elizabethan theory of the stage. My use of
montage is to enable the present reader consciously to
counter and question the critical predisposition towards unity
and decorum.

Different sorts of montage can be identified. The first is
diachronic—experienced in the passage of time, one action
following another—and works as an opposition between
scenes. For example, the end of *The Battle of Alcazar*'s
(1589/1594) Act III has the Portugese prince Sebastian calling
all to a 'rightful war, that Christians' God will bless' (l.977) to
aid Muly Mahamet. Next the Presenter speaks of Muly

Mahamet as 'this hapless heathen prince. . ... This Moor, this murderer of his progeny' (ll.978, 980), and he shows a bloody banquet with dead men's heads. The contrast qualifies the heroism of Sebastian who is allied to a murderer, and insists on the bloodiness of war that had hitherto been called rightful and blessed. Diachronic contrast works to undermine the truth of references to heaven again in *The True Tragedy* when a scene of Earl Rivers's imprisonment is followed by a speech by Richard accusing him as a Judas and attributing his detainment to the action of heaven, whereas the audience had already seen Richard's henchmen at work. Such contrast reveals and questions ideological statement, and there are many more subtle versions of it (I consider elsewhere the sequence in *Tamburlaine* of the killing of the virgins, the apostrophe to Zenocrate, the ransacked town).

A second form of diachronic montage shows parallel or duplicate actions represented in differing styles, usually 'high' style and clowning (see also Dessen, 1977, on visual analogues). A parallelism can be found at the end of *Wounds* when the tyrant Scilla penitently moans: 'O wanton world that flatter'st in thy prime' (V.v.164). Two clownish citizens enter, one worrying about his daughter: 'O vain world, O foolish men' (ll. 173–4), he begins, half-parodying Scilla. One of Scilla's soldiers is responsible for the daughter's fate, but Scilla disclaims responsibility since he has decided to live as a private man. The clowns think the resignation of office is simple-headed and ask questions to explore this stupidity; Scilla invites the audience to admire the new-found patience with which he bears this. The contrast works to create a different reading of the scene, however, for Scilla's patience and choice of life-style are part of the privilege of the ruler while clowns, being only citizens, still appreciate wealth and suffer the abuses of soldiers. The problematising of the concept of the ruler as private person could be seen to relate to the rhetoric of many counsellors and MPs, and particularly to Elizabeth's speeches to the Commons (see, for example, Neale, 1969, I, p.366).

A more famous, more thorough-going parallelism appears in *Faustus*, where the clowning action mimics in detail the action of the main plot; that has been dealt with enough.

Slightly different in duplicated action, as exemplified in *The Famous Victories of Henry V* where two clowns re-enact the previous scene in which Henry hits the Lord Chief Justice for punishing one of his men. Dericke gets John Cobbler to act the Justice and tells him he has to say the Justice's line: 'to teach you what prerogatives/Mean, I commit you to the Fleet' (ll.389–90); they repeat the scene until John asks the Justice's question 'who am I?' and Dericke forgets the play and tells him he is John the Cobbler. John says he is the Justice, Dericke agrees, and John says the line about prerogatives. The re-presentation of the action, as in the *Faustus* scenes, questions how much the style of presentation (writing and acting) constructs the value or importance placed on what is seen, rather than these being inherent in the event itself. The suggestion that value is not inherent but rhetorically constructed gives particular point to the deliberately repeated line about prerogatives, for the issue of royal prerogative—the inherent rights of personal rule—versus established law was debated not only by political theorists but, perhaps more importantly, in the House of Commons. Even more radically unsettling here is the jokey hiatus over John's acted identity because it foregrounds the activity of representation itself, so that the history is not seen as the exemplum of an absolute truth but as a manufactured representation (this changes later in the text). These undercuttings will be missed for as long as dominant critical discourse talks of clowns as 'comic relief', as if they are a gap in the main action rather than a balance to it: the editor of *Wounds* feels the play goes off at the end and the citizen scene discussed above is simply an effort to please the 'pennie knaves' (why is it that laughter is class situated?). (And anyway, why isn't comic relief necessary in *The Ten Commandments*, *Bent* and *Hi-di-Hi*?)

The foregrounding of representation itself is part of the effect of the third montage, synchronic, in which different elements of the performance text (speech, movement, costume, props, scenery), which are normally assumed to be combined to create a unified effect, may be set in contrast or opposition within a scene: a well-known example is Brecht's direction that the lights should change for the songs in *The*

Threepenny Opera, which gives them a status of non-diegetic commentary (I owe this whole formulation of synchronic montage to Mick Wallis, who puts it less clumsily). We know too little about Elizabethan performances to treat the full range of this montage, but some examples may be suggested. It may be that the scene of a town burning is continued throughout Act III, scene ii of *2 Tamburlaine* (1588/1590): it begins as part of the memorial effects for Zenocrate, but the speech changes to talk of war—if the flames continue, their juxtaposition to the words creates a new ironic meaning to the scene. Easier to locate are synchronic juxtapositions of performance style: in *Locrine*, the starving bleeding Humber has to share the stage with the clown Strumbo who is wearing a 'scotch-cap' and eating his breakfast. When the ghost of Albanact appears and draws a moral about the fate of those who 'intrude themselves in others' lands' (l.1678), although that moral may have important relation to Mary of Scots or the Spanish in the Netherlands, its authority and indeed relevance are limited by Strumbo's unmoralisable presence.

Related to performance style but clearer in written text are changes in speech style. Again modern criticism has tended to deny dramatic effects here by explaining changes in verse form as an immaturity of Elizabethan practice, in that attention is drawn to the words rather than the words simply transparently expressing real complex minds. But a change in verse can alter the way a scene is viewed and hence its meaning (see Elam, 1980, on speech acts): in Act IV of *1 Henry VI* (1590/1623) the besieged Talbot urges his son to flee; the scene that opened in blank verse suddenly shifts into stichomythia between father and son. Whereas the narrative action and Talbot's opening speech concentrated on the idea of haste, the formal change points up a moment that differs from the flow of 'real' events (like Brecht's lighting changes): it is the moment at which the historical Talbot becomes the figure of English mythology. It may be that different voices were used for different styles of speech, for the text of *Edward I* labels a speech 'Queene Elinors speeche' and in *The True Tragedy* after a long soliloquy Richard finishes and changes into prose with a new mood, this change being marked by the printer with a repeat of the speech heading. In both cases the typography seems to suggest that the printed text is thought of as a series of separate speech activities rather than a group of consistent characters expressing themselves through speech. This attitude may be informed by performing style.

Eisenstein claimed that 'it is precisely the *montage* principle, as distinguished from that of *representation*, which obliges spectators themselves to *create* and the montage principle, by this means, achieves that great power of inner creative excitement in the *spectator* which distinguishes an emotionally exciting work from one that stops without going further than giving information or recording events' (Eisenstein, 1968, p.37). We cannot know how Elizabethan audiences responded; for Eisenstein and his audiences much of the excitement of montage was presumably produced by its challenge to a dominant mode of realistic representation, which the Elizabethan theatre did not have. Such a theory does, however, make possible a more rich and exciting reading for the modern viewer than do theories of comic relief, immature incoherence and irresponsible joy in words, although many such arguments are legitimated by (highly suspect) assertions about the taste of Elizabethans and the spirit of the age. My last example of synchronic montage is chosen to suggest how the mode of representation (I use the word differently from Eisenstein) enriches the narrative of action.

To have finished with the example of *1 Henry VI* would have been to show montage being used, typically, by Shakespeare to mystify the nationalist hero Talbot. Since, however, I have argued that Elizabethan theatre can also be critical of dominant ideology, I shall take the scene from *The Troublesome Reign* in which Hubert attempts to carry out King John's order to blind his prisoner Prince Arthur. The sequence of events is Hubert instructing his flunkies, Arthur entering and being bound to a chair, Hubert threatening him then giving him the royal letter to read, Arthur debating with Hubert about his obedience and condemning him, Hubert feeling strife in his conscience. The episodes are marked by verbal style changes, although the action is continuous. When Arthur enters, prose is replaced by a blank verse that is full of

ironies, with Hubert's treacherous courtesy in inviting
Arthur for a walk and Arthur's delight in a change of scene,
not wanting to 'lose the pleasure of the eye' (1.1407[1]). The
ironies depend on noticing an untrustworthy relationship
between speech and reality. The attention to language
becomes an event in the diegesis, for Hubert threatens the
captive Arthur in alliterative verse: 'listen words of woe,/
Harmful and harsh, hell's horror to be heard' (1.1421–2), and
Arthur complains: 'thou wrong'st my youth with words of
fear:/'Tis hell, 'tis horror' (1.1430–1). This blatant alliteration
in fact does not say the central task that Hubert has to
perform, and he gives Arthur the letter to read. This is
followed by stichomythia debate about the legal status of the
king's command, which marks the scene as a study of the
operation of tyranny. But the speech montage foregrounds
not a legal issue but a clash between language and person,
more specifically between royal language and private person.
The cue phrase to seize Arthur is 'God save the king', a
conventional salute not an expressive utterance; Hubert
cannot *say* what the king has told him to do, and his
threatening alliteration is marked diegetically as hesitation (in
character terms) and redundancy—Arthur says: 'If it must
needs be done,/Act it and end it' (1.1432–3). The most
natural-sounding speech (because syntax tends to follow
everyday speech order) comes after Arthur has read the letter,
which sets up a major contrast between the royal command,
signalled as written object, and 'real' private thoughts. The
ideological effect of the scene is to privilege the personal real
against the absent and unreal (non-expressive) king. Thus the
legal debate over royal power does not convince Hubert, but
after Arthur curses him he is apparently so moved by an inner
force that his linguistic control falters:

> I faint, I fear. My conscience bids desist.
> 'Faint' did I say? 'Fear' was it that I named?
> My king commands; that warrant sets me free;
> But God forbids, and he commandeth kings;
>
> (1.1511–4)

The inspection of his own speech, together with the chopped
syntax, presents a picture of the personal 'real' which consists
of feelings that pre-exist speech but which recognise God.

When Hubert thinks the king's warrant sets him free, the speech montage has already shown that what it really does is to trap him personally into artificial speeches, to let an absent monarch suppress his private emotions. Thus freedom cannot be produced from royal warrants, but only from the private conscience that acts with God. This statement affirms the stance taken by those like Peter Wentworth who opposed Elizabeth in the name of freedom of speech in the Commons, or puritan ministers who claimed to act on God's word (and indeed on similar grounds Paulet, the gaoler of Mary of Scots, refused to act on Elizabeth's instructions to kill Mary secretly).

The discovery of Hubert's conscience is, however, complicated, for the speech in which Arthur curses him and invokes heavenly disapproval is highly rhetorical, a noticeable contrast to Arthur's private thoughts. Arthur could be said to be producing the right speech for the right occasion, as a good rhetorician. But this unsettles the discourse of the personal, because although Hubert claims really to feel God this claim is itself placed within a rhetorical strategy, something that is as much a construction as the king's letter (although it is not, of course, an object). The reality of Hubert's emotional response is not to be questioned, but its claim to be the real freedom is. The personal can be seen to be never free from rhetorical constructions: the scene thus potentially contradicts the ideological position that its project is to adopt. Arthur's rhetoric works as persuasion, whereas Hubert's threatening alliteration is crude and does not work. Within the economy of the scene Arthur is the one really qualified for rule because he can move his audience; the king is a document and a conventional phrase, and Hubert has problems with language. In its use of a rhetorical hierarchy the scene displays its unwillingness to affirm the implications of an ideology of the personal which questions the validity of any rhetorical and hierarchical structure.

It can readily be argued that an audience in general would not have noticed these problems foregrounded by structuring; we can't know either way. What I do think necessary is to move the discussion away from the events of the diegesis, where problems about rhetoric and appearance are the concerns of fictional characters, and to explore how far the audience/performance relationship is problematised and consciously investigated.

(iv) The audience looking back

There are plenty of narratives which present the audience/performance relationship. A famous one in *Friar Bacon* has Bacon show Prince Edward through his magic mirror how his far-off friend Lacy is wooing Margaret for him. Bacon is the Presenter: 'mark the comedy', the mirror shows the mimetic action, Edward is the audience. The mirror can show Lacy's innermost thoughts when he decides to woo Margaret for himself and it arouses Edward's passionate desire to stab the performers. Yet for the real, off-stage, audience their comic 'mirror's' picture is none too plain: when Lacy justifies his own actions by saying that Edward is only trying to trick Margaret, he is also making a proper critique of the prince who had already disguised himself as his own servant. The moral structure is not clear, but the power relations are: Margaret, the object of all the wooing, is the only one who knows none of the truth; all of the truth is known by Edward, who uses his princely wealth to persuade Bacon to stop Lacy and Margaret's marriage. Although he cannot stab the mirror, he can arrange the reality that the mirror shows. As Presenter, Bacon does more than show the mirror scene: he makes possible the princely intervention in real events. The whole scene suggests that debate about what theatre shows is finally controlled by the power structure of the society within which theatre is a small part.

The *Friar Bacon* scene is announced as a play-within-a-play scene, but scepticism about the visually or verbally presented is written into a number of plots. In *Edward I* the Welsh spy David wants to confirm English trust in him, so he instructs his friends, who have 'captured' him, during a siege that 'when you parle on the walls,/Make show of monstrous tyranny you intend/To execute on me' (ll.813–15). The stage directions in the next scene say David is stabbed in the arms and shoulders, shown hot pincers, has his nose cut; he yells in pain. The acting out of this makes it more or less indistinguishable from stage violence which is to be taken for real, except that the audience knows it is fake here. It raises problems as to whether David is 'really' hurt for the good of the cause or whether it is all illusion: the reality of stage violence depends more on the way an audience chooses to view it than on its own characteristics as representation. As with the *Friar Bacon* scene, illusion is situated within the power relations which are real. Thus, in another Peele play, *The Battle of Alcazar*, a dead leader is re-invented:

> in this apparel as he died,
> My noble brother will we here advance
> And set him in his chair with cunning props,
> That our barbarians may behold their king
> And think he doth repose him in his tent.
>
> (ll.1242–6)

Presumably they used the 'dead' real actor. An audience that did not regard themselves as barbarians would not mistake the illusion.

Peele's text here demonstrates how illusion may be used without actually fooling the audience. There are other instances when a spectacle is staged in all its apparent reality and plenitude, yet turns out to be something other than it seemed. For instance, the chivalric pomp and triumph of the entry from battle with Balthazar captive in *The Spanish Tragedy* quickly becomes a plain haggle about money and rank; the triumphant processions of the rival tyrants in *Wounds* soon fall into an ever-shifting sequence of victories and defeats; the emotional fullness of Tamburlaine's mourning pageant for Zenocrate switches into instructions about warfare. This method of working potentially teaches through experience in that it engages the audience with the spectacular fullness and then gradually alienates, empties, that fullness. Such an emptying happens literally at the opening of *1 Henry VI* when Henry V's funeral is interrupted by messengers from France and the mourners put off mourning robes and leave the stage. (Shakespeare's pageants are, however, ambivalent in that the later funeral processions for Salisbury, Bedford and Young Talbot bear the fullness of nationalist sentiment, uncritically (as they do in *Edward III*); processing and tableau kneeling are used as aesthetic organising devices throughout *Titus Andronicus*, creating a satisfyingly balanced whole but not investigating illusionism.)

The use of experience of the deceptiveness of pageants matches the use of experience to judge the truth of what characters say or report (which I looked at earlier). The scepticism is sometimes embodied in virtuous characters— Edmund, Talbot—who don't believe deception; the shifting meanings of words are foregrounded in the common dramatic technique of selecting and repeating key words—'policy' throughout *Jew* (see Babb, 1957), 'free' in its final moments, 'right' in *The Troublesome Reign*, perhaps 'terms' in *Tamburlaine*, 'pleasure' in *Faustus*. Such measuring of words and appearances against experience (as opposed to giving them automatic belief) may be said to be in line with the attitude of new scientific thought and of sceptical philosophy (see Hill, 1965 and Haydn, 1950). Machiavelli wrote of the political usefulness of keeping 'the semblance of the old forms' in the state because 'men in general are more affected by what a thing appears to be than by what it is, and are frequently influenced more by appearances than by the reality' (Machiavelli, 1531, I, p.272). Montaigne writes similarly of the mystery of law and traditional belief: 'Laws are now maintained in credit, not because they are essentially just, but because they are laws. It is the mystical foundation of their authority—they have none other—which avails them much.' (Montaigne, 1603, III, p.377) Many play plots would seem to encourage scepticism about appearances, especially the 'forms' of the state; their portrayal of illusion and lies within power relations may question the 'credit' that maintains the law, and may replace idealism and mystique with pictures of human competition. The sharp juxtapositions of triumph and defeat that the Elizabethan theatre imitated from Seneca present a world of continual flux and change: Cosroe exits triumphant in one scene and re-enters wounded and cowed in the next; of the defeated Abdelmelec it is said: 'of a manly man/Lo, in a twinkling, a senseless stock we see' (*Alcazar*, ll.1231–2). The Elizabethan theatre specialised in those 'twinklings' of transformation; change was a major source of its pleasure. Its technical innovations created sudden and shock effects, it continually explored new ways of using the stage space: *Titus* begins with a tableau above and below and progresses to corpses discovered in holes, Belimperia's letter suddenly falls from above, *A Looking Glass for London and England* (c.1590/1594) has an arbour spring up from the stage. In pageants and court plays the gallery was used for divine figures, in *1 Henry VI* it is repeatedly occupied by opposing armies, Earl Rivers and Belimperia are imprisoned in it, Marlowe puts devils in it. Where court plays addressed a chief spectator, complex groupings of asides simultaneously address different sectors of the audience. The technological advances of the courtly stage mainly concerned scenery, the devices used to create a sense of fixed specific place, with eventually Inigo Jones using perspective to align the whole show with one chief spectator. On the professional stage the images of the world were of flux, sudden change, impermanence.

But although a neat parallel can be made between stage practice and, say, Agrippa's sceptical suggestion that law and doctrine of manners are mutable, shifting in time and place, it is more difficult to argue that an audience was critically conscious of the act of representation. My examples so far have been diegetic, and it could be countered that an audience, wrapped up in the narrative, would be in no position to extrapolate from the problems of fictional characters. In other words, I need to demonstrate that the theatre reflects on itself as theatre, thus making that consciousness of representation. Examples are few, but there is a famous story of Tarlton the clown playing in *Famous Victories*. He stepped into the part of Lord Justice whom Henry hits on the ear: the actor playing Henry hit him hard, which made people laugh because they knew it was Tarlton. When he re-appeared in the next scene as the clown, he was told about the hitting of the judge and he improvised a reply: 'it could not but be terrible to the judge, when the report so terrifies me, that methinks the blow remains still on my cheek that it burns again' (Bullough, 1962, p.290). The interplay between actor and role caused much laughter: the audience's pleasure was derived from the combination of diegesis and metadramatic knowledge (see, too, Bullithrumble's joke about Corcut and his page: 'these are, as a man should say,

beggars' (*Selimus*, l.1970), which plays on the attributed
social status of actors). The written text of this same scene in
Famous Victories creates an opening for a similar interplay,
when Dericke forgets that John Cobbler is re-enacting the
role of Lord Justice and in answer to the Justice's question
'who am I?' tells him he is John the Cobbler; John has to say
he is the Justice and Dericke says 'thou saist true, thou art
indeed' (l.413). What John says is 'true' within their game, is
not true within the play-world, but possibly true in a theatre
that practised regular doubling of roles. A proper study of
doubling might, as I suggest elsewhere, make all sorts of
ironies: these ironies would depend on metadramatic knowledge operating simultaneously with interest in the diegesis.
(Sider, 1979, suggests that the boy actor of Arthur in *The
Troublesome Reign* doubles Henry, who is crowned king at
the end—so that in Henry's crowning an audience sees the
vindication of Arthur, who was persecuted by John; we
know that the Presenter actor doubled the Governor of
Lisbon in *Alcazar*, which gives more weight to the Governor's 'correct' censuring of Stukeley's expedition to win
Ireland from the English; in *Three Ladies* Love is doubled by
the actor of Lucre, and the effect aids the sense of a corrupted
Love in the play. See also Brooke, 1966, on doubling in
Cambises; and Holland, 1979, on the interplay between actor
and role on the Restoration stage.)

A different form of interplay is written into the words of
the Chorus in *Edmund Ironside*: he appears as if a soldier to
describe the battles of Edmund and Canutus:

> The way is long and I am waxen faint.
> I fain would have you understand the truth
> And see the battles acted on the stage,
> But that their length will be too tedious;
> Then in dumb-shows I will explain at large
> Their fights, their flights and Edmund's victory;
> For as they strived to conquer and to kill,
> Even so we strive to purchase your good will.
>
> (ll.967–74)

He begins by acting the part of an exhausted soldier and
representation is said to be truth; but theatrical necessity

requires dumb-shows, to admit which is another form of truth. The 'I' shifts from being a soldier to being a player; the battling Saxons referred to as 'they' are at the same time the group of players, 'we'. The 'truth' that the stage must show to the audience coexists with the 'good will' that must flow from the audience to the stage. This example does not make a jokey pleasure of the interplay between actor and role, but if we ask of it John Cobbler's Justice's question, 'who am I?', the answer is as uncertain.

I have raised the issue of the possible self-reflexivity of the stage because, if the critics are to say that Marlowe's texts are ironic (as they tend to do now), then they have to be able to argue that the irony was noticed. To take the case of *Tamburlaine*: the play could be seen as an ironic investigation of the construction of heroism, in particular exploring the idea that rhetoric creates personal reputation which can be found in the moralised biographies of *The Mirror for Magistrates*: 'belike quoth one, this Richard [Earl of Cambridge] was but a little man, or else little favoured of writers, for our Chronicles speak very little of him' (*The Mirror*, 1559–87, p.142). His stature depends on writers. Similarly Cambini says if Tamburlaine 'had with him some man of excellent learning and wisdom, who mought with his writing have celebrated the great enterprises that he did, there is no doubt but that he mought have been numbered among the chief and principal captains' (Cambini, 1562, p.5). The play has Tamburlaine publicise himself, and his rhetoric is powerful: when Cosroe meets him Tamburlaine outlines his ambitions in a speech full of grandiose imagery, at the end of which Theridamas points out to Cosroe: 'You see, my lord, what working words he hath' (II.iii.25). Although Cosroe wears the crown, the rhetoric projects Tamburlaine as the more powerful figure; what, of course, it does not do is to argue that morally he is to be approved of. Diegetically the rhetoric is offset against brutality; a developed scepticism about rhetoric and about the ability of words to invent the person would have to reflect on drama itself as rhetorical structure. But it is impossible to show that Alleyn the actor followed the practice of Tarlton the clown by creating interplay with Tamburlaine the role. On the other hand, the written text does set up occasions when separation between performance and representation could be marked. The prologue speaks, conventionally, of the play as 'tragic glass'; at the end Tamburlaine invites those on stage, and perhaps the audience, to see the corpses as 'objects fit for Tamburlaine,/ Wherein as in a mirror may be seen/His honour, that consists in shedding blood' (V.ii.411–13). Temporarily Tamburlaine the character becomes Tamburlaine the Presenter, referring to Tamburlaine in the third person (whereas a line earlier he spoke of 'my') and using the mirror image and the idea of decorum ('fit'): the lines have ironic effect, with the blood questioning the decorum, but that irony is extended to the whole practice of representing through the foregrounded split between character and Presenter—a split which, if the Chorus of *Edmund Ironside* is any guide, was always potential in the interplay between actor and role.

In performance conditions where an audience shouted back at the stage, all sorts of provocative posturing could be suggested; Theridamas's invitation to *see* (not 'hear') Tamburlaine's 'working words' could extend beyond the diegesis, could even taunt an audience to be seen to be hushed, could anyway point out the *performance*. Certainly the oppositions within the narrative would reinforce any self-reflexivity of the drama, and as such that constitutes a precise critique of a state that printed descriptions of its pageants and its tortures, that printed the sincere speeches of its monarch—after she had carefully corrected them. The Elizabethan state continually presented its own state discourse, but without reflecting on it as rhetorical strategy.

We have lost a further device which may have undercut or ironised representation, for *Tamburlaine* was originally presented with clowning scenes—and who knows but that they may have worked as the ones in *Faustus* do? Those clowning scenes were removed by the printer: 'I have (purposely) omitted and left out some fond and frivolous gestures, digressing (and in my poor opinion) far unmeet for the matter, which I thought might seem more tedious unto the wise . . . though (haply) they have been of some vain conceited fondlings greatly gaped at, what times they were showed upon the stage in their graced deformities: nevertheless, now, to be mixtured in print with such matter of worth, it should prove a great disgrace to so honourable and stately a history.' (Epistle, ll.8–17) All the factors of class, order and form emerge in this fascinating part of the printed *Tamburlaine* book. The printer, Richard Jones, is making a product for the 'wise', that is the literate; and in doing so he shapes it to observe the rules proper to its artistic kind, a 'history' or 'tragical discourse'. With Sidney, Jones cannot recognise mixed form as proper or coherent form. The shape that pleases fondlings, those who watch, has to be altered to suit the wise, who buy and read; the book is after all a class object.

In altering *Tamburlaine*, Jones was only doing what printers regularly did to plays in order to make them books. *Jocasta* (1566/1573) was printed with marginal notes said to be begun 'at request of a gentlewoman who understood not poetical words or terms' (p.159), but these notes are less concerned with poetical terms than with the moral meanings of the text. For the reader they fix a unitary interpretation. Similarly in the book of *The Misfortunes of Arthur* it was possible to print explanations of what the dumb-shows meant, and the play's main author, Thomas Hughes, uses the opportunity of printing to correct alterations made to the performance: 'where some of the actors either helped their memories by brief omission: or fitted their acting by some alteration' (p.224). The book of the play therefore becomes the most complete, most authoritative, version of the text, fixed for all time, ordered: not, in fact, a version but the real thing.

As a literate and upper-class man, Hughes could see to the printing of his own play. The plays of the professional theatres were not generally destined to be books, and were only flogged to printers in times of hardship. Their medium was performance. In making plays into books printers did more than fix them in print, they fixed them in meaning. The title page of *The True Tragedy* speaks of 'a lamentable end of Shore's wife, an example for all wicked women'. On the model of moralised biographies, part of the play is made into an exemplum; but the printer's title-page wording suppresses the sympathetic handling of Jane Shore within the narrative, and indeed the whole critique of moral hypocrisy. Other textual framing devices, such as prologues and epilogues, can also be printers' additions: *Locrine* was given an epilogue between performance and printing which praises Elizabeth, although the play has moments of political ambiguity; it may be that the verses prefixed to *The Troublesome Reign* which refer to *Tamburlaine* were added in the press; act division and title were imposed on the old play *The Wars of Cyrus* (1576–7) to make a *Tamburlaine*-type play of it when it was printed in 1594. In these cases additions are turning the playtexts into proper books, with a full apparatus of compliment and (possibly lucrative) intertextual reference. My last example is Danter's printing of the anonymous *Life and Death of Jack Straw*, in which a section of the text is isolated by being set on a new page, in a new fount and headed with a printer's colophon. This section is 'The King's Pardon delivered by Sir John Morton to the rebels': thus emphasised by its isolation from the narrative it becomes an exemplary text for the king's relationship with the commons. In the rest of the text, which would all be part of the performance, there is clowning parody of official royal language and fooling with the ideas of punishment and pardon. Against this, the technical resources of print are used to privilege one section of the text and thus fix an interpretation.

The efforts to make the authoritative text are continued now by academic editors rather than printers. The work to produce the best possible text involves selecting particular textual readings from other possible variants, which may for example consist of revisions made at different dates by anyone connected with the production process, or variations between printings; supposed interpolations may be excluded and conjectured phrases included. What is constructed is a text that may never have been performed, read or written at any one time; a text that exists for the first time in the book in which it is published. Decisions about interpolations and variants are often based on assumptions about theatrical form and literary decorum: thus the repeated efforts to marginalise or remove the comic scenes in *Faustus*, and others like them, by explaining them as interpolations by others unknown, or as unworthy attempts by the author to please groundlings. The contempt for the comic in particular and performance in general echoes Puttenham's snobbery (about class as well as taste): 'the common people, who rejoice much to be at plays and interludes, and besides their natural ignorance have at all such times their ears so attentive to the matter and their eyes upon the shows of the stage, that they take little heed to the cunning of the rhyme, and therefore be as well satisfied with that which is gross as with any other finer and more delicate' (Puttenham, 1589, p.82). The book-centred view continues in the undervaluing of performance work and the privileging of a mystique of 'scholarship' which becomes more apparent the higher you progress through academic institutions.

This insufficiently polemical reflection on books means to conclude a chapter that argues for the positive advantages of the denigrated mixed form of Elizabethan drama. It is possible to suggest that form not only addressed audiences as frivolous groundlings but also qualified them to make judgements about what was shown—judgements about a rhetoric that claims to be authoritative and pageantry that reflects the hierarchy of state, judgements about a vision of the world that says it is based on law, truth and order. These audiences were described in official documents as lewd, unchaste, disorderly, seditious. That description is part of the operation of a literary and social order which not only theorised about correct decorum but also chopped off the puritan pamphleteer Stubbs's right hand.

Note

1. The numeral in front of this and subsequent line references to *The Troublesome Reign* indicates the part number (ed. Everitt, 1965).

CHAPTER 3

Making Persons

(i) Signs of the private person

Dramatic characterisation in the 1580s is supposed to be a bit of a mess. The playtexts are seen to be caught between the didactic presentation of Moralities and the imitation of real psychology which Shakespeare invents. This argument is being put at the time I write by a series of television programmes by John Barton and RSC actors, in which extracts from pre-Shakespearean plays are read in silly voices to show how unreal they are, and extracts from Shakespeare are read earnestly to show how 'natural' and real is the achievement of his blank verse. What marks the real, apparently, is that the actor recognises what is portrayed and vouches for it, claiming a basic human feeling that transcends class, gender and history; the actor's (historically-specific) experience precedes the text. It is assumed that the play attempts to imitate human psychology, and that, hence, disrupted or incomplete characterisation, foregrounded writing in the text, repeated phrases or gestures, all constitute failed character-drawing.

To recognise a character or situation as real from your experience and to view all textual strategies as expressions of this convincing reality is to ignore the specific historical and cultural locations of a text. The written texts of 1580s plays were put together in a culture which had different ideas of the nature and politics of the individual subject than those of the people who currently interpret the plays for performance (just as there are differences of a lesser kind between an RSC interpretation and one, say, at the Vic Theatre, Stoke) (thankfully). The creation and interpretation of character in a text are loaded with various historically-specific ideological values; these values are not seen to be ideological by a reader who assumes them to be reality. In this chapter I do not want to argue whether characters are real or not, but instead to describe some of the devices which indicate subjectivity and then to discuss the values carried by these devices (see Williams, 1981, on soliloquy and Dollimore, 1984, on the problematised subject). Dramatic characterisation can then be located within ideological debate of the 1580s. This discussion is designed principally as an introduction to *Dr Faustus*, which is why it is an all too sketchy treatment of what is a large subject in need of rigorous theorising.

Morality-play figures will often represent single sins and virtues which influence a central figure of mankind, or everyman. The whole playtext displays the inner person as a moral battleground, but does not show any person within society or history. The central figure is a free agent, able to choose the correct moral course; the didacticism works by making the inner person totally knowable as a moral model. Similarly, in moralised biography such as *The Mirror for Magistrates* a person tells the reader of her/his life, attributing its shape to the operation of a particular sin: 'O cursed goods, desire of you hath wrought/All wickedness' says Owen Glendower (ll.139–40). The particular life becomes an example from which the reader can learn: 'note (as it is reason)/How wicked deeds to woeful ends do draw' (Richard Earl of Cambridge, ll.52–3). These speakers are named as real historical figures, so that history is explained not as political or economic power struggle but as the operation either of sin or of fortune on the individual. The dominant image of the mirror works in two ways: first, what it shows is true and complete. The speakers claim to speak from a specific place in history and directly address the editor of *The Mirror* or an author:

> So Higgins if thou write how this my fall befell,
> Place it in Baldwin's *Mirror* with the rest.
> From crazed skull sith here my mind I tell,
> Sith bleeding heart these rueful rhymes expressed,
> This mangled tale beseems my person best.
> (Nicholas Burdet, ll.602–6)

The speaker not only precedes the author but speaks with

complete expressivity: 'We claim as right in truth our minds
to break' 'I may full well on stage supply the place a
while/Till I have plainly laid before your view. . .' (*ibid*.,
ll.12, 16–17). The speaker has to be able to say everything,
otherwise, in this medium, the text would not exist—there is
no other way of telling the story. The mirror, secondly, is
metaphorically held up to the reader or watcher so that they
can examine how far the image in it reflects their own lives;
they make a moral comparison. This image lasts on through
Elizabethan plays: the *Looking Glass for London* presents a
fictional image of the city's corruption; characters in plays
speak of their lives as mirrors.

The presence of the actor on stage immediately complicates
the transparency of moral biography, for that actor is a
person who has an objective social life as the audience does.
This is known even when the actor is temporarily representing only a facet of a person, such as envy. The star's person,
in particular, will pre-exist and be greater than any individual
fictional role he takes on. The conditions of theatrical
production tend to insist on the individual as social being and,
through the presence of the actor, that there is always more to
a person than a necessarily selective fictional characterisation
presents. The social existence of the person is portrayed by
dramas that changed from Moralities to histories or tragedies
and comedies that are set in a material world. The actor can
do what the written medium of the moralised biography
cannot, namely present the actions, gestures, voice of a
person by imitating them. Potentially a contradiction arises
between the mimesis of a person in crisis and the overview
that analyses and draws out the moral lesson to be learned
from that crisis, between the imitator and the presenter. The
Elizabethan actor was both.

Before examining what the inner person is shown to consist
of, I shall look at the tension between mimesis and
presentation in the signalling of the subjectivity of an
individual. Mosby, alone, says: 'Disturbed thoughts drives
me from company/And dries my marrow with their watch-
fulness' (*Arden*, viii. 1–2). Individualism is frequently signalled by a contrast to a full stage, for example a pageant or
tableau: thus Edricus, the villain of *Edmund Ironside*, talks

while the rival armies of Canutus and Edmund march about
and he refers to them and his ambitions. The speech is
articulate and the plans are fully stated; the audience is
privileged to hear what no one else hears, a privilege and
authority announced by the classic villain line: 'no man hears
me'. This presentation of villainous plans is complicated in
Leir's solitary thought:

> O what a combat feels my panting heart
> 'Twixt children's love, and care of commonweal!
> How dear my daughters are unto my soul
> None knows, but he that knows my thoughts
> > and secret deeds.
> > > (*King Leir*, ll.204–7)

In the privilege of its knowledge of what no one else knows,
the audience may be expected to assess Leir's mistake in
placing commonweal second to children (*Gorboduc* and
Misfortunes of Arthur warn royal fathers against this). Yet the
mimetic detail of the 'panting heart' registers the strength of
the emotion, and indeed an audience cannot know *how* dear
the daughters are. The audience has already found the
daughters to be cynical and wicked, so Leir's emotion is both
irrational as well as forcefully present.

The 'panting heart' indicates the presence of an emotion
that is not fully articulated; this presence in the individual is
signalled as a distortion of the element of the performance
that alone carries the capability of moralising, the speech.
Thus when Constance enters there is a gap before she speaks
at all because 'her passions stop the organ of her voice' (*The
Troublesome Reign*, 1.1214), Queen Philippe says 'inward
passions will not let me speak' (*Edward III*, 1.2544). At the
end of her life, Edward I's wicked wife Elinor confesses:

> while this faltering engine of my speech,
> I learn to utter my concealed guilt,
> I may repeat and so repent my sins
> > (*Edward I*, ll.2400–2)

The confession may be expected to operate as moralised
biography, where the faltering speech simply indicates
sincerity. But Elinor says more than the audience so far

knows and more than her disguised husband (one of the confessors) wants to hear. Thus raising questions, it does not operate as the anticipated closure: the faltering has been caused by something hitherto unseen. The irruption of emotion is more startlingly shown early in the play, when at the end of Edward I's huge ceremonial arrival in England the Queen Mother suddenly faints, turning the triumph into apparent 'tragedy'. The faint is caused by extreme emotion in one who is a virtuous figure and had earlier fitly eulogised 'illustrious England'. It is a version of numerous scenes in which the individual feels unable to say anything in the presence of state occasion: here it is designed as surprise, a sudden upstaging of state by that which is inexplicable within the person.

Hooker's *Ecclesiastical Polity* suggests that all men (sic) are influenced by reason, that its text is written into them: 'those men which have no written law of God to show what is good or evil carry written in their hearts the universal law of mankind, the Law of Reason, whereby they judge as by a rule which God hath given unto all men for that purpose' (Hooker, 1593–7, I, p.228). The definition implies complete articulateness, as does moralised biography, and furthermore that in the innermost of the individual is that which is already written, already ordered. 'The general and perpetual voice of men is as the sentence of God himself' (*ibid.*, I, p.176): the voice speaks the sentence which has already been shaped, the judgement which has already been passed. Against this there is a stage practice which signals extreme emotion with speechlessness. When Lectorius prefaces his long speech about Marius's death with the apology: 'Though swoll'n with sighs my heart for sorrow burst,/And tongue with tears and plaints be choked up' (*Wounds*, IV.ii.171–2), Lodge is following a classical practice for labelling emotion; nevertheless, it suggests that the emotion precedes the verbalising and, as we have seen, that emotion can disrupt or even replace the verbalising. Moments of individual feeling are marked as discontinuities in the spoken, as speechlessness or silence.

It would be possible to argue that God's law operates in people through emotion, particularly in the choked speech of the penitent wrong-doer. In some circumstances the ordered discourse of divine law is only too apparent, but in others stage practice stresses that which is unforeseen or non-rational, such as the Queen Mother's faint or, more extendedly, the form of Hieronimo's madness. A clearer case of the inner person being moulded by some natural or divine law is when the individual's subjective feelings articulate with an audience's expectations. The rebellious Mordred, for example, says: 'I inwards feel my fall./My thoughts misgive me much: down terror: I/Perceive mine end' (*Misfortunes*, II.iv.81–3). The performance of terror is simply the label that Mordred is being worked on by the inexorable moral law, and there is not much stage space for its mimetic enactment. Compare, however, King John's apprehension of doom:

> Disturbed thoughts, foredoomers of mine ill,
> Distracted passions, signs of growing harms,
> Strange prophecies of imminent mishaps,
> Confound my wits and dull my senses so
> That every object these mine eyes behold
> Seem instrument to bring me to my end.
> (*The Troublesome Reign*, 2.135–40)

The chaos of the inner person is commented upon by the character, the passions are 'signs', he presents himself as an example. But the character's way of looking at his world is also made problematic: Mordred perceives clearly his 'end' (which is abstract) whereas John perceives in a new, troubled, way the 'objects' around him; there is the opening for the mimesis of a changed looking. The difference is between a character who says he is in turmoil, which he can morally analyse, and a character whose relationship with his world changes. The person can be posited as something more than the passive site of operation of divine law, the workings of which may be rationally described or presented; the person who acts out a different looking at the world is a person whose gaze cannot be shared by the audience, who becomes other, without the assumptions shared between presenter and those presented to. Richard III talks of the fearful shadow which pursues him: he is an example of a tyrant being satisfyingly punished, but his reaction to the shadow makes his inner life mysterious and opaque, in that the actor's performance of an emotional response designates the reality of precisely what the audience cannot see; thus the performance challenges the supposedly authoritative all-seeing look of the audience. Again the mimesis exists in tension with the presentation. A less mimetically developed version of such a scene preserves the presenter intact: when Porrex tries to demonstrate his grief for killing Ferrex he exclaims: 'Oh! would it mought as full appear to sight/As inward grief doth pour it forth to me' (*Gorboduc*, IV.ii.38–9). This admits the non-showing, whereas the Richard III actor claims he really can see shadows.

When the individual's looking at the world suddenly changes, or when emotion inexplicably irrupts, the assumption of inner order in the person becomes questionable. To draw together some of the signs for individual subjectivity, and to progress to another stage of the analysis, I want to look at an early scene in *The Troublesome Reign*. The brothers Philip and Robert are quarreling as to who is the rightful heir to their father; Robert accuses the older Philip of being King Richard's bastard. Philip is asked in this royal tribunal who his father is and twice he defends his mother's honour. On the third question he cannot answer: in this public gathering he is in a 'trance', a 'dream'. Then he begins a long aside, speaking in Latin at first. The foreign language is another marker, besides the 'speechless' trance, of the break between individual and society (when Scilla addresses his genius he uses Latin; when Jone discovers her bastardy she breaks into Italian). While Philip speaks there is no other action; the action is now within him, and it is signalled as inner because no one else on stage hears it.

Within the narrative the speaker's identity is a social problem. The text foregrounds this by disallowing the speaker a unitary subjectivity: 'What sayst thou, Philip?' 'Methinks I hear a hollow echo sound/That Philip is the son unto a king' (1.261, 265–6). The speaker addresses Philip as 'thou'; 'I' hears a message about Philip from an echo. Later in the speech the name is lost. The speech is constructed of two different modes: a steadily building series of paired lines ('The whistling leaves upon the trembling trees/Whistle in concert I am Richard's son' (ll.267–8), and similar natural images); then a set of questions ('Why, how now? Knowest thou where thou art?/And knowest thou who expects thine answer here?' (ll.282–3)) in which he worries about the loss of land if he denies his claimed father, and about his status in society and the rank of his audience. In the questions the speaker addresses himself as 'thou' but in the earlier section there is a sense of 'I', which is acknowledged by echoes, birds, leaves — by 'nature'. The discourse of paternity is spoken by natural voices, uniting the speaker with the person presented into the single 'I'. In the concern with matters of social position the speaker is split from the person presented, who is addressed as 'thou'. When 'Philip' tries to deny his bastardy he cannot speak: 'It will not out. I cannot for my life/Say I am son unto a Falconbridge' (ll.291–2): the presenter's articulateness is now conditional upon the fictional identity, the Bastard becomes real. When he has acknowledged his true paternity Philip talks much more fluently, his dialogue with his mother is frequently rhymed (with particular repetition, significantly, of 'shame' in her case and 'name' in his). Later in the play Philip the Bastard will be characterised by common-sensical plain speaking.

The scene shows how natural law operates in the individual, despite problems of social rank, and how it constructs identity. Philip would seem to have identity signalled by his speechlessness, his separation from the tableau. But that identity is the site of conflict between natural law and social hierarchy: indeed that identity cannot at first even be expressed by the unitary 'I'. De Mornay explains: 'there is in man a double speech; the one in the mind, which they call the inward speech, which we conceive afore we utter it; and the other the sounding image thereof, which is uttered by our mouth and is termed the speech of the voice; either of both the which we perceive at every word that we intend to pronounce' (De Mornay, 1587, p.267). For the Christian this duality is unproblematic, since God controls the inward speech. For one more sceptical there is nothing either fixed or articulate about the person: 'every human nature is ever in the middle between being born and dying; giving nothing of itself but an obscure appearance and shadow, and an uncertain and weak opinion' (Montaigne, 1603, II, p.364; for a more full account of Montaigne's significance, see Dollimore, 1984). On stage, the split is constructed into the performance, without prioritising the essential or authoritative discourse of God.

The performance of Philip both shows the character and is the character; there is a split between the 'I' who is the subject of what is spoken and the 'I' who does the speaking. This split is necessary to the making of the moralised biography which is spoken by its subject, for an exemplary traitor will describe his own death: thus Henry Percy in *The Mirror* mentions that he was executed: 'This was my hap, my fortune or my fault,/This life I led, and thus I came to naught.' (ll.132–3) The language of *The Mirror for Magistrates* reappears when Earl Rivers defies Richard in *The True Tragedy*: 'The Chronicles, I record, talk of my fidelity, and of my progeny,/Where, as in a glass, you mayst behold thy ancestors and their treachery' (ll.621–2). Earl Rivers is to be killed in the play and the moralising overview provided by the Chronicles exists outside the world of the play; the status of the 'I' who refers to the Chronicles becomes problematic, revealed, perhaps, as the 'I' who speaks the part of Rivers rather than the 'I' who pretends to speak as Rivers. On stage the split is materially apparent in that an actor takes the part of Rivers, whereas in *The Mirror* the speakers are textual fictions. The split is a common feature of Elizabethan dramatic writing. When Marius speaks alone in his exile in the mountains he begins by addressing himself as 'thou'/'thy' and then shifts to 'my'/'I': 'Old Marius finds a world of many hells. . . . But I will quell by virtues of the mind' (*Wounds*, III.iv.18, 20); similarly Acomat begins: 'Advise thee, Acomat, what's best to do', and changes to: 'then he think that I am factious' (*Selimus*, ll.804, 813). In all these examples there is a rationale in the shift. 'Acomat' talks confidently of wooing the Janissaries to his cause with money, but 'I' then wonders what Bajazeth and the bassos will think of the speaker: the change does not only mark doubt setting in, but a different estimate of the speaker's power relations with others: a shift from seeing people as servants of the will of the spectator (to be bought) to being 'other' or oppositional (having an opinion of him). The Marius speaker's 'thou' refers to a past life in society, the 'I' refers to the present solitary comparison of himself to nature; the alternation continues and the speech ends with an echo repeating some of Marius's words, as it were his language spoken by a voice that is 'personless'. Thus the melancholy scene is written as crisis in the identity of Marius, a discovery of new limitations on what is assumed to be 'Marius'. Lastly, Earl Rivers's reference to the Chronicles is produced by the necessity of making two orders of knowledge for the audience—the experience of Richard's acts of cruelty as they happen and the simultaneous judging of his place in history.

Within dominant critical thinking I would guess that the Rivers example would be seen as more clumsy or immature than the other two. More clumsy because the other two could be said to have explanations, consistent with the narratives, for the shifts in pronouns, whereas the Rivers speech unsettles the status of the representation itself. Such critical thinking says that only the portrayal of a subject that is unitary is realistic; and realism is valued as more serious than non-realism. Certainly the Elizabethan theatre did develop towards the portrayal of apparently more unitary subjects, but this development need not be seen as the necessary and inevitable progress of a drama that begins with split subjects. More importantly, the ideological construction and evaluation of the individual should not be seen as silent continuity but as a site of debate, change but not progress. If dominant critical thinking sees the development towards the portrayal of the unitary subject as progress, that says something about the ideological values of that thinking.

I shall first illustrate the change in representation from *Titus Andronicus*, a play that does make an intervention (not necessarily healthy) in Elizabethan practice. Titus, like Hieronimo, is moved by personal feelings and loyalties into a position of opposition to the state. In the great opening scene of Act III he pleads for his sons while senators and judges process by in silence: lying on the ground, 'in the dust I write/My heart's deep languor and my soul's sad tears' (III.i.12–13). Although 'The tribunes hear you not, no man is by,/And you recount your sorrows to a stone' (ll.28–9), Titus nevertheless continues to express his feelings. He admits that the tribunes would not listen to him or pity him anyway, 'yet plead I must'. His poetic speeches are defined not as persuasive rhetoric (there is no one to persuade) nor as narrative information, but as emotional expression which satisfies a need. The imagery works to fill the world with Titus's emotion:

> O earth, I will befriend thee more with rain,
> That shall distil from these two ancient ruins,
> Than youthful April shall with all his show'rs:
>
> (ll.16–18)

The tear-covered stones at his feet seem to weep with him. This filling and subjective transforming of the bare stage threatens, suggests Marcus, to go beyond reason. Titus replies with a metaphorical logic:

> If there were reason for these miseries,
> Then to limits could I bind my woes:
> When heaven doth weep, doth not the earth o'erflow?
>
> (ll.219–21)

The transforming effect of emotion is seen figuratively to redefine his own identity: 'I am the sea;' (l.225). Individual emotion is presented as something that has a logic of its own beyond the rules of reason, and that needs neither audience to listen to it nor social individual to speak it: the metaphor takes over the person. Yet at the same time Titus is a speaker, his speeches dominate the scene. And there *are* people near by to hear him, namely the audience. Lines that hitherto encouraged critical listening—'no man is by', reference to a lack of reason—now cease to have their former provocative metadramatic function. For Titus is not scheming and his emotion has a logic of its own; there is nothing to be judged. The audience is not recalled to a sense of its independent social existence, and the social identity of the speaker is denied. These absences are filled by the poetry which clearly misrecognises the real world yet has a metaphoric logic of its own, that indeed creates the feeling of plenitude of the scene, the sense that everything is expressed just as the stage is literally filled with Titus's words.

Where Titus is more obviously mad is in his dealings with public speech, for example the shooting of arrows with messages on them into the sky. Such an activity is pointless and politically inept; on the other hand, the Act III revelation of personal emotion is not felt to be pointless or powerless. Its point is the revelation of personal emotion: the expression is fluent and full, the inner Titus seems totally knowable. But the plenitude suppresses questions about what constitutes the human subject—what is the 'I' that needs to plead? Is it constructed by natural law or social relations or the interplay of sin and virtue? Why is it always able to express itself fully? Not only are the questions suppressed by metaphor ('I am the sea'), but the audience is not constituted as critical spectator. The poetry is clearly well organised, but its form is unusually consistent through the play so that the sharp contrasts of rhyme, blank verse, prose, etc., which I have argued motivate critical reading, are missing. Notably the audience is 'not there' at the high point of Titus's emotion: the provocative 'no one hears me' line is displaced from the central speaker to the rational by-stander. In place of a critical relationship with a split subject, the audience is offered a view into the non-problematic, depoliticised subjectivity of the central fictional character; and this view feels satisfyingly full because everything is expressed. The passive audience overhears it all, it gets something for nothing. This is the development to which *Titus* contributed; and it is not necessarily a healthy one, though it goes down a bomb at A level and Stratford.

(ii) Private and public persons

The problem with *Titus Andronicus* lies not with the political meanings of the story, but with the relationship between audience and text produced by its fictional strategies. (I am employing a distinction between story and mode of repre- sentation that Toril Moi clarifies in her review of the differences between Anglo-American and Continental femin- ist critics, see Moi, 1983). The story of a tormented individual (especially a father, for which see later) in a repressive state is what might be expected from the backlash of the late 1580s;

especially the imaging of the brutal censorship of speech in the person of Lavinia may be taken to typify the activities of an Elizabethan state that closed down printing presses, and imprisoned and interrogated those who defended freedom of speech. The concentration on the personal suffering of Titus may partly be shaped by the ideological construction of the 'rights' for which people suffered — freedom of speech, freedom of worship—as personal. But the representation of the story tends to make Titus's speech expressive and sincere and his inner person knowable; it tends not to foreground as a problem the definition of what this individual is and of how he is constructed in society. Yet the definition of the individual was an ideological battleground.

Writing from an Anglican position, Hooker said that all people were influenced by reason: 'The Law of Reason or human Nature is that which men by discourse of natural Reason have rightly found out themselves to be all for ever bound unto in their actions' (Hooker, 1593–7, I, p.182). Nature, says Wilson, 'is a right that fantasy hath not framed, but God hath graffed' (Wilson, 1560, p.32). Reason is made natural; its law can simply be discovered by any individual thinking rationally; all individuals find that they are linked together by a law that informs all their actions. They are indeed written upon by this law and are thus part of a whole text. The wrong individual is generally defined as one whose private desires or passions prevent her/him from hearing the discourse of reason or acting on it. Usury, in *The Three Ladies of London*, says 'Let country, pity, love, conscience and all go in respect of myself' (p.316). The placing of 'country' first in the list is important since the individual who denies the operation of the law of reason denies links with others and disrupts community. This is why *The Mirror for Magistrates* can explain rebellion in terms of a fault in the person, such as excessive greed or envy. *The Misfortunes of Arthur*, performed before Elizabeth, attributes the cause of civil war between Mordred (the Mary of Scots figure) and Arthur his father to irrational desire in Mordred:

> I hate a peer,
> I loathe, I irk, I do detest a head.

B'it Nature, be it Reason, be it Pride,
I love to rule:

(I.iv.112–15)

He is told he is destroying the realm he seeks to rule, increasing 'the rage that long hath reigned' (II.ii.60). Personal rage inflames state rage; personal metaphors describe politics and vice versa:

Peace hath three foes encamped in our breasts,
Ambition, Wrath and Envy: which subdued,
We should not fail to find eternal peace.

(III.iv.16–18)

Watching the performance was the monarch whose image was constructed by propaganda as disciplined, controlled, chaste as opposed to passionate or licentious.

Those who are virtuous behave in line with the interests of the community. Eubulus, the virtuous counsellor in *Gorboduc*, tells how the rebels were by 'common country's care, and private fear/Taught to repent the error of their rage' (V.ii.30–1). *Misfortunes* repeats the image when Arthur addresses his allies: 'to Arthur's cause you join/In common care, to wreak my private wrongs' (III.iii.103–4) (and it is ironised in *Edward II* when Warwick talks of 'our country's cause' (II.v.23)). The recognition of a 'common cause' suppresses description of the state as a contestable grouping of interests; not an inegalitarian hierarchy but something common to all. The individual who is virtuous is at one with the state's interests; under the rule of a tyrant, Turkillus and Leofric are 'Born Englishmen, but strangers to ourselves' (*Edmund*, l.360). When Philip the Bastard learns his true identity in *The Troublesome Reign* he becomes a champion of English arms against the French, and of Protestantism against the monasteries. On the battlefield Philip shows honest natural emotion in response to French bragging, and it is the naturalness of his identity which carries a central political message in the play. He sides with John against the barons who oppose him, he always fights popery though the barons may temporarily flirt with it: he is the guardian of a concept of Protestant English monarchy. His defence of the king is correct because John, despite all else, is the natural king. Against the barons who threaten to elect a foreign king, John says:

> A mother, though she were unnatural,
> Is better than the kindest step-dame is:
> Let never Englishmen trust foreign rule.
>
> (2.275–7)

The mother can never really be unnatural in that she is kin, but she may act temporarily against the natural law of her role. This is a defence of monarchy, clearly, and the caution against foreign rulers had particular point in the Elizabethan succession debates. More interesting is its reflection on the Bastard whose illegitimacy might seem unnatural but is in fact, once he owns it, an affirmed naturalness. It is this person, outside the grouping of barons, independent of established family, who makes kings and defends English Protestant nationalism. The independent agent defends the personal ruler and upholds the myth of nation, all of which is more 'natural' than the barons: it is an ideological affirmation of absolutist structures.

A definition of the person which opposes Hooker's stresses the motive of self-preservation in the individual. Bodin mentions its influence: 'in man mother nature engenders first the desire for self-preservation, then little by little due to awe of Nature's workings drives him to investigate their causes' (Bodin, 1566, pp.15–16). The viewpoint Bodin is essentially rejecting here, with his imagery of 'mother' nature and the awe, is that of Machiavelli, who denied the existence of natural law. To deny that individuals might share a communal understanding of good and reason, to deny that each individual may have written into them a moral intuition, is to knock away at the dominant ideology of quiescence within hierarchy. Instead, individuals fight to preserve or advance themselves in a world that is always competitive. Machiavelli defined the human will as anarchic and anti-social, which is why forms of government have to be invented in order to limit chaos. But that government has to be enforced by material means (though Machiavelli says that ideologies of liberty and religion play their part in strengthening a state against inner disintegration: Machiavelli, 1531, I, pp.220, 243ff.) and laws have to be specifically constructed. The relations between individual and state are not naturalised, law is not part of nature, all has to be constructed; thus human institutions are in a continual flux of decay and rebirth. Machiavelli's theories question the dominant ideologies of Elizabethan England, hence they were devalued, misrepresented and opposed (like communism now in Anglo-America). The stage Machiavel plays its part in the misrepresentation, for the individualist who stands alone on stage and plots is portrayed in opposition to community and is loaded with markers of evilness. Thus any dramatist who wished to explore Machiavellian ideas had to displace the theory from the individualist villain. A canny strategy is that of *The Jew of Malta* which has the Machevil of the prologue claim he is favoured by Barabas the Jew, which directs the audience to look out for Barabas's Machiavellianism. But a concentration on the Jew misses the method by which Ferneze preserves the state of Malta: his combination of military strength and treacherous 'policy', and his legitimation of these by reference to heaven, are rather more Machiavellian than Barabas, especially since they are not recognised as such. The whole play is arguably more influenced by Machiavelli in its study of the relationship between religion and state interests, and in its refusal to naturalise hierarchy or state, than in its portrait of Barabas. Again, a Machiavellian influence could be seen in those endings of texts by Marlowe and his contemporaries which refuse a sense of natural closure and fittingness and instead make pictures of compromise and foregrounded relations of power.

The Machiavellian theory of the individual is more materialist than Hooker's theory in that it stresses the determinants of economic and social power. Such an outlook may be of wider currency in the period than is generally allowed for: for example, in the Life of Nicholas Burdet, added to *The Mirror for Magistrates* in 1587, the speaker begins by talking of 'Fortune's guile' but ends by explaining his fall in battle in France thus:

In England was the fault, though we did feel the smart.
While they at home at bate for strife and honours were,
They lost abroad of Normandy the greater part.

                                              (ll.589–91)

His fall is not caused by a personal sin, but by a competition
for political power that is outside his control. (A world of
constant competition not ordered by natural law is what the
Turk plays show, as we shall see.) Ramus defines: 'A man is
the subject of riches, poverty, honours, infamy, clothes, and
of his train' (Ramus, 1574, p.31).

A third, and major, definition of the person is that of
puritanism. This has been described in detail elsewhere, so I'll
keep my remarks brief. Puritans (I speak in general)
acknowledged only the authority of the word of God as
contained in the scriptures; it was this divine law, rather than
a law of nature or government, which was to be obeyed. The
puritan emphasis on preaching, reading and debate within
congregations facilitated an individual understanding of this
divine law and personal answerability to it. In cases where the
laws of the state opposed puritan beliefs, as they did during
Whitgift's anti-puritan campaigns, the individual might, and
did, oppose the state on the authority of a personal
understanding of God's word. This opposition is constructed
within the discourse of conscience: 'the conscience of man is
internal, invisible, and not in the power of the greatest
monarch in the world; in no limits to be straitened, in no
bonds to be contained' (Neale, 1969, I, p.214). Thus
Aglionby spoke in 1571 in the Commons, and here was the
location of numerous battles of conscience, one of the most
famous of which was Peter Wentworth's campaign for
freedom of speech against the attempts of the queen's officers
to inhibit debate. Outside the Commons, puritans opposed
the Anglican episcopal order and the magistrates that
supported it. The puritan Robert Browne (1582) defiantly
said: 'The Magistrate's commandment must not be a rule unto
me of this and that duty, but as I see it agree with the Word of
God' (Allen, 1960, p.222). *A Looking Glass for London and
England* shows scenes of various sorts of social corruption
(usurers, lawyers, etc.) in which the corrupt practisers ignore

conscience. Almost halfway through, the play introduces the prophet Jonas who is sent to tell Nineveh of its wickedness; at first he avoids the task, arguing that God will be too strict to those who have not heard of him whereas his own country of Israel, that knows religion, is already sinful and it would go against his conscience to publish their sin to the world. Later he is forced to go to Nineveh, and 'prophets' are invited to see in him an example of necessary obedience to God. Here God's word is set against the individual's sense of patriotism and justice, and has to be acknowledged as greater. The play clearly refers to London as a corrupt city, where puritan ministers were often described as 'prophets'. It urges the individual sent by God to speak even against the will of the most powerful.

In the plays, conscience generally happens to villains, and when they experience its workings they step back into line with the expected natural order. Ragan has 'a hell of conscience' and is worried 'the world should find my dealing out' (*King Leir*, ll.2357, 2360); Richard III experiences a 'hell of life that hangs upon the crown' (*The True Tragedy*, l.1874). Because at these points the villains recognise the evil that the audience knows (the audience has already found out Ragan's dealings), their talk of internal hells is not highlighted as a problem by the texts. Yet Elizabeth attacked puritans because they preached 'they wot not what—that there is no Hell but a torment of conscience' (Neale, 1969, II, p.70). The burden of the attack is one that was continually repeated, that puritans are 'so curious in searching matters above their capacity' (*ibid.*). The idea of an internal hell is one that validates the conscience, and a stress on conscience is part of the puritan emphasis on the ability of the individual to criticise and oppose the state—hence Elizabeth's annoyance. The state's devaluing of opposition was conducted in terms of the discourse of truth, namely that the monarch and her officers spoke what was true and ordered and hence that any opposition was disorderly. Disorderliness in the person was described as the dominance of emotion over reason (for if reason was listened to the individual would admit the correctness of what the state spoke). Thus attempts of MPs to debate forbidden issues were described as frivolous or licentious; Mildmay drew a distinction: 'we may not forget to put a difference between liberty of speech and licentious speech' (*ibid.*, I, p.331). Closing the Parliamentary session in 1571 Sir Nicholas Bacon delivered Elizabeth's message attacking those who 'will thus wilfully forget themselves . . . by frivolous and superfluous speech spending the time' (*ibid.*, I, p.236). Similarly, Hatton spoke of puritans as 'men of a very intemperate humour' (*ibid.*, II, p.198).

By contrast with those whose personal passions were ungoverned, the queen projected herself as one whose private person was disciplined to answer the needs of the state. This strategy was used particularly in answer to criticisms about marriage and succession, 'personal' issues, in 1576. 'Let all men therefore bear their private faults; mine own have weight enough for me to answer for': the idea of a faulty person behind the responsible public self is set up. So she can go on: 'if I were a milkmaid with a pail on my arm, whereby my private person might be little set by, I would not forsake that poor and single state to match with the greatest monarch'. She is, however, a public person: 'for your behalf, there is no way so difficult, that may touch my private person, which I will not well content myself to take' (*ibid.*, I, p.366). The unwillingness to marry is stated but displaced onto the private person; what she will undertake to do is not stated explicitly, but instead is created a reassuring sense of a responsible public person who has others' interests at heart—the image replaces the answer. The apparent openness of the speech is, as in most of Elizabeth's, a product of a very carefully constructed prose. The presentation of the private person here departs slightly from the propaganda that saw personal rule as essentially unknowable, where what 'secret cause or scruple there may be in the hearts of princes, it is not for all people to know' (*ibid.*, I, p.194), where Aylmer (1559) justifies Elizabeth as a female ruler on 'some secret purpose' of God (Raab, 1964, p.13). For puritan rhetoric could also claim God's purposes working in the individual. It was not so much inner truth as obedience to public needs that supposedly divided the state from its opponents, yet of course the puritan conscience argued that an attack on corrupt public order was a responsible act by the individual who knew

God's truth. Hooker addressed himself to this problem of order versus private truth when he argued that private assertions of divine revelation were to be suspected since they would lead to chaos (Hooker, 1593–7, II, p.37): the important argument is the one of order: 'Because, except our own private and but probable resolutions be by the law of public determinations overruled, we take away all possibility of sociable life in the world' (*ibid.*, I, p.228). The private truth can always be questioned, whereas the public law is fixed. When he defended himself against his interrogators, Peter Wentworth accepted the ideological evaluation of private and public, but at the same time argued that he spoke in opposition as a public person: 'I am no private person: I am a public, and a counsellor to the whole State, in that place where it is lawful for me to speak my mind freely [the Commons] and not for you, as Councillors, to call me to account. . .' (Neale, 1969, I, p.326). The political tactic was not to defend the private, which was ideologically devalued, but to question the definition of what was private and what public.

The puritan could be a person of intemperate humour or a preacher of God's truth: the choice of definition depended on the political interests of the definer. The relation between private and public person connects, on one hand, to the discourse of political order in the state and, on the other, to the definition of what a person is. Is the 'I' that speaks a private or public person? is that 'I' told that it is a private or public person? When Robert Browne said: 'The Magistrate's commandment must not be a law unto me . . . but as I see it agree with the Word of God' the 'I' sits between the two texts which address it, the commandment and the word: is what it 'sees' true or false? Hooker's individual is addressed by only one discourse of law, which incorporates God, nature and social order; Browne's is addressed by two, between which 'I' has to choose. What happens when the 'I' that speaks publicly is told that it speaks privately? All of these issues add a political inflection to the dialectics of the person signalled in the performing style of the Elizabethan stage.

To explore these questions at work within a text, I shall offer an analysis of *Doctor Faustus*. The edition I am using does its best, however, to silence the problems. The cover illustration is a photograph of an actor (presumably) in a moment of high emotion (perhaps fear). This photograph could illustrate one of the three names on the cover: Doctor Faustus (biggest letters), Christopher Marlowe (middle-sized), or the editor John D. Jump (smallest). I take it that it's a photograph of 'Doctor Faustus' (since I am not presented with other images and versions of the doctor, then this must be *the* definitive Faustus—remove the quotes). The cover emphasises that Faustus is a real man who suffers. Inside the cover I learn that the Faustus of Marlowe's play is not a single person, that there is a tragic Faustus and a 'cheerful anti-papist wonder-worker'; I also learn that it is not all Marlowe's text. Like most students I learn that inconsistencies of characterisation are to be defined as 'problems' and that the authentic bit of the play, the bit I have to take to be by the named author Marlowe (rather than anonymous others), is concerned with the portrayal of deep emotion (just as the photo on the front has told me). It is just possible that the man on the cover is Christopher Marlowe deeply agonising about what other people have done to his Faustus; or even that it's John D. Jump agonising about Marlowe agonising about nameless others doing things to Faustus.

I take seriously that there are problems which complicate the portrayal of human character in the text; I also take seriously that if a reading is to be made of the text some bits will be prioritised and others dismissed, and that the selection will eventually be based on a set of political interests (though these may appear to me as that which is 'good', 'true', 'tasteful', etc.). I make these points because the strategies of the critical debate around the play adopt a 'scientific' scholarly stance on textual authenticity in order to legitimate evaluative interpretations. I have disregarded questions of textual authenticity, I am untroubled by how many people wrote the play, my reading is a provisional one based upon a text that is readily available in an edition that claims to be as authoritative as others: mine is *a* reading of the Manchester University Press *Faustus*.

In his first speech Faustus acknowledges the limits to his achievements so far: 'Yet art thou still but Faustus, and a

man' (i.23). The line suggests that the natural condition of
'man' is a point beyond which the ambition cannot go. Yet
the syntax creates a split between speaker and role: 'thou'
'Faustus'. When Edward Alleyn performed, the line presumably induced expectations that limits would be transgressed:
the presence of a performer noted for big roles participates in
the play of identities. Together with this, anyone who knew
the Faustus story might expect the split 'Faustus'/'man' to be
resolved by a deconstruction of 'man'. The 'natural' unitary
subject dissolves into uncertainties while the *name* 'Faustus'
becomes what is privileged and fixed, and binding.

Faustus tells Valdes and Cornelius that his fantasy has
helped convince him to pursue magic, he tells Mephostophilis
to be obedient to his 'will': most commentators have enough
evidence to read the play as a moral tale of an over-ambitious
egotist. Knowledge of other Elizabethan texts might produce
expectations that the career of Faustus will be presented
within a narrative that uses its theatrical devices to confirm
that the world is really ordered and thus to counter the appeal
of the central, disturbed but mistaken individual. In plays
with gods, human action can be explained with reference to
the divinities: thus when Bomelio in *The Rare Triumphs*
(?1582/1589) says 'now somewhat it is, but what I cannot
tell,/Provokes me forward more than wont to leave my
darksome cell' (p.175), the origin of the thought which is
unknown to him can be traced by the audience to the debate
between gods. Without an actual authoritative frame, the
human individual can still be shown to internalise the
language and values of an assumed general order: thus
Richard III claims: 'My conscience, witness of the blood I
spilt,/Accuseth me as guilty of the fact' (*The True Tragedy*,
ll.1405–6), carrying the structure of a metaphorical court
room within him. Frequently playtexts work to privilege the
audience with a knowledge of narrative greater than that
possessed by individual characters—Leir's secret thoughts are
public knowledge, Titus's dismissed dream does accurately
prefigure events—and this privileged knowledge places the
characters as vulnerable and judgeable.

While Ragan and Richard III claim to feel a 'hell' within
them, Faustus says hell is a fable. His inner life does not

reflect the debates which supernatural figures introduce—
there is no indication that he has heard the Good Angel's first
speech. When the inner person inflects supernatural debate, it
not only shows how the subjectivity is morally constructed
but that the moral language has emotional force. Faustus's
relationship with the angels is, however, problematic:

> Good Angel: Faustus, repent; yet God will pity thee.
> Bad Angel: Thou art a spirit; God cannot pity thee.
> Faustus: Who buzzeth in mine ears I am a spirit?
> Be I a devil, yet God may pity me;
> Yea, God will pity me if I repent.
> Bad Angel: Ay, but Faustus never shall repent.
> Faustus: My heart is harden'd, I cannot repent.
>
> (vi. 12–18)

The Bad Angel tells Faustus what he is; for Faustus that is
always conditional: 'Be I a devil. . .'. There is an 'I' which
can still repent, but that 'I' is made powerless when the Bad
Angel speaks of what 'Faustus' will or will not do. There is no
writing of an extended inner debate which precedes the
hardening, no illusion of an articulate choosing subject.
Faustus responds according to how he is addressed: the 'I'
subject is not unitary or fixed but shifts with the way it is
framed. This explores the Elizabethan ideology of a morally
controlled individual who nevertheless chooses freely the
right course of action. Faustus takes up the language that
addresses him but that language is not shown to be
naturalised by the subject's emotional response. The syntax
foregrounds a verbal patterning of 'pity' and 'repent'. From a
puritan point of view perhaps, it looks like the way the
Anglican Prayer Book sought to use its liturgy to constrain
the participation and the free understanding of the individual,
from another view it is a battle for the soul of a man who will
not hear the discourse of reason. But it's not a choice between
religious positions, it's a questioning of what the individual
is. 'God' is a word in no discernible authenticating relationship with 'heart'; most Elizabethan ideologies assumed
that God was real because it could be felt in the heart.

'Faustus' does, however, feel religious intuition: 'O,
something soundeth in mine ears,/"Abjure this magic, turn to

God again!'" (v.7–8). Later his conviction of his distressed
soul is sufficiently strong to lead him to call on Christ. Again,
outrageously, in the middle of a comic scene, the Horsecourser's 'now I am a made man for ever' prompts Faustus:

> What art thou, Faustus, but a man condemn'd to die?
> Thy fatal time draws to a final end;
> Despair doth drive distrust into my thoughts.
>
> (xv.19–23)

Thinking of divine forgiveness he can sleep, but while he
sleeps the Horsecourser returns and pulls off his leg with a
shout of 'Alas, I am undone!' (l.35). Technically, the legless
Faustus is also undone. The comic language and action play
on the idea of a constructed man. The Horsecourser is 'made'
by commercial gain, and uneasily unmade (because he too
wanted to explore 'hidden mysteries'). Faustus is 'a man
condemn'd to die': the law tells Faustus what he is, yet there
is also in the subject a belief that can dismiss these 'passions'.
The split is articulated in the writing: 'Despair doth drive. . ..
Confound these passions with a quiet sleep' (l.24). The sharp
change of tone, the writtenness of the alliteration, the absence
of inner debate—all make the thoughts inexplicable in origin
and unsettle our view of the speaker as a fixed unitary subject.
In *Selimus*, when Bajazeth 'thinks some voice still whispereth
in my ears/ And bids me to take heed of Acomat' (ll.1252–3),
he is told dismissively that it is just his 'overcharged' mind.
But he is proved right when evidence of Acomat's cruelty
enters. The intuition has a rational project in foreseeing the
narrative, it cannot be accounted for as a personal disorder.
Faustus's intuitions of Christ, however, are serious and
sudden, but dismissed by the same mind that articulates
them. They go nowhere, have no authorisation of a narrative
place; expected, in the context, but random. This might be
said to correspond with Montaigne's view of the endlessly
deconstructed human intellect: 'Since the senses cannot
determine our disputation, themselves being so full of
uncertainty, it must then be reason: and no reason can be
established without another reason: then are we ever going
back unto infinity.' (Montaigne, 1603, II, p.363). The

difficulty is in certainly defining the 'real' Faustus as the one
who feels the call of Christ but who generally suppresses it
beneath an ambitious will or fantasy. 'Faustus' is addressed
by moral law but 'I' has passions. Identity is made and readily
unmade (just as the more evident devices of Elizabethan social
control literally unmade the unitary subjects addressed by
ideology, by pulling guts from body, chopping head from
shoulders—mutilating natural private bodies to keep the
public body politic whole).

The only sign of heaven is also an emblem of state control,
a throne, an inanimate theatrical machine. The play raises the
problems about divine texts that Bishop Andrews located
when he said to Barrow: 'The word of God cannot speak:
which way should it decide our controversies?' (Allen, 1960,
p.172). The Good Angel encourages Faustus to read scriptures, but reading in the play is marked as a problem. Faustus
is a scholarly authority because of his skill in books but he
reads books given him by devils (and it's parodied in the
comic plot). When Mephostophilis shows the book of spells
and planets, the audience sees characters reading; the contents
of the book are obscured from the audience, there is no sense
of shared knowledge—the book is not necessarily an authoritative guarantor of truth. Later the book is used in popish
rituals. When puritans attacked the mumbo-jumbo of the
Prayer Book they had their own authority of scriptures. No
single voice addresses Faustus with a claim to authority; yet,
like Barrow, he needs to be spoken to.

In the uncertainties of the human world the bond with hell
acquires its status. When Faustus first starts to write with
blood, it congeals: 'Is it unwilling I should write this bill?'
(v.65). It seems as if 'nature' instinctively follows true
religion, despite the ambitions of the brain. Faustus settles his
doubts with a question: 'is not thy soul thine own?' (l.68).
The ideology, the 'rights', of ownership overcome instinctive
morality. In another sanguinary mishap he finds 'Homo fuge'
written on his arm: an image of the person inscribed by divine
law. But the same problem with written text recurs, that the
subjectivity is not totally controlled by the received text: 'My
senses are deceiv'd, here's nothing writ.—/O yes, I see it
plain; even here is writ,' (ll.79–80). After the devils' show,

Faustus reads his deed of gift to the devils: 'full power to fetch or carry the said John Faustus, body and soul, flesh, blood, or goods' (ll.109–10). In the text he becomes the 'said' John ~~Faustus, no longer the sayer.~~ The end of the bill ties together the feeling 'I' with the named 'Faustus'—'By me John Faustus' (l.112). The bill acquires a power by naming Faustus and situating him in a social bond. This, together with its authority as written document, makes it a fixture in the world of speculation. What is shown is the power of ideological address as well as/rather than the power of magic.

An alternative guarantor of certainty in some Elizabethan thinking was experience, and the play problematises this. It is Mephostophilis who suggests that experience can change the mind: Renaissance scientists emphasised the value of experience/experiment in discovery; the Italian theorist Castelvetro (1576) said: 'experience is a greater demonstration than is reason' (Charlton, 1913, pp.25–6). The problem in *Faustus* is that language cannot fully express the truths that are by definition beyond human knowledge: 'No mortal can express the pains of hell' (xviii.47). Faustus speaks of 'our' hell before he experiences it, but when he does experience it his expressivity is undercut. Most of his visions at the end cannot be shared by the audience: 'See, see where Christ's blood streams. . .'; 'see where God/Stretcheth out his arm. . .' (xix.146, 150–1). The audience has been told to expect 'desperate lunacy', 'idle fantasies', self-demeaning; all that can be seen beyond Faustus is a stage gallery full of devils. There is nothing to confirm the truth of Faustus's visions beyond the power of his poetry: the scene is typically that of the deluded individual. The audience has a choice of belief and that responsibility is constructed by the staging: the audience watches Faustus, the devils watch Faustus, possibly the devils watch the audience watching Faustus; the audience's privileged seeing is complicated for they watch with devils and possibly they watch a show put on by devils. Conventional expectation would assume that the author is showing the erring man coming round to repentance; the presence of devils suggests that the show may not be put on by the trustworthy author but by fictional devils. There is no moral fixed point in the sceptical questions set up by the staging; but there is the strength of Faustus's poetry. The empathy for the individual is in tension with the distancing sceptical staging. The assumption about the social power of expressive truth-telling language is questioned, for there is only the individual truth—and that is as questionable as it is powerful. The speaking/showing dialectic at the end draws together the doubts about truth, language, the transparency of the unitary subject. The sceptical thrust of the text may be measured against de Mornay's attempt to naturalise religious belief: 'the universalness of this consent [in Christian principles] showeth that it is nature, and not instruction, imitation or bringing up, that speaketh, and the voice of nature is the voice of truth' (de Mornay, 1587, p.199). *Faustus* shows how seemingly natural ideas and feelings may be constructed, how the voice of truth is difficult to identify. Consent itself, as we shall see, is the problem area.

It is a danger in interpreting *Faustus* to make a coherent reading which replaces and obscures the unsettling play of contradictions and gaps in the text. Precisely the religious figures in the drama attempt to impose on Faustus a pattern of coherent behaviour, but the character seems moved by an endless interplay of desire and dissatisfaction—which could be taken to be an application of Machiavellian theory to characterisation. Seen in this way the Chorus's final quotation from *The Mirror for Magistrates* ('Cut is the branch. . .') becomes deeply ironic in that it offers a theory of the individual which has been disputed by the whole text.

(iii) Truth and pleasure

So far I have allowed the assumption that individuals will be affected when addressed by the state's law or the word of God, without exploring Elizabethan ideas about *how* the individual responds to textual address. Theorists of rhetoric and drama claimed that words could move their audience. In poetry and drama this moving is brought about by empathy; Nashe speaks of 'brave Talbot' who has 'his bones new embalmed with the tears of ten thousand spectators at least' (Nashe, 1592, p.113); on stage there are scenes in which spectators are moved by what they watch, for example the soldiers who witness the death of Antony in *Wounds* (IV.ii), or Faustus distracted by shows arranged by devils. Bodin says: 'there is no limit to our desire for pleasure' (Bodin, 1566, p.29), and pleasure, which should be taken in its widest sense (Castelvetro argued that there was a pleasure in sadness), is assumed to be sought by all. The problem was that not everybody would take pleasure in what was improving: Gosson noted with disapproval that audiences cheered trickery. The force of Castelvetro's theories, based on Aristotle, was in the separation of history from poetry, facts and utility from pleasure and delight; thus an audience would take pleasure in the aesthetic organisation of an artwork irrespective of its morality and indeed a poet should only write to produce pleasure.

Where pleasure operates irrespective of morality it becomes necessary to sanction only certain modes of its operation. The language of sin written into the City authorities' response to the theatres performed the function of devaluing the pleasure of audiences. Similarly, in Parliament, disallowed debate could be called improper private pleasure: the queen asked MPs in 1571 'to speak of matters already proponed only, and not to make new motions, every man at his own pleasure' (Neale, 1969, I, p.221). In *Wounds*, the Captain censures his soldiers who are moved by Antony's rhetoric by speaking of their 'presumptuous praises'. The legitimate pleasure is one that is moved by that which the state approves, that which is said to be moral, ordered or true. Bodin noted the 'danger that while we revel in too great appreciation, we may overlook the utility (although in delight, also, there is use)' (Bodin, 1566, p.12). Pleasure that ignores utility is formulated as emotion that ignores reason.

In his defence of plays Nashe presents two arguments for utility in theatrical pleasure. One is that pleasure aids social control by distracting: for example, 'corrupt excrements' such as soldiers in peacetime, who may threaten public order: 'it is very expedient they have some light toys to busy their heads withal cast before them as bones to gnaw upon, which may keep them from having leisure to intermeddle with higher matters' (Nashe, 1592, p.112). Similarly in the afternoons, 'wherein men that are their own masters . . . do wholly bestow themselves upon pleasure', plays are preferable to drink, whores and gambling (*ibid.*). In *Faustus*, a text that I suggest deals centrally with pleasure, a show is early on used as a controlling distraction. When Faustus is having doubts about signing away his soul, Mephostophilis goes to 'fetch him somewhat to delight his mind'. Devils appear, dance and give crowns. Faustus asks what it means and Mephostophilis replies: 'Nothing, Faustus, but to delight thy mind/And let thee see what magic can perform' (v.82, 84–5). Clearly there is a meaning, in that they offer crowns and thus imply power: Faustus is asked only to delight in what magic can do. The operation of 'delight' is doubly insidious in that it distracts from Faustus's doubts and then pretends not to make the meaning it does make. Pre-eminently it inverts supposed power relations between spectator and showman since Faustus is flattered by the performance that suppresses his doubts about his own action. He is weakened by the magic he is told he can control.

This scene early in *Faustus*, unlike later ones, privileges the audience to see the connection between theatrical delight and relations of power. Faustus is silenced by his pleasure, the delight could be said to effect his consent. I introduce the word 'consent' deliberately to invoke a political formulation of Hooker's: 'strifes and troubles would be endless, except they gave their common consent all to be ordered by some whom they should agree upon' (Hooker, 1593–7, I, p.190). This consent could be satisfied, supposedly, by institutions such as Parliament and monarchy: Smith said that 'the consent of the Parliament is taken to be every man's consent' (Smith, 1583, p.49) (—but Parliamentary debate was inhibited). But consent also operates ideologically, beyond areas of conscious agreement. Law's 'seat is the bosom of God' and angels, men and creatures 'all with uniform consent, admiring her as the mother of their peace and joy' (Hooker, 1593–7, I, p.232). The reference to 'mother' makes the relationship to law one of natural bonding; men are seen to revere law naturally alongside all the rest of creation. This idea of consent specifically envisages social ordering, but it is order maintained without force—the relationship with mother law is natural and joyous. An analogy may be drawn with Sidney's account of the moral operation of epic poetry: 'Who readeth Aeneas carrying old Anchises on his back, that wisheth not it were his fortune to perform so excellent an act?' (Sidney, 1595, p.41). The emotional response to the picture may be taken to be natural, primarily unforced, consent to the moral ideal. A connection between political/ religious consent and theatrical delight is made by de Mornay (1587): 'Insomuch that although thou be not acquainted with the story, yet the art which thou perceivest and the end which thou expectest make thee both to bear with the matter and to commend the thing which otherwise thou wouldst think to be both unjust and also cruel in the governor of the stage. How much more oughtest thou to refrain thy misliking if thou considerest that the world is a kind of stageplay, conveyed to a certain end by a most excellent maker?' (quoted in Battenhouse, 1941, p.126). That plays teach, through delight and empathy, moral lessons applicable to society is Nashe's second point about the utility of dramatic pleasure.

Cynically seen, consensual pleasure, especially as de Mornay talks of it, involves delight as repression, pleasure as deception. A suspicion of the honied words of rhetoric was strengthened by the movement for plainness in speech and writing; Ramus argued that pleasure could deceive, that rhetoric could be used to control recalcitrant pupils. This control is spoken of in interesting imagery by the Presenter of *The Battle of Alcazar* when he tells the audience: 'Like those that were by kind of murther mummed,/Sit down and see what heinous stratagems/These damned wits contrive' (ll.21– 3). There follows a dumb-show in which two young princes are smothered. The selected metaphor of murderous silencing seems to connect with the smothering. The pleasure in seeing what heinous wits contrive is obtained only after agreeing to be silenced/murdered. *Alcazar* does not follow through the problems of spectacle, so I should like to turn back to *Faustus* to explore the relations of delight and control, and particularly the position of the audience. For example, the show of the Seven Deadly Sins is apparently a moral pageant which has reference to the corrupt human condition and is spoken in the familiar terminology of Elizabethan social satire. The audience also knows that this pageant is offered by devils as a pastime to entertain Faustus who has been calling on Christ: 'Talk not of paradise or creation, but mark the show' (vi.110). Instead of talking of Christ he is invited to questin the Sins, at the end of which he feels delight and is told that hell is all manner of delight. Because the Sins are so hackneyed I suspect an audience did/does not feel a similar delight to Faustus's, and the discrepancy foregrounds his response. The show is an appropriately moralistic piece of theatre, but more significant are its (diegetic) conditions of production. It is arranged by devils to distract Faustus and limit the questions he asks. The familiarity of the contents of the show, the old Morality-style performance, makes it less interesting in itself than the part it plays in the narrative. The scene, I would argue, shows an audience that conditions of production are more important than the show itself, and that delight in the show does not recognise the repression built into its production relations. The point of danger is not in the morality that is shown but in the power that does the showing.

In the supposed source for the play, when Lucifer appears to the distressed Faustus he comes with 'certain of his hideous and infernal company in the most ugliest shapes that it was possible to think upon'. Lucifer reminds Faustus of his vow and offers to show him 'hellish pastimes'; Faustus asks to have the skill of transforming himself and Lucifer gives him a book (quotations from Manchester U.P. edition, p.128). In the narrative source it is possible to moralise the delight by balancing pastimes against ugliness, pleasure against threat and by making sober the descriptions of the pastimes, or omitting them. Marlowe's version is a play not a book, its theatrical spectacle is, morality apart, spectacle: what delights Faustus can delight the audience (and not just in the pope scenes). An audience is placed to expect new theatrical surprises from Mephostophilis, like a Presenter; Faustus's inner turmoil is almost upstaged by devils; the comedy scenes invite laughter at devils. As I suggest elsewhere, when the pope curses souls to hell an audience tends to laugh with the devils at the pope, to enjoy Faustus specifically when he becomes an 'actor' in this 'show'. The spectacle gains its force from a contrast with books: Faustus's progress in magic is presented as a movement from static, book-surrounded, stage action to the spectacular first appearance of the devils. When Mephostophilis shows Faustus a book of spells the audience cannot share what Faustus sees in it; the book is an object at which the actor peers: in spectacle the audience too sees the sights. The audience may not feel the pleasure Faustus shows when he looks at the book; similarly they may not share his feelings in the opening speech with its 'learned' Latin. Books do not offer theatrical pleasure, and in the pope scenes spectacle takes revenge on the book and the symbol of authority becomes laughable: the cardinals are to be charmed asleep over their 'superstitious books', then Faustus invents fake decrees by 'statutes decretal', and comic confusion follows over the synod's book of law.

As the play of *Faustus* develops the audience is offered shows in which it can take pleasure, delight closes the critical distance. At the same time the pleasure in spectacle is located within the strategy of social control. Faustus requires from the Emperor 'dumb silence' for viewing his show; his magic skills can silence sceptics such as Benvolio. When he is with the Duke of Vanholt he manipulates the lower-class figures as a 'good subject for a merriment' (xvii.53); when these figures start to accuse him he charms them dumb. The Duke and Duchess watch the performance that exploits and silences the lower-class figures. Thus the play enacts some of the suspicions about deceptive pleasure but, most importantly, it simultaneously shows the dangerous strength of that pleasure by trapping the audience within it.

In *Faustus* an audience takes pleasure in what, viewed critically, would appear repressive. Such a political function of pleasure is described by Machiavelli in a passage I have already quoted (in Chapter 2) and which now needs re-examination: it is useful, he says, to keep the 'semblance of the old forms' of the state on the basis that 'men in general are more affected by what a thing appears to be than by what it is, and are frequently influenced more by appearances than by the reality'; similarly religion should be fostered, for Livy tells of soldiers who behaved devoutly because 'they heard the answer they wanted the goddess to give and had taken for granted when they approached her' (Machiavelli, 1531, I, pp.272, 244)—thus consent operates. The problem still remains to explain why people are 'affected' by appearances and why appearances can have as much influence or authority as realities. To take the second question first: poetic theorists and historians argued that verisimilitude can be constructed. Castelvetro said that poetry should tell a fable 'as it ought to be' and that verisimilitude performed the function of convincing the reader of the possibility of events that could happen. The theory of dramatic unities was an attempt to ensure that the play had the conviction of verisimilitude: 'there is no possibility of making the spectators believe that many days and nights have passed, when they themselves obviously know that only a few hours have actually elapsed: they refuse to be so deceived' (Charlton, 1913, p.86). The picture of an audience that is permanently conscious of where it is, and who it is, is a useful corrective to assumptions about generalised empathy and suspended disbelief which are made by much modern criticism. It is that consciousness which makes the truth-effect necessary, for only with verisimilitude does the stage gain its authority for what it shows. A similar authority of truth has to be created by the historian, whose job it is to select and arrange the material in order to construct a true history out of the mess of chronicles (which mess, said the historian Grafton, allowed all sorts of private interpretations). Higgins takes time off in his life of Nicholas Burdet in *The Mirror* to describe the proper historian who 'should so place each thing in order due,/As might approve the stories to be true' (ll.405–6). The apparent transparent expressivity of truth-speaking, which state utterances claimed, was something writers had to construct: once constructed, 'a feigned example hath as much force to teach as a true example' (Sidney, 1595, p.36).

When Higgins describes the historian at work he says he should 'both supply the wants, correct that is not right:/He should have eloquence, and full and fitly write' (ll.396–7). Not only is the history thus decorous ('fit'), but it is also 'full'. The historian has made a text that fills in the gaps that are found in less ordered records of human activity. It is this sense of fullness, I suggest, that makes the 'appearance' authoritative and enjoyable. In Machiavelli's Italian the word translated above by 'affected' is 'pasce', which is also used of feeding, or of cattle grazing: as if people are ideologically nourished, as if appearance is pleasurably consumed. In his defence of history plays Nashe suggests that they not only offer exemplary heroes, as instruction, but they enable their audiences to participate in the heroism: thus the audience 'imagine they behold [Talbot] fresh bleeding' and they embalm him with their tears; the whole play then offers a 'reproof to these degenerate effeminate days of ours' (Nashe, 1592, p.113). In the absence of real heroism the audience emotionally participates in that of the fictional Talbot. The language of Puttenham's justification of the necessity and naturalness of pleasure envisages a plenitude of emotion: 'yet is it a piece of joy to be able to lament with ease, and freely to pour forth a man's inward sorrows and the griefs wherewith his mind is surcharged' (Puttenham, 1589, p.47). Art constructs the satisfaction of full emotional response.

The desire for pleasurable satisfaction is seen by Bodin as a part of human nature: 'because nature has engendered first in every being the desire for self-preservation, the earliest activities of men are related to things impossible to forgo. Later they are directed to matters without which we can, indeed, live, but not at all comfortably; or if comfortably, not splendidly; or if splendidly, still not with that keen joy which delights the senses most sweetly. Hence the desire to acquire riches.' (Bodin, 1566, p.29) Economic development relates to a continual desire, which makes the present dissatisfying: the effort is always to experience a fullness of delight. This analysis may be related to Castelvetro, in a very different context, discussing the thrill of tragedy, particularly its heroes: 'In order to feel such pleasures, and before they can feel them, they must have fallen from their high estate, or at least be in danger of doing so. For then only have they anything before them to hope for or take pleasure in' (Charlton, 1913, p.108). Loss or threatened loss is the precondition of experiencing pleasure. Both authors, in their different ways, link pleasure to lack: for Bodin there is always an effort to reach a supreme delight, and present circumstances are always discovered to lack this delight; for Castelvetro

the consciousness of pleasure is only created by experiencing (threatened) lack of it. In both cases the mind is looking
for some means of evading a sense of lack, of filling a gap.
Thus, to return to Machiavelli, it could be said that
appearances of old forms may satisfy the ideological appetite
because they evade the prospect of realising the lack of them.

An appearance that satisfies because it claims the authority
of truth and promises to guarantee a fullness of pleasure has
relevance, clearly, to theatrical practice. In the Induction to
The True Tragedy Truth promises to add 'bodies' to the
'shadows' invented by Poetry; Truth will make the insubstantial substantial, offer real bodies to perform rather than
something known to be shadows, fill the threatened human
absence. The mirror scene in *Friar Bacon* looks at the
promised truth and fullness of theatre. It is where Friar Bacon
shows to Prince Edward in a magic glass the wooing of his
loved Margaret by his friend Lacy. By the end of watching
what Bacon calls a 'comedy' Edward is so furious he attempts
to stab them, forgetting that he watches only a scene in a
mirror: 'Choler to see the traitors gree so well/Made me think
the shadows substances' (vi. 129–30). The filling out of the
'shadow', the making substantial, comes from the desire of
the watcher: Edward's emotion leads him to forget the
artwork, the absence of the real bodies—his desire to be
satisfied in revenge made him think them present, just as the
desire to share Talbot's glories makes his imaginary wounds
seem to be full of real blood, or Hieronimo's seeing in the
Old Man the 'lively image' of his own grief when the Old
Man 'names' his son (*Spanish Tragedy*, III.xiii). It is,
perhaps, the desire for a sense of plenitude, not the contents
of the show, which is important.

To apply these ideas again to *Faustus*: Faustus has to
remind the Emperor that the figures in the show of Alexander
'are but shadows, not substantial' (xii.55). The Emperor
describes his thoughts as 'ravish'd', he forgets himself, leaves
his 'state': identification with shadows leads to a hierarchic
disordering. The spectator is also internally frustrated: 'since
I may not speak to them/To satisfy my longing thoughts at
full' (ll.59–60)—speech here would be satisfying expression
but theatre frustrates because it simultaneously excites desire

and refuses consummation. The form of consummation it may allow, however, is a fetishism of the person: the Emperor is allowed to inspect Alexander's paramour but he may not talk to her—the theatrical fetishism enforces gender power relations, with the male showman inviting the male spectator to gaze at a fictional silent 'woman'. The theatre can prove true that Alexander's lover had a mole but it cannot offer the satisfaction of mutual speech: a silenced audience is one of the conditions of its pleasure, and its power. It is his necessary recognition of the difference between his substantial humanity and the shadows of theatre that the Emperor finds frustrating. Knowledge comes from dissatisfied desire, not from satisfied fullness. (Similarly Lodge (1596) says of 'Christian believers': 'they only that know the world truly trust it not in well knowing it' (Hattaway, 1970, p.69)). Later in the play Faustus asks to 'glut the longing of my heart's desire' (xviii.91): he wants the satisfaction of desire to obliterate thoughts that remind him of the terms of his own existence. He wants 'heavenly Helen' 'Whose sweet embraces may extinguish clear/Those thoughts that do dissuade me from my vow' (ll.94–5). To embrace shadows, to experience a sense of theatrical plenitude is here to proceed ignorantly to the devil. By extension . . . the pleasures of the spectacular or patriotic sections of the play thus tempt the audience.

Insofar as it can be read as a text about the politics of pleasure, *Faustus* reveals the power relations operating within the theatrical pleasure and empathy that are common to other plays. There is always the possibility of noting both presence and absence where the performer both presents a character and mimetically is the character. The common 'behold my tragedy' line promises a fully expressive statement of inner emotion, both true and full, yet also reminds of the circumstances of presentation in the theatrical image of 'tragedy'. Not real emotion but show; show containing fictional emotion that an audience desires to be real: the tension potentially creates knowledge. Thus the audience at the end of *Faustus* is left with an eminently privileged sharing of the main character's inner life but simultaneously an awareness of watching a show; the unresolvable choice makes a political knowledge in that one response is always conditioned by its opposite—to watch with devils a man demeaned, to sympathise with a man damned and going to devils. Other experiments with expressivity make the emotional speech in some way difficult—either unintelligible or consciously theatrical (as with Kyd's Hieronimo, as we shall see): this again undercuts the sense of full expressivity, by reminding of what is not expressed or of the fact it is a show. A sense of absence or difference again makes a knowledge about what is watched.

The duality of presentation/mimesis disappeared in a movement towards fuller expressivity. When Porrex in *Gorboduc* says: 'would it mought as full appear to sight/As inward grief doth pour it forth to me' (IV.ii.38–9), the audience that does not share the vision may view Porrex as a presented example of the penitent brother. Were the emotion fully to appear to sight, the audience would share it and be less able to judge Porrex. The operation of full empathy may complicate the clear moral lessons. In *The True Tragedy* Richard III says he is haunted by shadows, in Shakespeare's play the audience sees the ghosts he sees. Titus's early arrogance is lost sight of in the full poetic expression of his tortured subjectivity. What happens politically in the case of Titus is that while an audience hears the voice repressed by the state, it experiences a plenitude in hearing that voice. There is no problem of the status of 'I', no battle within the subjectivity. There is no difficulty in the theatrical relationship of privileged watcher and tormented victim (against this compare the embarrassment about Hieronimo). When the King of Scots says of himself 'fear and love hath tied thy ready tongue/From blabbing forth the passions of thy mind' (*James IV* , I.i.85–6), in the middle of a twenty line speech, the necessary silencing is a political image but the audience experiences it not as a silencing but as a fullness of communication. Here, as with Titus, full expressivity is a trustworthy revelation of the inner person; it is not treacherous. But it can be treacherous, as Tamburlaine's apostrophe to Zenocrate shows, for to concentrate solely on the issues expressed in that speech is to ignore the conditions of its production (the slaughtering of virgins). The words create an illusion of plenitude (Tamburlaine fully expressing his feelings) while in fact they are produced in an emptiness (the absent or dying women).

Willing identification with the fullness of Tamburlaine's speech would be mistaken consent. The Emperor has to learn that silent shadows cannot satisfy his longings, Faustus deliberately embraces illusions to forget the conditions of his life. In the play's narrative overall it is loss which teaches value: Mephostophilis valuing Faustus's 'glorious soul' before he has it, Faustus only taking it seriously when he is about to lose it. Theatrical delight offers a plenitude that satisfies and silences its audience. *Faustus* seems to show specifically what is endemic to Elizabethan theatrical practice, where the very theatricality of presentation offers a knowledge not just about the person represented but about the conditions of viewing that person. This knowledge vanishes when the audience loses its distancing awareness of show and takes pleasure only in the illusion of fully expressive persons that is constructed by later Renaissance drama.

CHAPTER 4

Messengers, Prophets, Scholars

These three common Elizabethan dramatic figures are all associated closely with language in spoken or written form. All lack the social power derived from property, wealth or government. Their social place and their inner lives are shaped by the texts they handle.

Usually placed on the margins of dramatic action, the messenger and prophet originate as devices which communicate narrative information and sustain narrative shape. The gradual allocation of an inner life to a messenger figure could be taken to be part of the general movement of Elizabethan drama as it 'matures' into psychological realism. My analysis wants to interrogate the assumptions behind this idea of dramatic process, to which end I have sought to contextualise these figures historically and to look again at matters of dramatic language and pleasure. Links are made between history and art in an attempt to present these figures as 'typical' in Lukacs's sense: they embody and clarify specific aspects of the structure of Elizabethan social relations. The roles of messenger, prophet and scholar connect with the theatre's foregrounding of elements of its own practice, in the relations of drama and narrative, subjectivity and 'truth'. In two places the case studies act as prefaces to studies of Marlowe: overall, they contribute to my effort to chuck out the window the belief that Elizabethan drama was simply a clumsy stage in theatre's growing up towards psychological realism.

(i) Messengers

In Senecan and classical drama the messenger or *nuntius* is a useful device for telling the audience about what cannot practically be shown (often because of distance in place or time). He is not a character involved in emotional exchanges, his text has the status of narrative alongside the 'drama'. Sidney helpfully provides us with a distinction here between 'reporting' and 'representing': 'many things may be told which cannot be showed, if they [playwrights] know the difference betwixt reporting and representing. As, for example, I may speak (though I am here) of Peru, and in speech digress from that to the description of Calicut; but in action I cannot represent it without Pacolet's horse; and so was the manner the ancients took, by some *Nuntius* to recount things done in former time or other place.' (Sidney, 1595, p.66)

Modern audiences tend to find the messenger device crude because realism, to which they are accustomed, claims to be able to represent all that it wishes to report. The reporting-representing contrast does, however, make its own particular meanings: for example, in *The Misfortunes of Arthur*, which is a court play about rule and the problems of succession, there is a message about the correct personal discipline of the monarch; the passions of Arthur and his son are to be assessed for their part in making history, and to this end they are framed by dumb-shows and messenger's narrative, seen not as something natural and inevitable but as exemplary. The juxtaposition of report and representation locates the personal alongside (but not necessarily in) history.

The technique of *Misfortunes*, of the late 1580s, looks back to the much earlier didactic court play *Gorboduc*. Its use of the messenger thus contrasts with professional playtexts where representation was by now the dominant mode, and where the messenger's role was smaller—simply the announcement of unexpected news. When Canutus and his court are gloating over two young men they have just maimed, a messenger brings news of military defeat. The dramatist constructs the sharpness of impact by insisting on the laughter that precedes the entry. The unseen outside world suddenly impinges on what seemed so secure. Here that impinging in fact creates a new sense of moral security, in that tyrannical cruelty is deservedly punished by providence, but in a scene such as the famous opening of *1 Henry VI* the stability of the state is unsettled. A tableau of aristocrats surrounds Henry V's coffin, Bedford is invoking Henry's

ghost when his speech is cut off by a messenger's announcing
the loss of seven French towns. Two other messengers
follow, the aristocrats put off their mourning robes, the
dialogue increases in volume, the stage movement gets faster.
The ceremonial of the state funeral seems fragile, ignorant of
the events of an outside world. The fullness and stasis of the
stage imagery disintegrate under the pressure of what is
presented as historical necessity. The invocation of the dead
monarch's ghost is replaced by a final image of a more or less
unattended bier on a bare stage. This structure is similar to
that of the death of King John in *The Troublesome Reign*: a
messenger requests admittance for John's son and the barons,
John himself is rendered speechless by his disability; the
barons seek to crown young Henry in John's presence and as
they do so he dies. The dying monarch loses power of speech
even while the text of historical necessity is spoken, his death
is almost upstaged visually by the attempted crowning. After
his death, which is very quickly followed by the noise of an
approaching messenger, news is brought of the French army;
John's corpse is forgotten. As with Henry V, the old king and
the emotion surrounding him are redundant. Instead of
privileging the audience with a full report of what is not seen,
the messenger's presence disrupts the representation: it
dismantles the fullness of the stage picture with its tableaux
and high emotion, empties the stage, shows the emotional
focal points to be useless corpses that are no longer fetishised,
temporarily decentres human beings from the process of
historical events. It is not just that within the narrative the
apparent stability of state crumbles, but that dramatic
pleasure is also unsettled, for, as in the case of John, the
leading actor is upstaged by a supernumerary, the large death
speech thwarted not just by disability but by an apparent
concern for events that are neither represented nor fully
reported (you can still find productions of *Hamlet* that want
to end with the hero's death, especially where he's an
important actor).

The messenger brings the narrative of history into present
human relations. The increased stress on representation
means that the moment of intervention of the message can be
scrutinised (where report to the audience would simply be

transparent communication): the message is a text seen at its point of entry into a social group. Many playtexts endorse the traditional idea that a benevolent ruler treats a messenger well and a mark of a tyrant is that s/he does not:

> In mischiefs, such as Ferrex now intends,
> The wonted courteous laws to messengers
> Are not observed, which in just war they use.
>
> (*Gorboduc*, II.ii.42–4)

In the late 1580s such princely benevolence is given a nationalist inflection: 'though Spain use messengers ill,/'Tis England's guise to entreat them courteously' (*Three Lords*, p.467). While Richmond welcomes a messenger, Richard III demands he be searched for weapons (*The True Tragedy*); Ragan hits an ambassador, Acomat has one blinded and mutilated. As well as proposing a contrast between the conducts of rulers, these scenes exhibit the operation of class power—after Ragan hits the ambassador she calls him a 'base and vulgar peasant' (*King Leir*, l.1972). The text of *The Wounds of Civil War* experimentally shifts the point of view in the message scene to see it with the messenger: the messenger is branded, one of Cinna's 'barbarous swains' (II.iii.45), called slave and peasant; he hesitates before identifying himself but explains to the audience why he does it, so his consequent joy at finding Young Marius—which is inexplicable to the recipient—is clear to the audience; he then talks of the hardships of his journeying. Only after the social interaction, with its careful placing of the audience, is the letter opened and read. By making the message into a letter, a written object, the scene draws on the opposition of spoken to written in its presentation of the messenger as a figure in class society: the bearer of the *written* communication of a higher class. Subservient to the message he carries, the messenger's body can be mutilated, marked, as it were written on (as this messenger is already branded), by the recipient who dislikes the message. The messenger is turned into message in a world where one class owns the language.

Not all recipients are, however, powerful and we get scenes where the messenger is seen as the intrusive agency of a tyrannical power. Thus Richard III's messenger breaks into the intimate scene of the queen and her children, 'with thy ghastly looks presseth into sanctuary, to affright our mother queen' (*The True Tragedy*, ll.812–13). Goneril hires a messenger to carry letters to Ragan and abuse to her their father; Ragan offers him money to kill their father, and he readily agrees. In the service of these two the messenger becomes murderer, yet he begins in the play as a more traditional messenger on his way to Leir. Goneril stops him on his journey, and offers him her protection: he turns out to be good at railing; Ragan thinks she may use him and he admits to being pitiless; she offers him money and he undertakes murder. The traditional messenger is transformed by patronage and payment; the new order of Goneril and Ragan creates its own professional agents. No longer the sufferer for someone else's text, this messenger is seen to be a courtly talker, good at flattery and railing; he prides himself on railing his neighbours out of the parish—a detail which sets his articulate, professional individualism against older values of community.

This element of the text of *King Leir* seems to lay bare a structure of social relations which Peter Wentworth and some of his fellow MPs were trying to identify from the mid-1570s onwards. Elizabeth made frequent use of royal messengers to inhibit debate in the Commons, especially on the banned topics of the royal succession and religion. As the years wore on, both topics became more pressing, especially in view of the campaign against puritan radicals masterminded by the comparatively new man, Whitgift. In his famous speech in the 1576 Parliament, Wentworth identified the two main ways in which the queen controlled the Commons: first, there were rumours about her approval or not of matters under discussion, and second, 'sometimes a message is brought into the House, either of commanding or inhibiting, very injurious unto the freedom of speech and consultation.' (Neale, 1969, I, p.320) He urged MPs 'from the bottom of your hearts to hate all messengers, tale-carriers, or any other thing, whatsoever it be, that any manner of way infringe the liberties of this honourable Council.' (*ibid.*, p.324) Ten years later Wentworth was still fighting, asking the Speaker a series of questions about freedom of speech in the House, the Speaker's right to interrupt, to 'rise when he will', to overrule, and 'Whether it be not against the . . . liberties of this House to receive messages either of commanding or prohibiting, and whether the messenger be not reputed as an enemy to God, the Prince and State?' (*ibid.*, II, pp.155–6). He was identifying the regular tactics of royal control: Elizabeth and Whitgift received reports of debates (which Wentworth saw as an illegal practice), the Speaker would be summoned to court in order to cut short debate, those who opposed the royal will would be interrogated if not imprisoned to set an example (one of Neale's sources speaks of the horror aroused by Bell's reappearance after interrogation by the Privy Council), royal messages through the Speaker would forbid certain discussions. There was a power struggle between the Commons and the royal administration, expressed in the terminology of freedom of *speech* against the prepared message, the elected individual against the messenger in service. (The terms are, however, ideological not factual: many MPs wrote down the speeches they spoke.)

Tale-tellers and messengers were the evidence of a power structure outside the control of a 'democratic' Parliament. There had always been Walsingham's spy network, agents of which may have trailed Marlowe to his death, but Whitgift's campaign against puritanism employed the Court of High Commission, using ecclesiastical law rather than the secular law made in Parliament. In 1590 a man on trial for shooting a messenger of the High Commission who was sent to arrest him claimed that the Court had no right to imprison, so the messenger was committing assault: he got off the murder charge, but it's an illustration of the ways of state (Russell, 1971, p.240). The text of *King Leir* presents its messenger as the servant of a new sort of regime—murderous, not bound by traditional respect; Wentworth argues that free speech in Parliament is a traditional liberty to be defended against new administrative controls. In the ideological argument the messenger typifies the operation of repressive order, what Anderson sees as the centralised bureaucracy, the administrative machine, so necessary to be set up by the monarchy with pretensions to absolutism (Anderson, 1979).

Messenger scenes in plays are more than a reflection of contemporary politics, for the form of the artwork encourages a view of the power relations around the message text different from that proposed by the royal messages. I have already noted that the Senecan *nuntius* addresses the audience whereas the drama develops to a situation in which the audience watches someone on stage being addressed by the message: the audience is still addressed here but it is possible to shift the point of view, and hence sympathies, in the scene. The Senecan *nuntius* has an authority based on his superior historical knowledge, he tells the story not of a character but of History. In the Commons, when the Speaker (the title is so important) returns from court with a message to inhibit religious debate he asks: 'Who is so important whom the presence of such a majesty would not appal?' (Neale, 1969, II, p.274). The authority of his message is acquired from the aura of the presence; the Commons are recipients, the Speaker simply a voice for the speaking presence that lies elsewhere (intentional pun). In the drama of representation, however, the people addressed are more interesting than the messenger. Certainly news has a powerful effect on the scene, but there are two orders of story—the narrative of objective realities and the revelation of subjective realities; and the hierarchy of importance among the performers conflicts with the supposed hierarchy of the narrated events: the messenger has no high emotion and is a supernumerary. The dramatic text invites us to be interested precisely in what the royal messages marginalise, the language and responses of the recipients. In 1593 Puckering pointed out that 'her Majesty granteth you liberal but not licentious speech', and went on: 'so will there be no good conclusion where every man may speak what he listeth, without fit observation of persons, matters, times, places and other needful circumstances'. A message to the 1576 Parliament had condemned those who 'make new motions, every man at his own pleasure' (Neale, 1969, II, p.248; I, p.221). The policing language condemns what is personal and emotional and recommends what is 'fit', disciplined, linguistically (and hence politically) law-abiding. On the stage the interesting moment is when the formulaic utterance breaks down, when something new happens.

To oppose 'fit observation' against speaking as one 'lists' is to impose language laws on human emotion; it is like using messengers to spy on or disrupt intimate scenes. While this writing/speaking discourse certainly posits the essential reality and expressiveness of the spoken, it is possible to suggest that some playtexts envisage times when writing so pervades human relations that nothing can be seen to be expressively spoken. I describe elsewhere the scene in *1 Hieronimo* where father dictates a letter to son while he dresses himself, a parallel which suggests that the speech is already preplanned, of the status of ornament not plainness. A different case is Mortimer's letter ordering the death of Edward II where the completeness of the writing cannot be expressed in speech: to read the letter aloud requires the selection of only one of its two possible interpretations. There may be situations where there is no expressive presence that agrees to be the ultimate source of the real meaning of the message. The repressive state that writes human relations denies responsibility for its texts, just as Elizabeth so outrageously punished Secretary Davidson for delivering the order for Mary of Scots' execution which she herself had signed (Elizabeth I's *Belgrano*, perhaps).

All of these remarks about messengers are intended to serve as preface to an analysis of *Edward II*. The play is not structured simply as the moralistic tale of a 'humorous' (dangerously emotional) prince. Shakespeare's later way of dealing with such a figure in *Richard II* (1595/1597), with which *Edward* is almost always disadvantageously compared, was to increase the focus on the prince, giving him lyric language and self-aware reflections on monarchy, thus producing a close relationship between audience and pathetic monarch. Marlowe's text questions the concept of the 'personal', which combined with the structuring makes the work seem 'difficult' or even, as the literary academy has it, incompetent in its effort to present the liberal humanism which we all know Shakespeare believed in.

The first scene locates the personal relationship of Edward and Gaveston within the traditional estates structure of society: poor men, king and nobles, king and favourite, king and bishop; and within an idea of the 'personal', which is not just expression of private feeling (Gaveston's solo speeches, Edward's desires), but a mode of political interrelation: poor men ask Gaveston's personal favour, Gaveston uses Edward's personal desires to manipulate him. The letter from Edward, the requests of the poor men, both foreground at the play's start the idea of patronage. The whole act continues to sustain in parallel the 'public' and the 'personal' discourses: scene ii balances the Archbishop's opposition with Isabella's private distress, both useful to the barons; scene iv begins with a contract between barons limiting the king's 'will' and ends with a marriage sustaining their 'rights'.

There are scenes of sending and receiving messengers, writing and reading letters; there are transactions and negotiations. These all have two major effects, the first of which concerns the 'nation'. The large number of characters contributes to a sense of a confused, almost unknown 'world' of the play. Incidents and lines are repeated: young men given titles, people acting in the 'country's cause'; yet after scene i we don't see who is ruled, nor what the country is. The structuring permits few ideological images of wholeness, 'little England'; no such scene as that of the allegorical gardeners in *Richard II*, with its sense of a real England somewhere beneath the temporary unnatural turmoil. Specifically the affairs of England are pursued in neighbouring nations, with appeals to the pope, emissaries to France, letters to Ireland, ransom notes from the Scots. Unlike other history plays, especially those of the early 1590s, which inflect the vigilante policy of internal security (see, for example, *Edmund Ironside*, *The Troublesome Reign*), 'England' is not portrayed as a discrete entity or spiritual continuum. The playtext questions thus the rhetoric of both sides in the foreign policy debates of the late 1580s, with the military expansionists urging that England fulfil 'her' role as leader of Protestant nations, and those with other interests arguing a defensive, Fortress England line to make the country 'most secure and dreadful to her neighbours' (Camden, quoted in Read, 1960, p.308).

The other effect of structuring concerns the 'personal'. Words and syntax are repeated so that meanings become unfixed, absolutes mere utterances; everything is debated over, contested. Messages are not transparent expressions of emotion or political will, but untrustworthy and manipulative. Edward's niece enters with a letter from her betrothed, Gaveston, and she addresses it as if it were Gaveston: 'What need'st thou, love, thus to excuse thyself?'; she claims it 'argues the entire love of my lord' (II.i.59, 62). Yet the audience expects Gaveston's primary loyalty to be to Edward, a male bonding that precedes the engagement to the niece—this is confirmed when she receives a letter from Edward, bidding her meet Gaveston at court. She is a woman controlled by male writings, vulnerable because she takes them to be sincere expression. The penetration of the written into her love empties, for us, its emotional fullness; the possession of letters marks the absence of human contact. The niece has to believe Gaveston's intentions, although she is unconscious of the choice she makes, unlike the readers of Mortimer's more cruel murder letter who *have* to choose what it intends even while they are conscious of an alternative and opposite meaning. These messages make problematic the expression of human intention, and show the gender and class relations produced by such expression.

While messages claim to facilitate human contact, they also reify it. Mortimer sends with Lightborn a token to ensure his death; Isabella sends Edward, deceitfully, a ring 'as witness of my love' (V.ii.74); Edward gives Lightborn a jewel to make amends for his suspicion. King and peers haggle over who has to pay the ransom for Mortimer's uncle. This picture of human interaction relates to the play's foregrounded activity of patronage, in which everyone is paid, from Gaveston to the Mower who betrays Edward. To show his love for Spenser, Edward gives him money to buy land; he promises the barons 'We will requite your love' (I.iv.385). Mortimer tells the Mayor of Bristol: 'Your loving care in this [bringing the Elder Spenser captive]/Deserveth princely favours and rewards' (IV.v.64–5). 'Love' is one of the text's repeated words. It is usually mentioned with treasure or reward; structured by monetary relations. Bodies are thought of as owned. Gaveston and Isabella each 'rob' the other of Edward; Gaveston the prisoner is 'delivered' to a keeper; young Edward 'is my charge; redeem him.' 'Edward is my son, and I will keep him.' (V.ii.118–19)

It is part of my general hypothesis that Marlowe's texts work to make knowledge of the ideological language of the state. Therefore I would suggest, here, that it is important to note the use of 'love' in the quarrels between monarch and Parliament. A royal proclamation of 1571 promises that 'Her Majesty would have all her loving subjects to understand that as long as they shall openly continue in the observation of her laws. . .' she will not 'have any of them molested by any inquisition . . . being very loth to be provoked by the overmuch boldness and wilfulness of her subjects to alter her natural clemency into a princely severity' (Neale, 1969, I, p.192). If the subjects are 'loving', why do they have to be warned off 'boldness'? Note, too, that clemency is 'natural' to her, as suggested by the text. A royal message of 1589 speaks of subjects' 'loving affection' and then firmly prohibits debate. From the other side, Wentworth, in his oppositional free-speech stance, claims it is his 'love' for her that compels him to utter Elizabeth's faults, and that it is dangerous for a monarch to oppose herself to 'most loving and faithful nobility and people' (*ibid.*, p.322). The word enters Hooker's theory of the Anglican state, where ecclesiastical and secular authority reinforce one another: 'the reverend authority of the one might be to the other as a courteous bridle, a mean to keep them lovingly in awe that are exorbitant' (Talbert, 1962, p.60). The language naturalises obedience, constructs absolutist authority within desire and consent—the loved personal rule. But in *Edward II* when characters speak of love they exhibit a power relation; when events are described (often) as being unnatural, there is little clear sense of the natural.

Although it deconstructs the political notion of personal rule, the text does not reduce the personal totally to the determinants of money and class. Approximately the central scene of the play is structured by four arrivals. Elder Spenser in 'person' comes to defend the 'royal right'; he provides troops and will be rewarded with land, both expressions of 'love' in the personal patronage system. Isabella brings news of the quarrel with the French king, and she and her son, the closest of kin, are 'employed' as emissaries. Arundel, next in the sequence of steadily worse news, comes to relate

Gaveston's death, and since the audience already knows what has happened the interest centres on Edward's response. His emotional pathos contrasts with Young Spenser's suggestions of vengeance. The scene apparently discovers for us, as in other messenger scenes, the sincere response of the troubled individual. (It's an expectation partly constructed by the depersonalised, prepared rhetoric that marks Arundel's speech.) But there are problems with Edward's outburst. His passion first of all makes him act becomingly as a king along the lines already suggested for him by Spenser. Then there is the apparently *real* deflation of the role as he embraces Spenser: 'Spenser, sweet Spenser, I adopt thee here;', giving him Gaveston's titles 'merely of our love' (III.ii.147, 148). Yet this gesture is consistent with his expressions of love earlier, in that it sustains the relationship produced by patronage. The property evaluation of persons fixes Edward's power as a constant whether he expresses vengeance for Gaveston (he will 'have heads and lives for him as many/As I have manors, castles, towns and towers!' (ll.135–6)), or love for Spenser, who gets titles. Similarly, in his passionate final scenes, he gets comfort from wearing the crown, he rages when asked to resign it. He loses the power to speak while the messengers wait for their token, the crown. The fetishised object controls his responses. (And in this scene the passion is useless as a force within human interaction; but of that more elsewhere.)

The central message scene presents an already constructed emotion where we might expect spontaneity or 'natural' instinct. The raging follows Spenser's suggestions, the loving obeys the patronage relations. The response to Arundel's prepared text is itself an already shaped text. His defiance of the final arrival, the barons' messenger, is not so much a revelation of homosexual obsession as an affirmation of status quo: 'see how I do divorce/Spenser from me' (ll.179–80) (embracing him). Spenser is placed in the Gaveston role; permitting Edward to exercise his love he continues the structure of his power. The scene, I would suggest, does not show a basically real person dressed as a monarch sending and receiving messages, but shows the sending and receiving role structuring the person. By implication, say, Elizabeth has no 'natural' emotion beyond her role of message-sender.

If the social role and its texts do construct the person, then *Edward II* questions the concept of the mis-advised monarch. The barons' herald tells Edward to 'have old servitors in high esteem,/And shake off smooth dissembling flatterers' (ll.171–2). The distinction between wise old counsellors and deceitful flatterers is an ideological analysis produced by competition for royal favour under personal rule. Marlowe's text shows little of either of the two Spensers' corruption, and makes the barons unattractive, which unsettles our agreement with the herald. At the root of such an outlook is the concept of a monarch free to choose counsellors and companions, so that when the bad are stripped away the real, naturally good, king re-emerges. *Edward II*, however, posits a monarch whose nature is inseparable from the social structures he reinforces. To extend the patronage that confirms his power Edward looks for loving recipients. Although their presence is felt as a need, that need is shaped by a political system. There is, we might argue, no real monarch outside the one that needs favourites. Personal rule is not a function of person but of rule.

(ii) Prophets

Prophecies have to be distinguished from prophets. An example of the prophecy is Exeter's in *1 Henry VI* when he reflects on the feuding nobles:

> now I fear that fatal prophecy
> Which in the time of Henry named the Fifth
> Was in the mouth of every sucking babe,
> That Henry born at Monmouth should win all
> And Henry born at Windsor should lose all
> (III.i.196–200).

Similarly, Friar Bacon looks forward at the end of his play to the reign of the 'matchless flower' Elizabeth. The dramatic character looks beyond the temporary problems of his own time to the larger scheme of history, a story in which everything has its proper place. The dying King John sees 'a catalogue of sin/Wrote by a fiend in marble characters' (*The Troublesome Reign*, 2.1102–3). As he dies he assesses his own place in the moral chronicle of history and foresees the 'kingly branch' that will threaten Rome. At the momentous event of royal assassination the audience is directed instead to the chronicle of history where everything is already written, where temporary chaos is revealed to be eternal order.

This use of the prophecy in historical plays suggests that men do not make their own history. The chronicle's events are always already known, as the audience knows the events that Exeter looks forward to. History is seen to have pattern and moral order which do not originate in human beings and are not controlled by them. It may help to clarify some of the issues raised by prophecy if I employ here Benveniste's distinction between history and discourse: history is always presented as 'a story from nowhere, told by nobody, but received by someone (without which it would not exist)' (Metz, 1981, p.230), as opposed to discourse where the speaking position is identified.

Against the ordered providential history may be placed Bodin's suggestion that 'human history mostly flows from the will of mankind, which ever vacillates and has no objective' (Bodin, 1566, p.17). This is the effect of the text that now constitutes *The Massacre at Paris*: we have been taught to see its incompleteness in a negative way (the mangled text) not positively, with the suppression of the coherent sense of nation and of moral order as a counter-statement to providential histories. Such a position is perhaps more easy to see when it is placed in the diegesis rather than suggested by the form. *Tamburlaine* and the plays it influences show heroes refuting predictions of their downfall: Corcut warns his brother Selimus: 'There lies a book written with bloody lines,/Where our offences all are registered' (*Selimus*, ll.2153–4), but without replying Selimus has Corcut strangled and is still alive himself at the end of the play.

Cynical new men making their own history differ from the ancient monarchs who could be influenced: Nathan made David 'as in a glass see his own filthiness' (Sidney, 1595, p.42). The world, as Sidney views it, no longer gives public authority to the poet-prophet. The playtexts insist on the low status of their full-time prophets: Joan of Arc is 'by birth a shepherd's daughter' (*1 Henry VI*, I.ii.72), Peter the Prophet is followed by a 'rabble', 'To him the commons throng with country gifts' (*The Troublesome Reign*, 1.1599), Ralph the Cobbler remains treated as a cobbler despite his new gift of prophecy. In his study of prophecies, Keith Thomas shows how popular risings used prophecies to strengthen their case and to keep alive their cause; indeed, prophecies were used as 'justification' at all levels, both by the government and against it. Many prophecies were specific to popular unrest—a Leicester embroiderer, Edward Sawford, a Catholic, in 1586 foresaw a time when 'all those who racked rents, hoarded corn, or otherwise oppressed the poor, would fall before a rising of "clubs and clouted shoes"' (Thomas, 1973, p.482). Ralph tells the Country Gentleman:

> The widow's woeful cries,
> And babes in street that lies,
> The bitter sweat and pain
> That tenants poor sustain
> Will turn to your bane I tell ye plain
>
> (*Cobbler*, ll.324–8)

Ralph is a comic figure, not seen by the text as a problem. Joan and Peter, on the other hand, are located as difficulties. The French claim Joan has the 'spirit of deep prophecy' (*1 Henry VI*, I.ii.55) and she claims a sacred profession; Talbot, the English champion, calls her 'that witch, that damned sorceress' (III.ii.38), and indeed the playtext shows her conversing with fiends. The opposition of plain English rationality to French (Catholic) superstition is clear; but the text does not disallow that Joan has supernatural contacts. Peter is greeted as one who talks with 'a power replete with heavenly gift' until he says the wrong things to King John, when he is rejected: 'False dreamer, perish with thy witched news!' (*The Troublesome Reign*, 1.1691, 1724). The interest is in John's attempt to censure, since it is primarily his own religious position which is the difficulty. The Bastard, like Talbot, has no illusions: 'a dissembling knave, that deludes the people with blind prophecies' (ll.1381–2)—again the firm, plain Protestant English viewpoint. But the playtext does not totally share this plain certainty, for Peter interprets an on-stage apparition of five moons: the capacity of the stage to make 'miraculous' effects unsettles the diegetic insistence on a favoured rationality.

When Talbot and the Bastard reject prophecies as witch-craft, they employ a familiar distinction which is formulated in the Prologue to *The Peddlar's Prophecy*(>1594/1595) as an opinion of St Augustine: 'That the true Prophets in Scripture "Prophets" are named;/Divinators are reproved, condemned and blamed' (ll.28–9). The separation of true from false, prophet from divinator, is the political lesson offered to 'magistrates' in *The Mirror*'s Life of Owen Glendower: 'Bid Princes fly Colprophet's lying bill:/And not presume to climb above their states' (ll.236–7). That second line makes an important qualification, for it is the bad ruler who listens to false prophets:

> False prophecies are plagues for divers crimes
> Which God doth let the devilish sort devise
> To trouble such as are not godly wise.
>
> (ll.173–5)

Thus the French king in *Edward III* is clearly labelled when he misinterprets a prophecy to his own advantage. The scepticism of Talbot and the Bastard acts out the Tudor governments' discouragement of belief in prophecy. An Act of Henry VIII had made false prophecies a felony and, although it was repealed (for three years) under Edward VI and again under Mary, it was re-enacted in 1563: 'divers evil disposed persons, inclined to the stirring and moving of factions, seditions and rebellions within the realm, have been more bold to attempt the like practice in feigning, imagining, inventing and publishing of such fond and fantastical prophecies, as well concerning the Queen's Majesty as divers honourable personages, gentlemen and others of this realm' (Taylor, 1911, pp.105–6). The problem with the false prophecy is that common people are inclined to believe it: false prophecies are 'things of men's fantasies,/Invented to deceive the ignorant and rude' (*The Peddlar's Prophecy*, ll. 11–12). Dominant ideology saw the common people as of their nature inclined to believe rumours, with no discrimination about truth: where the state utters 'truth', a prophecy was a text originating outside the control of the state and thus challenging that truth; hence it was seen as lies.

·The warning against false prophecies was used most widely in the ideological campaign against puritans. As we have seen, what was at stake in this battle was the hierarchic control of bishops, priests and magistrates, and each side claimed to speak with 'truth'. The puritans' Word of God was opposed to the state's authority. Thus the puritans compared themselves to prophets: the man of God was defined in *A Part of a Register* (1593) as 'a prophet to speak in such sort that when the unbelievers and unlearned come in before him, they may be rebuked and judged, and so the secrets of the heart made manifest with true repentance and faith' (p.203). (The connection of the prophet with radical social analysis and opposition was of long standing, and is to be seen in prophetic poetry from the middle ages onwards (for details see Norbrook, 1984).) Puritan meetings at which there were discussions as well as worship were known as 'prophesyings' and Elizabeth had them suppressed, sacking Archbishop Grindal when he disagreed with her over this. Prophesyings were meetings for which no provision was made by Anglican liturgy, and the campaign to silence puritan opposition by imposing Anglican authority was ideologically seen as Prayer *Book* against the speaking of the *Word*. Launching the all-out assault in a public sermon at Paul's Cross on 9 February 1589, Whitgift's henchman Bancroft called puritans 'false prophets'.

The Prologue to *The Peddlar's Prophecy* seems to reiterate the anti-puritan line, saying that God's prophets

> did not only of things to come prophesy,
> But they spake of one truth in one sprite,
> Which was fulfilled in their times openly.
>
> (ll. 52–4)

The stress on a unitary truth is close to Elizabeth's expressed wish that puritans 'minister the sacraments according to the order of this Realm and preach all one truth' (Neale, 1969, II, p.70). Yet, against the rest of the play, the Prologue looks as if it might have been added for publication in 1595, for the figure of the Peddlar goes through the play making criticisms of social abuses and professions that are very much in line with Elizabethan social satire, including some horrible attributions of all economic ills to the presence of aliens (a viewpoint from which *The Jew of Malta* radically diverges), and this figure is not only seen as right (far right) but lower-class. He is called a 'runnagate' and his speech 'licentious' by those who are (again rightly) implicated by what he says; when he confronts the guardians of religious and social 'truth', the Interpreter and the Justice, the Peddlar is the true-speaking figure. The Justice says it is very grievous 'To have a tinker or a cobbler to minister to us' (l.1339), a complaint against puritans which may be exemplified by the queen's attack on 'newfangledness': 'to have every man, according to his own censure, to make a doom of the validity and privity of his Prince's government, with a common veil and cover of God's word' (Neale, 1969, II, p.100). But the Justice here is the wrong party, as too is the Merchant when he attacks the Peddlar: 'Such fellows going abroad the country,/Make many simple folks them to believe' (ll.774–5)—it is important that the audience does believe the Peddlar. The Peddlar's prophecy later in the play is very much in line with puritan attacks on the Anglican church: not only does he say of bishops and priests that 'In one day they shall be consumed both great and small', but he attacks 'new unlearned ministers' and those whose garments vary as their ministrations do (which I take to refer to vestiarian controversy) (ll.1286–8, 1314–20).

The Prologue to *The Peddlar's Prophecy* seems either added or conscious disguise, for its low-class popular prophecies are 'true'. A similar theatrical strategy for making social criticism is used in *A Looking Glass for London and England* where the prophet Oseas is instructed by an Angel to record the sins of Nineveh and then broadcast them to Jerusalem. Already the differences with *The Peddlar* are marked, for the prophet is biblical not low-class and neither Nineveh nor Jerusalem are explicitly London (though the abuses are clearly problems of English society). Yet there is much that may link with puritanism, especially in the figure of Jonas who is distressed by the 'irreligious zeal' in Israel and sighs to 'see thy prophets so condemn'd' (l.922). There is sufficient about the tyrannical Rasni's priests of the sun to hint at Anglicanism or at least ritualistic religion: they enter with mitres on their heads, talk of their gods' statues and blood on their altars—idolatory and ritual. Jonas is reprimanded for trying to evade his allotted task as preacher, but he becomes effective at getting conversions; Oseas is told by the Angel not to fear 'to preach the word' (l.1755) in Judea; Jonas addresses 'ye nations bounded by the West,/Ye happy isles where prophets do abound' (ll.2048–9). The end of the play constructs Elizabeth as the shepherd against Romish Antichrist, but that is an evasion of the issue of anti-state prophecy foregrounded by the narrative. The play uses all the technology to give authority to the prophets, from the Angel that instructs Oseas to the thunder and lightning that burns up Remilia, the flame that consumes Radagon, the hand out of a cloud with a burning sword. On the one hand there is the theatrical pomp of a tyrant's court, on the other, destroying it, is the iconoclastic imagery and theatrical technology that backs the puritan-type prophets.

In *Looking Glass* there is little of the Protestant nationalist scepticism to oppose to the prophets' effects. The staging gives authority to Oseas and Jonas with its Angel figure, but the narrative also firmly places them as preachers rather than miracle-workers. When Jonas first appears he is given very personal inner anguish, a private emotional response to religious corruption; God releases him from the whale after hearing his *voice*. As a preacher he speaks from a personal urgency, a sense of truth felt inwardly. Oseas, too, is given an important label: told to record the sins of Nineveh, he moralises but adds: 'I speak, although I write not' (l.1735). The stress on speaking as against writing, and on personally motivated speech, ties in with the definition of false prophecy. The authority of the privately felt truth, the personal consciousness of God's word, is devalued when private speaking is seen as possessed, fanciful, witchlike. Whitgift (1584) said he required subscription to his articles of religious uniformity 'in that meaning which those that be in authority . . . do set down, and not in that sense which everyone shall imagine' (Collinson, 1967, p.254). The opposition of that which is set down in writing to that which is privately imagined informs the typical utterance style of prophets—the rhymes spoken by Ralph the Cobbler or the 'feigned rhymes' referred to by Glendower indicate less sophisticated, less ordered speaking (the Peddlar, significantly, claims to have read Latin books and to know 'ancient sayings'). Joan of Arc is characterised with an untrained 'wit', Ralph as not being able to write.

The ideological opposition of speech and writing was not on its own an effective basis of guarantee of truth. In practice, puritans depended greatly on printing presses, a well organised network of preachers and congregations, and good knowledge of scriptures; the state might be seen to fail in debate (in 1577 Whitgift could not answer Cartwright; see Marprelate, 1588–9, p.21) and to use the techniques of breaking up presses and calling in banned books. In material terms there was no way of authenticating utterance, simply strategies of propaganda and repression. This problem about the authenticity of the personal or 'imagined' is indicated in plays that censure prophets, for Joan's devils and Peter's moons are *seen*—they are in that sense true for the audience. At the same time their truth is of a different order from the presaging of history: it is 'personal' as opposed to the visions of those aristocrats whose forward looking may be confirmed by an audience as historical 'truth'. The aristocrat who presages speaks what is known, it is true because it is historical fact; the aristocrat is not defined by his ability to foresee. The prophet is on stage only as a speaker of that which challenges what is known to be; the source for the prophet's vision is identified, with its supernatural effects or inner feelings. The prophet speaks discourse with a clear point of origin, the aristocrat presages history; history is to be taken as truth, whereas discourse is not. This is marked in *Edward III* where an anonymous 'woman' speaks of a 'prophecy abroad,/Published by one that was a friar once' (ll.1274–5) of a lion carrying away the fleur-de-lis; although the prophecy has all the characteristics of what is to be suspected—low-class, rumour, speaking—it is in line with the nationalist project of the play and the known outcome of events. Its status as history, but more importantly its correspondence with the desired outcome of the play, give it truth. Again, when the son of the French king turns up with a written prophecy, as if from nowhere, the audience knows that it relates to English success and that the French, because of their own subjective ambitions, interpret it wrongly.

Beneath the opposition of speaking and writing there is the opposition of discourse and history which constructs the truth effect (for the construction of truth, see Foucault, 1980, pp.131–2). The authenticity of what is said lies not so much in what authorises the speaker as in the outcome that is predicted (thus *The Peddlar*'s Prologue stressing the need to have the prophecy fulfilled openly). *Edward III* enables its audience to understand the prophecies to be true simply because they fit with dramatic expectations; similarly, *Looking Glass* authenticates its prophets with its Angel. Both these texts make the truth status of prophecy unproblematic by using the devices of theatre to pre-select the true; they create an 'authority' either of God or history to legitimate the speaker, so that what is said is not viewed sceptically as discourse. In this sense, both texts from their differing viewpoints sustain the ideology which in the practical operations of the state was all too often challenged, for a cynical view of the campaign against puritans would see the discourse on neither side as true or false, but maintaining its authority only through superior political organisation or brutality. I introduce such a cynical view, which no one may have shared, in order to give importance to the problematising of the relationship between discourse and history, prophecy and fact in *Tamburlaine*. Tamburlaine the bandit claims his *deeds* will prove him to be a lord; the deeds do in fact make him a lord, but the truth of his lordship is always contested by hereditary rulers. By the middle of the play he can claim: 'I that am termed the Scourge and Wrath of God,/The only fear and terror of the world' (*1 Tamburlaine*, III.iii.44–5): in a world in which the Spanish invasion of the Low Countries was explained as God's punishment, Tamburlaine takes on the authority of divine agency, a prophesied doom. Yet he himself presents himself this way: there is no clear God in the play, no one is seen to 'term' him—his authority is simply asserted. The person makes discourse that claims to be history: 'I that am termed. . .'; the tension lies between the pronoun and the passive tense. When Marlowe used the image of a chariot drawn by captive kings he may well have borrowed from a dumb-show in *Jocasta* the tableau of King Sesostris that allegorically depicted Ambition. In *Jocasta* the tableau is a given, spoken by no one in the narrative world, it is History; in *Tamburlaine* the tableau is invented by a self-publicising character, its source is shown, it is discourse. But as discourse it still has power, because when Tamburlaine claims to be a scourge he has the troops to back him up; when he claims to 'hold the fates bound fast', his military success confirms his assertion. His prophecy is proved by material means, troops give authority to what only has the status of discourse. Thus Marlowe's text sidesteps the battle to prove an essential authority of truth in the utterance of state or prophet, to depersonalise the utterance so it speaks as God or history. In *Tamburlaine* the relations of discourse and history are blurred and truth is constructed by material power. This seems to have a bearing, if fortuitous, on the activities of the Elizabethan state.

(iii) Scholars

When the clown Strumbo enters as a scholar ('in a gown, with ink and paper') he says: 'Either the four elements, the seven planets and all the particular stars of the pole Antastic are adversative against me, or else I was begotten and born in the wane of the moon, when everything, as saith Lactantius, in his fourth book of Constultations doth say, goeth asward. Ay, masters, ay: you may laugh, but I must weep; you may joy, but I must sorrow' (*Locrine*, ll.311–18). The joke derives not only from the clown's pretension but from the picture of the typical scholar with the 'technical' words and involved syntax. Puttenham says that everyday language is not to be found 'in Universities where scholars use much peevish affectation of words out of the primitive languages' (1589, p.144); scholars' language is regularly described as 'inkhorn'. The pleasure in Strumbo's performance comes from the clown's construction of community with his audience, through direct address and physical fooling, to which the scholar's learning is alien and irrelevant.

The strangeness of the scholar's language is the marking of his otherness; he is also socially isolated: Bomelio has a secret cave with his books in it; Sacrapant is discovered alone in his study, as—playing on the type—is Faustus. In entertainments for Elizabeth, Hemetes the Hermit receives his sight and George Gascoigne dressed as a Savage Man is tamed by her presence. Gascoigne the author performs his own redundancy, the eccentric figure in a text he had himself authored (for the entertainment at Kenilworth, 1575); at the centre of the text's economy is Elizabeth, the civilising force because she has not learning but power. This siting of the intellectual is most fully stated in the Introduction to *The Misfortunes of Arthur* where the captive law-students (in reality those being groomed for real social power) defend Astraea's contempt for poetry against the attacks of the muses: the students are to be sidetracked by 'No eloquence, disguising reason's shape,/ Nor Poetry, each vain affection's nurse' (ll.68–9). Reason, truth and 'use' are opposed to eloquence, poetry, 'various history'; conspicuous learning or scholarship is an irrelevance and eccentricity. The poet who greeted her at Elvetham (1591) was booted 'to betoken that he was *vates cothurnatus*, and not a loose or low creeping prophet'; the green clothing and garland served partly to mark his *naturalness*, unlike the bookish scholar (Nichols, 1823, III, p.104). The division between 'learned' mumbo-jumbo on the margins, and rationality and 'truth' at the centre of power is similar to that described by Debray (1981) in his work on modern French intellectuals: he finds an early example of the competition between the University and the Academy in a text of 1658 where Princess Rhetoric and her Academy rout Captain Twaddle 'an obscure man from the dregs of society' who commands a 'seditious Sorbonne' (p.56). Such a marginalising of the scholar is produced by the centralising project of absolutism.

The ideological assault on conspicuous learning bit deep:

Wilson's conservative opinion—'they which speak otherwise than truth is, mind not the commendation of the person, but the setting forth of their own learning' (Wilson, 1560, p.14)—is echoed by the oppositional *A Part of a Register*: 'many preach themselves and not Christ Jesus, and study to leave an admiration and fame of their learning behind them . . . rather than a godly edification of the inner man' (p.207). In both cases learning obscures the transparency of human truth; the reality of the human subjects precedes intellectual ideas. *Faustus* is to complicate the relationship of person, ideas and truth. In the language of dominant ideology the intellectual is seen as an individualist who disrupts consensus. Puttenham attributes the corruption of ordinary language to 'clerks and scholars or secretaries long since, who, not content with the usual Norman or Saxon word, would convert the very Latin and Greek word into vulgar French' (1589, p.117). Against what is 'usual' the scholar is 'not content', moved by 'peevish affectation' (Puttenham repeats the phrase); the authors of *Misfortunes* say poetry is 'vain affection's nurse'. As an individual the scholar is prey to 'personal' feelings: Sacrapant says 'Each thing rejoiceth underneath the sky,/But only I whom heaven hath in hate' (*Old Wives Tale*, c.1590/1595, ll.337–8); this informs the joke of Strumbo's 'you may laugh, but I must weep'. When his books are burnt by his son, Bomelio goes mad: the display marks the scholar's unhealthy vulnerability to emotion and his isolation from rational consensus.

When the scholar places personal feeling before community he pursues individual interest, which is a possible political threat. His apparent peacefulness has to be regarded with suspicion. Ateukin offers himself to James IV as a poor scholar, who cannot be a flatterer and whose 'nature cannot brook of blood' (*James IV*, I.i.253)—yet he is the treacherous deceiver of the play. *The Cobbler's Prophecy* sets up a debate between Scholar, Courtier, Country Gentleman and Soldier; the Scholar praises contemplation, adding 'with my pen [I] hurt more than thousands do with pikes; I strike him that sees me not' but 'my contemplation is only of the life immortal': the Courtier replies: 'But you would be glad to creep in credit in the Court, Scholar' (ll.351–2, 363–6). The language of magic that so often comes into pictures of scholars specifically devalues their learning, presenting it as conspiratorial, self-interested, designed to entrap and conceal. Such is the language of the witch hunt of the Ralegh circle: *An Advertisement written to a Secretary of my L. Treasurer's of England* (1592) speaks of the 'School of Atheism' and 'the conjuror that is Master thereof' (Shirley, 1974, p.23). It is against this ideological representation of the dangerous magical other that Marlowe's *Massacre at Paris* presents Ramus killed by aristocrats who show contempt for both his learning and his class origins; the repressive role of the aristocrats is added by Marlowe to what he found in the sources, thereby foregrounding the power relations of class. There are similar scenes in *The Wounds of Civil War* where the military tyrant Marius orders the execution of the scholarly Mark Antony and in *Selimus* where the villainous central figure rhetorically challenges 'schoolmen' who are 'prepared/To plant 'gainst me their bookish ordinance' (ll.299–300). These texts make an association between plainness and brutality which highlights the relations of power suppressed in the ideological presentation of truthful reason versus individualist or magical scholarship.

The victim-scholar image tends to propose the scholar's devotion to truth, his innocence of power struggle, thereby reversing the notion of a truth-loving consensus threatened by a self-interested magician. Sited differently, but essentially unchanged, is the opposition of truth versus self-interest; but this opposition is precisely problematised by *Faustus* where the scholar's project of knowledge is shaped by the material values and interests of his society. When Faustus speaks of learning it is of 'a world of profit and delight,/Of power, of honour, of omnipotence,/Is promis'd to the studious artisan!' (i.52–4); spirits can 'Ransack the ocean for orient pearl' (l.82). What Faustus desires is formed by the discourse of Elizabethan imperialism; he shares Burghley's interest in the 'signory of Emden'. He enjoys the 'obedience and humility' of Mephostophilis, and this is parodied in the comedy. His conception of learning is not independent of but determined by a role in competitive society. The arrangement whereby he sells his soul is explicitly commercial: he is to 'buy'

Mephostophilis's service, not to 'hazard' his soul but to 'bequeath it solemnly/And write a deed of gift', for Lucifer wants that 'security' (v.33–7). It is all· commercially logical: why does Lucifer want Faustus's soul? it will 'Enlarge his kingdom'; what does Faustus get? a 'slave' in Mephostophilis. When Faustus later calls on Christ, Lucifer points out: 'Christ cannot save thy soul, for he is just;/There's none but I have interest in the same' (vi.87–8). The justice of Christ is like the justice of traditional rule: both are now replaced by law and commercial bonds. It is worth recalling here that the great epistemological break made by the absolutist theory of Bodin in the political sphere was that sovereignty *imposed* laws on subjects rather than governing by traditional justice; government was clearly in the interests of those who governed and the preservation of private property was the rationale of this system.

Faustus the 'typical' scholar, with his base parentage, his ambition and his study and books, follows an economic logic. There is little sense of the freedom of thought which might notionally be attributed to the intellectual, for the real relations of the state and its intellectuals are formed by a system of patronage which privileges the patron rather than the writer. Faustus's shows celebrate 'state majestical'; the Emperor expresses his approval in acquisitive terms: 'in this sight thou better pleasest me/Than if I gain'd another monarchy' (xii.67–8). While grapes are provided for a pregnant Duchess, protesting clowns are struck dumb. Scholars were used to produce state propaganda: Thomas Norton was employed to describe the tortures of Campion. It was neither the pursuit of truth nor the fear of magic which motivated Elizabeth and Burghley's interest in Edward Kelly—it was love of money. For Kelly, who had been made 'golden knight' by the Emperor, supposedly had a formula for making gold; this formula the mathematician John Dee was urged to bring back from the Continent. Burghley (1591) wrote to Kelly: 'I do conjure you not to keep God's gifts from your natural country, but rather to help to make her Majesty a glorious and victorious prince against the malice of her and God's enemies. . ... Let no other country bereave us of this felicity' (Read, 1960, p.476). All the discourses of true

religion, nation and monarchy work hard to pressurise the
wealth-making 'scholar' into service. Kelly, of course, was a
complete charlatan, but the interests and values that operate
in this little story of rulers and magic men form a nice parallel
with *Faustus*.

When dominant ideology spoke of the typical scholar, it
spoke of one that was outside, other; and thus it devalued any
systems of thought that might deviate from the thinking of
the centre. In professional theatres, however, University-
trained writers were in new conditions of production; no
longer necessarily placed as competing individuals within
centralising patronage systems, they worked as part of a
company which sold its artworks. Marlowe took a crucial
step towards securing his own intellectual independence
when he chucked in an expected career in the church to
become a theatre writer. It is not, perhaps, surprising to find
the re-examination of the scholar in professional theatre texts.
They give us the murdered Antony, the murdered Ramus,
Faustus, while court plays have the lonely Sacrapant, the mad
Bomelio. It is precisely the material situation of the theatre
writer, I think, that forms the 'scholar' into the man who puts
on shows; the image becomes more interesting when joined
with its variant, the discontented man or revenger who
chooses to put on a show to articulate his feelings about
dominant society: Hieronimo and Titus (in that he exploits
for himself Tamora's fiction) are invented alongside Faustus
and Friar Bacon.

Greene's *Friar Bacon* considerably differs from *Faustus*,
but it seems to argue a new site of social intervention for its
scholar, which would end the otherness: the trajectory of its
central figure moves from the magical cell to the public
nationalist prophecy. Bacon has books and 'secret cell', he
talks Latin, he looks 'lordly' as well as learned, he puts on
magic shows for which he is royally rewarded. The conjuring
allows space for stage spectacle and trickery, but it is a
sanitised magic: Bacon the conjuror is called 'jolly friar', he
upholds national honour in a magic contest (like Common
Market negotiations) and ends the play prophesying the
glorious reign of Elizabeth. He is situated within the
discourses of English nationalism and Tudor benevolence.

The text draws its audience into the excitement of 'magic' spectacle but sentimentalises the relations of patronage. Bacon's activities combine theatrical pleasure with the accepted truths of the regime's national myth, to produce a sense of enjoyable and 'natural' fullness which is simultaneously quiescent. Thus the play effects a closure on the disruptions of pleasure and the central ironic strategy of *Faustus*, which in its early stages presents a recognisably typical scholar and promises voyages into an unknown, and wrong, devil world that turns out to be a world all too close to the ideological structure of contemporary England. Faustus's thinking is described as 'blasphemy' and 'damned art' by an angel and another scholar, but instead of the audience hearing something strange and unfamiliar they are confronted with discourses similar to those of English colonialism: 'search all corners of the new-found world/For pleasant fruits and princely delicates' (i.83–4) and Protestant war aims: 'chase the Prince of Parma from our land/And reign sole king of all our provinces' (ll. 92–3). Leicester indeed tried to chase away Parma from the Netherlands, and accepted the governorship that had been offered to Elizabeth. The 'infamous' Valdes outlines schemes for spirits: 'From Venice shall they drag huge argosies,/And from America the golden fleece/That yearly stuffs old Philip's treasury' (ll. 129–31)—like the aggressive privateering plans of Drake.

The play apparently speaks a discourse of English Protestantism from the first appearance of Mephostophilis ('return an old Franciscan friar,/That holy shape becomes a devil best' (iii. 27–8)), to the pope scenes. Faustus swears by the 'kingdoms of infernal rule' when he expresses his wish to see Rome, and a portrayal of the Catholic church as devilish was a stock part of Protestant propaganda. The pope humiliates 'Saxon' Bruno, threatens to depose and excommunicate the Emperor, claims to possess 'all power on earth'; Elizabeth was likewise threatened by the papacy. The appeal of seeing the Anti-Christ pope baited may well have dominated over any misgivings about Faustus's use of devil skills to do so—it is so much in line with propaganda and theatrical fooling. Similarly, the produced spectacle of the 'heavenly beauty' of Helen, who is admired by scholars on stage, and Faustus's

courtly poetry to her (admired by scholars since) offer
themselves within a tradition of male appreciation of female
beauty which again serves to obscure the devil element in the
pleasure. And the punishment of the mean-minded 'sluggard'
Benvolio fulfils the expectations of comic revenge, a fulfil-
ment again achieved by the devilish powers. As much as the
nationalist references, the various episodes bring with them
their own generic expectations and pleasures, so that instead
of setting off to explore an unknown devil area the narrative
returns its audience to that which they can recognise as
familiar, and the recognition is pleasurable.

At all points the scholar's skills are said to be devilish. The
Emperor 'comes to see/What wonders by black spells may
compass'd be' (xi.40–1), but the audience may also have
pleasurable expectations about the 'wonders'. When the pope
curses people's souls to 'hellish misery' (twice) it is as likely
that an audience is laughing at his blustering (I find this stage
action predominates over the possible moralistic emblematis-
ing, the banquet of sense, etc.). It is, of course, the boorish
Benvolio who sceptically rejects the devil's magic, and his
attempt to send Faustus's soul to hell is upstaged by Faustus's
resurrection. Those who damn Faustus are morally accurate
but at the moment of their damning the moral sense is
weakened by the counter-pressure of comedy: the damners
are the targets of tricks from which delight is produced by the
audience identifying with Faustus in his comic business. The
tension between delight in and moral judgement of the
scholar Faustus's acts is emphasised after the Helen appearance, when the first scholar says 'for this glorious deed/
Happy and blest be Faustus evermore' and the Old Man says:
'O gentle Faustus, leave this damned art,/This magic, that
will charm thy soul to hell' (xviii.35–6, 38–9). The Old Man
has an emblematic authority, partly because he is so
peripheral to the narrative action, yet that authority has to
compete with delight engendered *in* the narrative. The
tension between the remarks also notes that there are others
besides Faustus who find the 'damned art' pleasurable, or
indeed politically useful: the scholars, the Emperor, the Duke
and Duchess of Vanholt—and the list might be extended to
include the audience. That audience has already been included

in the devil's gaze when he says 'This is hell', they are again to be situated in parallel with devils when they watch Faustus's final agony; their pattern of expectation and gratification has shown them always to be already in hell emotionally, despite all the apparatus of moral choice or quest that accompanies the action of the play.

Faustus advances himself as a scholar by agreeing to the proffered economic relationship and operating within a preferred theatrical relationship; both are proposed by devils, both recognisable from Elizabethan practices. The problem for Faustus is that, unlike Bacon, he does not secure a situation within the state, and once his term has run out he is disposed of and forgotten. His power never had any material base. The audiences who enjoyed his shows and whose interests he furthered are not implicated in his punishment, for it is only his soul that has been sold. The discrepancy between the fates of the passive viewers and the central actor (a discrepancy Walsingham had bemoaned as an 'actor', see p.xvii), the focus on the act of individual selling out, together indeed with the questioning of where hell actually *is*, all seem to relate much more closely to affairs in contemporary England than to issues of abstract morality. I would place the play in a context of re-invigorated state repression in the late 1580s, the show trials of puritan activists, the breaking up of presses. Whitgift's repressive campaign was compared by Burghley to the operation of the Spanish Inquisition (Neale, 1969, II, p.22); it was carried out in the name of the Anglican church whose bishops were described by Martin Marprelate as horned and Luciferian (Marprelate, 1588-9, pp.25, 28); Whitgift compelled puritan ministers to sign his articles of faith, and signing the bond is a central act in the play; finally, Faustus offering to burn his own books, his *last line*, foregrounds the precise feeling of error in a state that banned and burned books, and he gets torn limb from limb, like an advanced form of the rack. Alleyn apparently played the part in 'a surplice/With a cross upon his breast' (Manchester U.P. edn., p.lviii), which labels the religious association of Faustus. In the presence of God Faustus feels his tongue stopped, his arms held down, like one of the 'dumb ministry' that the state repression was creating. The (religious) intellectual who at first has schemes which benefit the nation is misled into signing an agreement which apparently promises him a better life, but he only gains knowledge of the full extent of repression in which he has acquiesced when the delusory pleasure comes to an end.

But it is difficult to see Faustus simply as a victim of repression, or one who unfortunately sold out, if for no other reason than that he himself claims to feel guilty and to describe his fate as punishment. The external repression is reproduced subjectively. Far from being free to act, there is a debilitating uncertainty of the terms upon which one acts. The Good and Bad Angels offer a clear choice; but the devil skills produce shows that give audiences, both on and off stage, pleasure, and the humiliating of the pope is politically useful. Indeed, the state specifically forbade an individual to claim her/his own knowledge of true or right action, for the state said what truth was. Thus Whitgift said that Martin Marprelate had to be told 'that his spirit is not the spirit of God, which is the spirit of truth, but the spirit of Satan, the author of lies' (Marprelate, 1588–9, p.55). Nor can experience give Faustus any reliable knowledge: 'No mortal can express the pains of hell' (xviii.47); Mephostophilis cannot disprove that hell is a fable 'till experience change thy mind' (v.129), at which point it becomes too late to be useful knowledge. Without experience to test his knowledge, Faustus is left only with a set of prohibiting or encouraging addresses towards him. The difficulty the play has made can be seen by comparing Faustus with Bomelio, who goes mad when his magic books are stolen. Bomelio's magic is anti-social, unhealthy, exceeds the bounds of human activity, is a personal problem; it is easy to accept the punishment of Bomelio, whereas Faustus's end is distressing not only because of the moving poetry, but because of the involvement with his pleasures earlier in the play. Bomelio's son can easily decide to burn the 'vile blasphemous books' and asks: 'What gain can countervail the danger that they bring,/For man to sell his soul to sin, is't not a grievous thing?' (*The Rare Triumphs*, p.218). Dominant ideology offers a simple answer; *Faustus* also begins by looking as if it is going to affirm the ease of that answer. But the action of the play makes the selling of the soul into a problem: in a state which defines the truth, when does one lie? Is an audience that acquiesces in repression already in hell? Is one ever free to sell a soul?

The examination of the relationship of scholar and society sees truth defined by power, and the innocence or freedom of the independent thinker to be illusory. The problematic Marlowe worked within forced him to focus on the inevitable crisis within individual subjectivity, for he was examining relations of individual and state. One solution to the fictional Faustus's crisis was, however, found by puritan dissidents: 'though every man hath some grace of God's spirit in himself, yet it is greatly increased by conference' (Bownd, 1595, in Collinson, 1967, p.372). It was, indeed, precisely the *group* organisation of puritanism that the state wanted to smash, for the group, the 'conference', could sustain the individual in opposition. Faustus, however, tries to make his way alone: individual power is apparently promised by the authorities that address themselves to him (like the state) but the real terms of that promise lead inevitably to the individual's inner collapse.

CHAPTER 5

Turks and Fathers

There was a fashion for plays about Turks (and other Islamic nations) in late Elizabethan drama. Similarly, many plays centred on the figure of a father, whereas after the 1590s young men become central. Turks and fathers are topics specific to the Marlowe period, although they are not necessarily connnected; I have connected them in this chapter because both are figures associated with rule. My intention is to describe how I think each figure is used in political discussion, but, by way of contrast to Turks, I have focused the very wide topic of fathers into a discussion of personality.

(i) Turks

Turks, Moors, Tartars, even Persians, constituted the infidel powers which neighboured and threatened European Christendom. The word 'Turk' was mainly used in two ways: as a generic name for an Islamic state with its own characteristic institutions of government and military; and as a description of behaviour or character—the Turks 'being of nature cruel and heartless'—which may be applied also to Christians. The idea of cruelty was probably produced by the Turks' distant foreignness combined with an absence from their lives of comprehensible Christian ethics, but more importantly by their military threat: 'They were (indeed) at the first very far off from our clime and region, and therefore the less to be feared, but now they are even at our doors and ready to come into our houses' (Newton, 1575, Dedication). By the time Newton wrote this the Turks had been defeated at Lepanto, but the scare remained, so that in 1586 Whetstone says the Turkish kingdom 'at this day is multiplied, to the terror of the whole world' (Whetstone, 1586, p.69).

The purpose of Newton's allusion to the Turkish scare is to appeal for 'unity, peace and concord among the princes, potentates and people of that little portion of Christendom yet left', for their 'division, discord and civil dissension' have attracted Turkish incursions (Dedication); Cambini's *Commentaries* (1562) makes the same explanation of the growth of Turkish power. The work Newton translated as the *Notable History of Saracens* called for a crusade against 'this arrogant and bragging hell-hound, triumphing over us, laughing at our misfortunes, rejoicing to see us thus lie together by the ears' (sig.C1v). He dedicated it to a man who commanded troops, the Lord Admiral, Howard of Effingham, offering him a justification of amity with Spain and a new imperialist project: 'if they would join in one and live together in Christian League, no doubt Constantinople might be again recovered and annexed to the Roman Empire' (sig.B4v).

Historians saw the European divisions as a sign of the decay of Christendom which the Turks had been sent—as the scourge of God—to punish: thus Luther (at first) recommended only passive resistance to them. *A short Treatise upon the Turks' Chronicles* (translated by Ashton in 1546) says the Turks are a scourge for Christian sins and gives three reasons why their soldiers are more praiseworthy: 'The first is, that they so readily obey their captains, which among our men is seldom seen. The second because there is no danger of life so manifest that can cause them to draw back or shrink in fight. . ... [which is attributed to a belief in predestination] The third, that they can live without bread and wine very long content with rice and water, yea oft-times they be well pleased and content to live without flesh' (sig.R5r-v). (That last point connects to a plea for proper food supply for troops.) The first point is the most important: the Turks are an anti-image, united and disciplined against divided and insubordinate Christendom. *Strange and memorable things* (1574) says: 'There is no sedition amongst them, no tumult' (Chew, 1937, p.107); *The Traveller's Breviat* (1601) attributed their success to numbers, military discipline, organised provisions. The point about military might that flourishes irrespective of religious correctness was put neatly by Greville; for him the Turks become exemplars of Machiavellian theory about the real relations of religion and power:

> The Turkish empire thus grew unto height,
> Which, first in unity, passed others far;
> Their church was mere collusion and deceit,
> Their court a camp, their discipline a war;
>   With martial hopes and fears, and shows divine,
>   To hazard only, they did man refine.
>   (Greville, *A Treatie of Wars*, 1633, st.64)

While religion needs only to be shows, real power derives from unity and discipline. This reverses, of course, the dominant ideology of Christendom.

The Turkish model of efficient empire building had particular relevance to England in the late 1580s, with its blunderings of a poorly-equipped, half-starved army in the Netherlands and its vastly underfunded ships and lines of defence along the south coast. The Spanish had successes in the Netherlands campaign and could put together an Armada; even after the lucky defeat of that Armada, English troops achieved few successes, and foreign policy was split by divisions of opinion at the top. It was the second meaning of the word 'Turk' that led to its use in the more immediate issues of foreign policy: Protestant propaganda could describe the alleged cruelty of Catholics in general and Spaniards in particular as Turkish: 'As from the Turk, so shield us, Lord,/From force of popish power' (John Phillips in Chew, 1937, p.102). Foxe spoke for many Protestants when he located the real problem for true Christians nearer home than Asia Minor: 'the Turk with his sword is not so cruel but the Bishop of Rome on the other side is more fierce and bitter against us. . ... Such dissension and hostility Satan hath sent among us that Turks be not more enemies to Christians than Christians to Christians, papists to protestants' (Foxe, 1575, sig.O8v). By insisting on the corrupt Catholic religion as the fundamental enemy a useful, ideologically justifiable, rapprochement between Islam and Protestantism could be constructed: in 1577 Elizabeth's ambassador to Morocco, Edward Hogan, said the king bore 'greater affection to our nation than to others because of our religion, which forbiddeth worship of idols' (Hakluyt, 1598–1600, VI, p.289).

In practical terms, Turkish rivalry with Spain for Mediterranean power suited England well as a distraction for their greatest enemy. Thus despite all the imagery of cruel Turks and Hakluyt's gory accounts of battles, Elizabethan politicians were setting up trading relations with the Turkish empire. In 1575, the year Newton's translation was published, two English merchants started commercial negotiations and in the year of *1 Tamburlaine*, 1587, the vessel *Hercules* made a profitable trading voyage to the Turks. Clearly the two senses of the word 'Turk' were far apart: while Leicester fought 'Turkish' Spaniards in the Netherlands, he had dealings with the court at Constantinople (and Turks encouraged the Netherlands' resistance to Spain). In the word 'Turk' there was a potential contradiction of meanings which, if consciously articulated, could lead to a knowledge of the discursive operation of 'faith' and 'infidel' within material economic and political practices. Peele's *Battle of Alcazar* does, I think, articulate the contradiction. It presents a power struggle between two Moors; the wrongful one is aided by Sebastian of Portugal who offers, the Presenter says, to 'aid with Christian arms the barbarous Moor' (l.6); in a dumb-show this Moor, Muly Hamet, 'Turkishly' murders his two younger brethren. When Sebastian argues his case for intervening he speaks of the 'kingly favour' that is requested from him, and Muly Hamet's promise 'to surrender up/The kingdom of Moroccus to our hands,/And to become to us contributory' (ll.578, 583–5).

The text makes the Christian hero Sebastian into a problem. He is always referred to as Christian, honourable and brave, but his motives are also imperialist and his trust in Philip of Spain mistaken, as is the support for Muly Hamet. Anyone trained to see Peele simply as a patriotic writer will have problems with Sebastian and so too any reading wanting unitary 'truth' will be unsettled by the play of Peele's text which here, as elsewhere, ceaselessly shifts in style and form; the problem was marked in original performance by having the star Alleyn play the wicked Muly Hamet, not the brave Sebastian. Sebastian's intervention, his 'bravery', ends as is foreseen in the battle which kills off all three major leaders. But Sebastian, honourable and valiant or 'proud invading', is not just a problem within the story-line. The text metadramatically links with recent English policy, Sebastian being associated with an army whose 'payment in the camp is passing slow,/And victuals scarce, that many faint and die' (ll.1008–9): recalling perhaps the main complaint to Elizabeth from the army in the Netherlands. Sebastian tries to make an ally of Philip of Spain, who sent the Armada against England, and with whom some politicians were secretly negotiating even in Armada year. Yet Sebastian also makes a lengthy eulogy of Elizabeth in the middle of the play. The language of Christian honour is made ambivalent by his actions; the eulogist of Elizabeth is the same fictional character who makes mistaken alliances. Peele's sources show a Sebastian who intervenes to set one Moorish faction against another, but the playtext, in place of the schemer, creates the brave Christian prince: it is precisely the brave image that the text makes into a contradiction, and hence potentially offers a knowledge, relevant to Elizabethan state propaganda, of the ideological function of religious and chivalric language.

By contrast, the Moorish characters of the play conduct a political discussion of which the issues are articulated only within the diegesis, a fictionalising that makes possible the fullness of the discussion. Their debate is the common (and prohibited) one: royal succession. The rival groups of Moors both claim to be lawful but each organises succession differently: the evil Moor intends to hand power to his son while the good Moors try to hand power to each of four brothers in turn. At the date of performance (c.1589) it was impossible that Elizabeth, last of three royal siblings, would produce an heir. The uncertainty over succession was creating what some called 'ticklish' times, with Catholics and foreigners commenting on English rule, and rival candidates being backed. In the play the wicked Muly Hamet already has the power and the good faction calls for outside help: 'To sow the lawful true succeeding seed/In Barbary' (ll.98–9). The seed metaphor is conspicuously an attempt to present as 'natural' what is deliberate armed intervention (Wentworth's pamphlet on the royal succession was to argue for the establishment of *right* of succession rather than natural line, Wentworth, 1598, p.23). And, since the Turks are called on, the traditional image reappears: 'Amurath hath sent scourges by his men,/To whip that tyrant traitor king from hence' (ll.107–8)—difficult times require tough solutions. The Turks point out that they are not 'mercenary men' but come as 'sure friends': Elizabethan rulers were not very successful with mercenaries on the Continent (pay proved a problem), though they had been used to put down domestic rebellions (like Home Counties police in the Notts coalfield), and Machiavelli advised against them. The Turks are, significantly, friendly, and the play argues that their intervention in a succession struggle is useful. It argues thus at a time when English affairs are ticklish, and some even might see the 'new man' imagery around the Turkish arrival, the 'glorious comet that begins to blaze' (l.95), as a glance towards James VI or indeed Essex, whose career was built through military, as opposed to Robert Cecil's civil, administration.

The Moorish story of *Alcazar* questions the alleged basis of royal power when two rulers claim to be lawful and when military might is the only decider. 'Turkishness' was constructed in ideology as a denial of the principles—natural law, divine law—that founded and legitimated the monarchies of Christendom. Bodin says: 'The King of Turks is called the Grand Seignior, not because of the size of his realm . . . but because he is complete master of its persons and property' (Anderson, 1979, p.398): there are no inherited rights or property. Smith views it as an absolutism, where the Turk rules 'an infinite number of slaves or bondmen among whom there is no right, law nor common-wealth compact, but only the will of the Lord and segnior' (Smith, 1583, p.21). Histories of Turks say they only became united under a single ruler from the time of Mahomet or Ottoman, before that being tribes or marauding companies of horsemen: 'Neither hath one the regiment and governance over all, but every tribe to have their proper king, after whom his own son should not succeed in the kingdom, but the first that was born of the seed of a right noble man and woman, after he were saluted king, was kept and brought up as heir apparent to the crown.' (Newton, 1575, p.3) These accounts portray a monarchy that does not exist from time immemorial, that is an office created by human decisions, where the form of government is shaped by economic and social needs. This is a more materialist analysis than the Tudor myths of origin, which trace monarchs back to Arthur and New Troy, a rule blessed by Christ and permanent as nature, always already there. The successful Turkish empire could manage without kings, for they 'appointed to every faction and country his governor, and in this sort governed for a long time, having among them neither king ne any man endued with title of sovereignty other than of captain' (Cambini, 1562, p.1).

The administration run by military officers was seen as a meritocracy, the operation of which would contradict the traditions of sacred kingship and inherited private property which Christian political theorists named as the bases of the state; the Mamalukes 'observing this order for ever after, that the son should not succeed his father in the crown and regal diadem neither that any more account should be made of the blood royal than of any other. . ... Neither might any of them claim to enjoy his father's inheritance as in the right of descent, neither look to be advanced and preferred to any commodity or honour, unless his deserts and service should be thought well worthy the same' (Newton, 1575, p.117). Traditional social rank was not operative: 'Ottoman (a man of base lineage)', says Whetstone, 'got the favour of the people and was made their K[ing]' (Whetstone, 1586, p.70). What Whetstone suppresses is the place of money and material reward within the structure of loyalty: 'through [Ottoman's] liberal distributing of the preys and spoils that he gat from the Christians to his soldiers, his power was so increased through the pleasantness of gain and reputation that his people had, that he (seeing himself chief of an army which desired to live licentiously and was apt to accompany him in whatsoever enterprise he should take in hand' made himself prince (Cambini, 1562, p.1). The immorality of the fighting force affects neither their loyalty nor their efficiency. Such examples of the inefficacy of the moral order within history (a theory propounded by Machiavelli, though the connection isn't made) are far from English moralistic histories (Whetstone attributes the fall of all kingdoms to Envy—so unlike the demeanour of his own dear queen).

Some of these reflections on morality, conquest and heredity are activated in *Tamburlaine*, whose low-born hero has the military skill to trounce the hereditary kings of Persia and Turkey, a bandit become monarch. Historians of Turks commend his discipline and order and personal virtue; both plays show his success, which they simultaneously ironise. The first *Tamburlaine* seems to have been very popular and highly influential, and, while it is impossible really to know what audiences found pleasure in, examination of the relations of text and context may suggest some reasons for the success. (Discussions of its morality or theatrical glamour only defer the question about context—why does an audience like what it likes when it does?) Clark (1965) has posited Tamburlaine as a figure for Ralegh—lowish birth, atheism, imperialist schemes against (Turkish) Spain. This analysis is not as batty as some, but it is highly reductive and has little idea of artwork. It may be more useful to employ a theory of typification, and to show the more general ideological attitudes which the fictional individual is constructed to reveal.

Tamburlaine has imperialist ambitions, which he achieves with an efficient army; that efficiency is signalled by his rewarding the 'virtues' of his captains, who are his friends, with crowns. He tells Theridamas that the gold he sees comes from Jove 'As if he meant to give my soldiers pay' *(1 Tamburlaine*, I.ii.183), and that line may well have had topical overtones after the recent Netherlands campaign in which funds for the army were so slow in coming through that Leicester had to pay soldiers out of his own pocket (he also founded a hospital for the wounded). Theridamas is asked to compare the military effectiveness of Tamburlaine with the hopelessness of his own king, Mycetes, and his decision to change sides foregrounds the attractiveness of the imperialist adventuring. This was the policy which divided ministers not only over the Netherlands but in all their dealings with Spain. Leicester's expedition to the Netherlands acquired the status of an anti-Catholic crusade (Strong, 1964, p.33), Ralegh and Drake set up privateering voyages, but against them was Elizabeth and Burghley's caution about money. (The division between gentleman-adventurers and conservative peers was later figured in the Elvetham pageant in 1591 (Boyle, 1971).) Similarly, some London merchants sought peace if not trade with Spain, whereas others backed privateering voyages against Spanish trade fleets. The Netherlands debacle had passed before *Tamburlaine* was performed, but nationalist Protestant feeling had a focus in the campaign for the execution of Mary of Scots (she was executed early in the year *Tamburlaine* appeared — 1587). A propagandist image for Mary and Catholicism was the Hydra (see *A View of the Romish Hydra*, 1588) and Bajazeth the Turk compares his power to 'the heads of Hydra' (III.iii.140), which presumably reinforces the sort of champion Tamburlaine is. Elizabeth, again, was cautious about dealing with Mary, keeping her imprisoned but trying to avoid execution.

Marlowe adds to his sources the rhetorical skill and poetic taste of Tamburlaine, for Tartars were apparently without 'eloquence or sophistical subtleties' (guided only, ironically, 'by a natural justice engrafted in them') (Newton, 1575, p.109). Also, where the moral histories talk of Tamburlaine's fury or his death in a raving fit (Whetstone; Byshop), Marlowe gives him a self-mastery which Elizabethan psychological tracts teach their readers to admire (Anderson, 1927). The playtext makes a courtly-spoken, self-disciplined hero, a new man successfully fighting decadent or tyrannical hereditary orders, a man seen by Christian historians as a deliverer from the Turks: 'May we not be glad to hear tell that Tamburlaine took the great Turk Bajazet prisoner and all his life after used him like a vile drudge?' (Ashton, 1546, Epistle). In the year before the Armada, with worry about Catholic (tyrannical, 'Turkish') threats at home and on the Continent, Marlowe's play presents a courtly military adventurer who was famous for delivering his people from Turks. With the uncertainty about succession and Elizabeth's policy of pacifying where possible, the ideology of Protestant aggression produced the need for heroes: Leicester tried for the role with his processions and acceptance of governorship in the Netherlands, and under his wing he had Essex, on whom many hopes were fixed after Leicester's death in 1588.

But the *Tamburlaine* text is constructed so that the

glamorous adventuring is shown but is not pleasurable—Tamburlaine produces corpses but without the excitement of battle scenes. When Cosroe invites his aid against Mycetes, he opens the way for a force he cannot control (similarly in *Selimus* Bajazeth seals his doom by using Selimus against Acomat). I see the text as problematising the contemporary hero ideology in trapping its audience between the success and the cruelty of Tamburlaine, between stable rule and the means that maintain it, between civil and military. In the 1580s this tension was given specific focus: first, in the Bond of Association, an initiative from Protestant gentry in the years of crisis around Mary of Scots—those who signed the Bond effectively agreed to fight against any attempt on the crown in favour of Mary or her son. The prospect of armed gentry taking the law into their own hands was a potential threat to the Renaissance monarch, whose bid for personal power required the discouraging and weakening of the private armies of other aristocratic families: these Protestant defenders of Elizabeth undermined her strategy for absolutism. But she was also weakened in her inability to head a national army when this became necessary. Elizabeth's attempt at absolutist rule was maintained by propaganda that linked her person with the fate of the nation. This worked in peace, but the Netherlands crisis produced conditions that required a national army to fight beyond English shores. The commander of this army would therefore be in a powerful position, and Leicester precisely indicated this power when he accepted the governorship of the Netherlands, an office only Elizabeth should have held (for absolutism, see Anderson, 1979, and for aristocratic armies, Stone, 1967). In two instances, then, the necessary saviours could have overthrown what they were supposed to be saving (the Protestant gentry would probably not have seen this; one imagines Leicester did—he always kept a private fortified castle at Kenilworth). In *Tamburlaine* the weakness of the old orders has to give way to the new man and the Turkish tyranny can only be defeated by the new man; that new man also comes with his own cruelties, and makes his own terms.

The final irony of *Tamburlaine*'s reflection on the Elizabethan need for heroes, both domestically and abroad, is

that the new cruelty is eventually not an opposition to but a
completion of the old order. Tamburlaine receives the
Soldan's permission to marry Zenocrate, the new man weds
the established family and makes a financial deal with its
father. The man who overthrows Turks himself has a
'Turkish' cruelty, and both the heroism and the cruelty can be
accommodated to the old order of the Soldan. It is a sardonic
view of the ideology and practice of absolutism, the
operations of which might be seen in the specific case of
English attitudes to Turks: the ideological hatred of that
which was infidel and brutal, yet the trading relations and
necessary alliance against Spain; the moralistic caution about
an empire organised by professional officers which in fact
offered a model for rather than an antithesis to the pursuit of
absolutism. Tamburlaine offers his truce to the world/the
audience only after the deals are made; the audience realises
throughout the play that it has a place on neither side (my
only evidence for this is the regular complaint about lack of
dramatic conflict and hence no emotional involvement with
the play), it has a sense of powerlessness. The story of the
disciplined hero seems constructed to produce ironic disbelief
and perhaps anger in response to his rule, that cynicism and
emotion which the authorities condemned in theatre audiences (by contrast, Greene's *Tamburlaine*-like play *Alphonsus* (1591/1599) naturalises and sentimentalises its hero by
giving him genteel birth). A final irony of the contextual
relations of the play is that the authorities urged the same sort
of self-mastery that the hero shows, whereas the only positive
response to his truce is to boo.

The follow-up play takes the next step, from establishing
rule to the problem of maintaining it and making a successor.
Tamburlaine inculcates cruelty and hardness to train his
successors, for the effeminate son's presence shows that
natural lineage alone does not guarantee an appropriate heir.
The play ends without showing what the histories tell of the
sons' quarrels and the division and decay of the empire.
Succession is not fully focused in *2 Tamburlaine*, and it is
another *Tamburlaine*-influenced play, *Selimus*, which uses
the distance of 'Turks' to discuss the issue so close to home.
The ageing defeated Bajazeth has three remaining sons (the

favourite has been killed); he feels threatened by soldiers, upstart critics and his sons' ambitions. The sons 'set the law of Nature all at nought'; Selimus has none of the filial duty 'Which nature hath inscrib'd with golden pen,/Deep in the hearts of honourable men' (ll. 114, 214–15). Unlike the dutiful inhabitant of a Christian commonweal as Hooker would see him, Selimus is not written on by natural law; there is only vicious competition for power. Bajazeth fears him because 'The Janissaries love him more than me' and his own royal power is vulnerable where 'the soldiers overrule thy state,/And nothing must be done without their will' (ll. 95, 101–2). The play foregrounds the political role of the army and counsellors. Mustaffa is instinctively loyal but other bassos find limits to 'love': 'Yet will we not for pitying his estate,/Suffer our foes our wealth to ruinate' (ll. 873–4). While Bajazeth sleeps, the counsellors discuss 'love' and loyalty: Mustaffa 'loves' Bajazeth because he was given the king's daughter to marry, but he is 'loyal' to Selimus whose cause he prefers to his brothers' for the love 'unto my country's good'.

Some arguments here are similar to those of Wentworth on the succession (the tract was printed only after his death, but his views were well known). Wentworth urges the queen to name a successor in order to ensure security. He dismisses the fear that 'subjects are given naturally to prefer their new master before their old mistress' (Wentworth, 1598, p. 54), for wise men honour the ruler who has already benefited them; so too Mustaffa explains his 'love' for Bajazeth. Halibassa argues that if the father can lawfully take arms against the rebel son, 'Why should it be unlawful for the son/To levy arms 'gainst his injurious sire?' (ll. 887–8); Mustaffa mocks the idea that it is lawful 'for a subject prince/To rise in arms 'gainst his sovereign,/Because he will not let him have his will' (ll. 890–2)—Selimus owes loyalty because he has been given an empire. The problem is debated by Wentworth thus: a named successor, far from endangering the ruler, 'must of necessity confess and take himself so bound to you therefore, as though you had (even) given him the kingdom' (pp. 64–5); the real danger lies with he who knows he has the best right to succeed, for the more this is suppressed and concealed the more 'it will stir the coals of wrath in his heart, and the sooner it will cause him to put forth himself, lest he should (by silence) miss of that which he accounted his right' (p.84). This description fits the career of Selimus.

The necessity to revenge himself on another rebel son, Acomat, forces Bajazeth (on the advice of Mustaffa) to use Selimus to lead his army. Bajazeth now experiences how his rule, which seems personal, is in fact delimited by the officers who carry it out. He wants the satisfaction of revenge 'I care not how', which he gets, but he also has his power removed. His 'captains' crown Selimus 'Knowing thy weak and too unwieldy age,/Unable is longer to govern us' (ll.1650–1); they threaten to kill him if he witholds consent. Bajazeth willingly resigns the crown, and becomes an increasingly pitiable figure with lengthy expressions of inner grief. But these expressions happen when the stage is empty; when bassos discuss succession he sleeps. His emotional life and the pity are redundant in the course of political necessity. Selimus is unlawful, 'unnatural' but necessary. Once crowned he institutes a reign of terror, which might be expected of 'Turkishness'; at the same time this sensationalism offers a challenge to Wentworth's position for, brave and radical as he was in his attempt to discuss political issues openly, he was still writing within an ideology of reasonable natural law: thus, 'if there be but common reason and nature in him [the named successor], it will bind both his heart, tongue and hands from ever continuing anything to your peril' (p.65). *Selimus* posits a world where people are not written on by natural law.

The necessary Selimus is labelled Machiavellian when he talks of making his empire secure by fear, claims religious belief 'disgraces man', rejects traditional beliefs of 'schoolmen'. This contrasts with *Tamburlaine* where the strategy was to make the hero's presentation initially pleasurable, and then to question the pleasure; Selimus is set up as a villain expected to fall, but he doesn't. His 'villain' speech is, we learn, the preface to success. His account of the origin of monarchy and private property is not so much Turkish (Ponet, 1556, says Turkish rulers did not respect private property (sig.E7r)) as drawn from the theorist of absolutism,

Bodin:

> Then first the sacred name of king begun;
> And things that were as common as the day,
> Did then to set possessors first obey.

(ll.321–3)

Selimus says how 'names of Gods, religion, heaven and hell' (l.329) were devised to make men obey laws. This is a notorious Machiavellian idea, the *Treatise of Treasons* (1572) defining the Machiavellian state where civil policy is 'not limited by any rules of religion, but the religion framed to serve the time and policy' (Raab, 1964, p.60). Selimus's image of religion as a 'bugbear' occurs in a poem of Ralegh's and the cynicism about religion may be paralleled in that circle, especially in the 'atheist' Harriot who, following Bruno, says belief in heaven and hell 'worketh so much in many of the common and simple sort of people that it maketh them have great respect to their Governors' (Shirley, 1974, p.13). The Ralegh circle was witch-hunted in the early 1590s and *Selimus* may cash in on that; but the play breaks with anti-atheism in showing that Selimus *succeeds*. For the persecution of a few scapegoats, the Ralegh circle, suppressed knowledge of a wider cynicism about religion among rulers: Stafford wrote to Burghley (1587–8) about the negotiations over Henry of Navarre's religion: 'It is a thing most certain that religion is but a colour and worldly pride and ambition the bottom of their hearts' (Read, 1925, p.212).

The unpunished holding of these ideas is of a piece with the play's speaking about topics prohibited by the state, an act foregrounded in the scene of the counsellors' discussion while Bajazeth sleeps behind curtains (the real Elizabeth was all too vigilant). It is tempting to reduce the play to a set of identifications, if only to show the relevance disguised as 'Turkishness'. Bajazeth's lines may evoke Elizabeth: 'What prince so'er trusts to his mighty power . . . If he were in the place of Bajazeth,/He would but little by his sceptre set' (ll.831, 835–6). The sons are contrasted thus: Selimus, the youngest, is favoured by soldiers and seeks to lead the imperial army; Acomat is 'pompous', married and puts off effeminate robes to take to the battle-field; Corcut is scholarly and religious. Here is the reduction: Selimus the young Essex, Master of the Horse, reading Marprelate pamphlets; Corcut the clerkly Robert Cecil, his rival; Acomat James VI of Scotland, married and with his own court. A quotation from James in 1592 indicates one sense of the times: he will not invade England but 'In the meantime I will deal with the Queen of England fair and pleasantly for my title to the Crown of England' (Willson, 1962, p.111), but after her decease if his title is not recognised he will obtain it with the sword. Acomat musters arms 'to prevent all sudden perturbations' (l.763) and writes to Bajazeth demanding he keep his promise to give him the empire. Walsingham, writing to James VI political advice in 1587, says: 'Princes are not so ready in these days to embrace other men's quarrels but where they are extraordinarily interested in their own fortunes' (Read, 1925, p.184). Conscious of the errors in doing so, I make these parallels really to indicate how much I feel the play connects with contemporary issues; the main point being that 'Turkishness' shows attitudes that are familiar but that cannot be ideologically recognised as natural to the politics of England—a power struggle in which monarchy is not sacred, where divine and natural law are fictions and military power is real. In the event, Essex did make a desperate, hopeless, attempt at armed intervention; alongside the immediate economic determinants of that (for instance, his aristocratic debts), the ideological possibility of it may have been presented in the early 1590s, in plays such as *Alcazar* and *King Leir* where 'foreign' military intervention is useful and favourable, in plays such as *Tamburlaine* and *Selimus* where the new man at the head of troops is necessary and irresistible. While the Commons was inhibited, the plays, I would argue, publicly discuss the problem of the relation of ruler, counsellors and army that was endemic to the absolutist project of the Tudors.

(ii) Fathers

The story of the father-king who makes mistakes about his

children and realm is repeated in numerous Elizabethan plots. Fathers of English mythology—Arthur, Gorboduc—are faced by internal strife, fathers of English history—Edward IV, Henry V—die to leave corrupt or divided regimes. The association between the father story and the central problems of Elizabethan polity was set up in the earliest and archetypal text, *Gorboduc*. There the issues are not simply succession and national unity, but the relations between monarch and counsellors. The specific reality of the problem by the 1580s potentially challenged the ideologies of personal rule and legitimation by Nature within which the stability of the monarchy was guaranteed, for there was no natural successor to Elizabeth: the institution of a 'personal' monarchy could be ensured only by the compliance of its officers, and the 'natural' royal line continued only by negotiation over the rights and suitability of possible candidates. The end of *Gorboduc* affirms the myths: the secure ruler needs to 'display by long descent/A lineal race to prove him lawful king', but God will protect—'yet must God in fine restore/ This noble crown unto the lawful heir' (ll.199–200, 276–7). In the late 1580s-early 1590s, many looked to James VI to take over, but as the son of Mary of Scots many tried to disqualify him in the mid-1580s, so he was not obviously 'lawful'; likewise in the 1584 Parliament Burghley had drafted a bill to set up a Grand Council of Privy Councillors and officers to rule 'in the name of the Crown of England' in the event of Elizabeth being murdered—she banned the bill, but its idea showed doubt about the efficacy of leaving everything to God. The ideology of succession was being tested by material circumstances, and while debate in Parliament on succession was prohibited the playtexts constantly returned to the effort to articulate the ideological tensions that were arising. In particular they focused on the figure of the father and, given the developing interest of the Elizabethan theatre in emotional mimesis, this figure is presented not just as a type of a ruler but as a person moved by what happens around him: the individual becomes the site of ideological struggle and affected by that struggle, and the meaning of the father, even in patriarchy, becomes unsettled.

One of the marks of Selimus's villainy is his attack on

the foolish names
Of father, mother, brother and such like:
For whoso well his cogitation frames
Shall find they serve but only for to strike
Into our minds a certain kind of love.
For these names too are but a policy,
To keep the quiet of society.

(ll.340–6)

It is evil to describe what is 'natural' as policy, cynical to articulate the connection of the personal with the political and argue that 'natural' love makes the individual submissive. Selimus is a Turk, cruel, vicious, a rebellious son; his attack on the family paves the way for an attack on his king. Reverence for the father was central to dominant Elizabethan ideology: 'all those to whom any authority is given, as magistrates, ministers of the church, school-masters; finally, all they that have any ornament, either of reverend age, or of wit, wisdom, or learning, worship, or wealthy state, or otherwise be our superiors, are contained under the name of fathers; because the authority both of them and of fathers come out of one fountain' (Nowell, 1570, p.130).

There are three points with which I want to preface my limited discussion of the large topic of fathers. First, that the imaging of monarch or social superior as parent has the effect of portraying as naturally given a power relationship that is, otherwise, open to negotiation (monarchs' powers can be limited, structures of wealth can change). Wentworth wrote of monarchs' duties to people as 'gods and natural fathers and mothers' (Wentworth, 1598, p.6). In the 1584–85 Parliament, the Speaker brought a royal message that inhibited discussion of church reform: 'therefore, of her great and tender favour, she could not choose but as a mother over her children eftsoons to warn you to forbear any further proceedings in this course: the rather for that . . . it pertained least unto them, being the lowest of the three estates' (Neale, 1969, II, p.74). The command implements hierarchical discipline, and at the same time refers to motives that are instinctive ('could not choose but') and a relationship that is natural ('as a mother'). The ideology is affirmed when its terminology is used by the Commons against the queen: they petition for the execution of Mary of Scots: 'She is only a cousin to you in a remote degree. But we be sons and children of this land, whereof you be not only the natural mother but also the wedded spouse. And therefore much more is due from you to us all than to her alone' (*ibid.*, p.116). The parental image not only constructs mutual obligations but suppresses any reference to Mary as a sovereign queen with divine privileges. This terminology constructs a place for the individual subject in the ideological order; as Vives put it, a prince should be addressed as if he 'were already furnish'd with the parts he should have, especially in affairs of state' (Talbert, 1962, p.82). The language used in political affairs works not to express a 'truth' but to make an ideological summons, an interpellation perhaps, which Bacon defines as: 'by telling men what they are, they represent to them what they should be' (Bacon, 1625, p.156; see also Talbert, 1946).

My second point draws a distinction between mother and father. Elizabeth was addressed as a mother because of her sex, but often the country is spoken of as a mother while the prince is the father. Ponet writes of the monarch's 'well beloved wife, England' (Ponet, 1556, sig.L4r), where the male is active, the female passive. More complexly, Nowell's *Catechism* calls the country 'the most ancient, sacred and common mother of us all, which ought to be dearer unto us than ourselves, and for whom no honest man will stick to die to do it good', and the prince 'the father of the country itself, and parent of the commonweal' (Nowell, 1570, p.133). The subject 'us' is split in that there is an 'I' that can love the mother and love the self; this mother offers a love which promises a community, which is the original community from which the self split off; the honest man will die, will choose to give up any sense of his separate identity in order to benefit the mother. The mother country offers the reassurance that we can all be one, that our socially constituted selves can return to that original unity with the mother. The father, by contrast, has nothing to do with the construction of the self; his authority is over a political unit, the commonweal. The division between father and mother enables Ponet to suggest that the body politic—the unity of country and commonweal—has power greater than that of the ruler, who

occupies an office for which s/he is selected and within which
s/he can make good or bad laws. The prince can invent
grounds—'gay painted words' (sig.G2r)—for seizing property, but beyond her/him is the law of nature which is 'not
written in books but graffed in the hearts of men: not made
by man, but ordained of God; which we have not learned,
received or read, but have taken, sucked and drawn it out of
nature: whereunto we are not taught but made; not instructed
but seasoned' (Ponet, 1556, sig.G6r). The image of the
mother suckling the baby affirms a relationship which
precedes the learning of language and the reading of books;
the written and taught language can be misused by the bad
ruler (the 'gay painted words') but mothering nature creates
her subjects before language. Of course, what is uninspected,
the 'natural' law is laden with political values when it places
its subjects in social degree, appropriate subservience, personal discipline—all of which are negotiable and could be
changed. Which is why Machiavelli attacked the whole
concept of natural law, and why that attack was so shocking.
(The figure of the mother behind changing male rulers is
ironised in *The Massacre at Paris*; and it may glance at
Elizabeth as 'mother'.)

My third point concerns the specific political authority
of the father. His government is not instinctive or pre-
linguistic; he maintains subjects in association with each
other, rather than offering the individual subject a place in an
original natural community: 'God willeth his magistrates not
to spare either brother or sister or son or daughter or wife or
friend' (Neale, 1969, I, p.270). It is the father who is seen as
the magistrate, not creating individuals but subjecting individuals to law. The father controls the social life, upholds the
connection between individuals and the property they own.
The influential Bodin made the role of the father central in his
political theory: the shape of the family arose inevitably from
the needs of human nature and thus formed the basic unit of
the state; it is impossible therefore to think of the human
individual without the family, and in all families authority
resides in the male because (says Bodin) the woman is the
physical, moral and intellectual inferior (may he rest in pain).
Furthermore, all families naturally have property of some

sort, so the father has always had responsibility for the security of a social and economic unit—that is his natural role. This patriarchal theory sees private property and gender inequality as guarantors of the stability of the state: 'It is impossible that the republic will be worth anything if families, which are its pillars, are ill constituted' (Bodin, 1576, in Allen, 1960, p.409; my translation). Men have natural authority but the father is an image of God. Bodin suggested that the decay of paternal authority had produced political disorder; the solution was 'in a well-ordered republic to grant to fathers the power of life and death that the laws of God and nature give them' (*ibid.*, p.409; my translation). The great Anglican apologist Hooker repeated Bodin's stress on the father in his own political theory: 'To fathers within their private families Nature hath given a supreme power'; fathers have 'natural superiority' (Hooker, 1593–7, I, p.191). The monarch was as a father, the father as a king or magistrate in his own household (see Hill, 1966, p.443 ff.). Even critics of monarchy repeated the idea: Hotman says: 'the king has the same relationship with the kingdom as a father with his family, a tutor with his student, a guardian with his ward . . . but . . . all these latter are appointed for the former, so the people are not found and procured for the sake of the king, but rather the king for the people' (Hotman, 1573, pp.399–401). The interesting point, as we shall see, is what happens to the father when the family collapses; whether he precedes the family or whether the family constructs him.

Bodin's theory can be extended into structures of language and emotion. The idea that man's superior reason should control women's susceptibility to appetite is all too familiar. Christian teaching is largely responsible for the concept that women are 'naturally' more emotional and influenced by their passions (Eve); this was given historically specific validation in the attacks of the puritan exiles on the reign of Mary Tudor (Goodman, for example, said female rule was a 'monster in nature'); and this attack was sustained by Elizabethan propaganda which figured Elizabeth as a uniquely chaste (and therefore male-spirited) female ruler as against the depraved misuse of power guided by passion that was exhibited by most other women rulers, in particular Mary of

Scots. Thus the words all link up in Merbury's statement that good commonweals have 'tenderness over the subjects, as good fathers have over their children: And the corrupted and usurped governments (like unto unnatural mothers) have no regard, but of their own lusts and licentiousness' (Merbury, 1581, p.11). The woman is given to emotionalism and hysteria (a fit of the 'mother' being a hysterical attack), whereas the male, particularly the father, speaks the language of reason and necessary government. When he defines those who lament excessively—through their undisciplined 'affection'—Wilson speaks of 'such as are subject to passions, and furthest from fortitude of mind, as women commonly rather than men, rude people rather than Godly folk' (Wilson, 1560, p.77). (The connection of women and 'rude people' is interesting: gender and class.) Gosson repeats the terminology when he claims that tragedies 'drive us to immoderate sorrow, heaviness, womanish weeping and mourning, whereby we become lovers of dumps and lamentations, both enemies to fortitude' (Gosson, ?1590, sig.C6r)—emotion breaks proper discipline, and that emotion can be engendered in anyone by such things as plays.

The father is the magistrate who speaks his 'sentences', he is the corrector: 'forsomuch as children and servants be often careless in attending unto the word of God, the very fear of rebuke or correction at their father's or master's hands will make them learn somewhat' (Udall, 1596, in Collinson, 1967, p.378). This picture of the father potentially contradicts the image of a mother nature whose shaping of an individual preceded the language of instruction. The problem lay in the weight that was given to natural law, and puritans, whose position often opposed the given 'natural' hierarchy, tended to stress only the authority of the Word. The presentation of the father as an individual subject consequently becomes problematic, in the tension between reason and nature; political crisis—the loss of control over state or family—means that the language of the magistrate which constitutes the subject 'father' becomes ineffective or non-meaningful, and thus there is a crisis in the subjectivity.

This inner crisis is explored by the father plays that develop from *Gorboduc*. That earliest play works as an exemplary lesson, with its explanatory dumb-shows and choruses, its consistently present counsellors. Gorboduc mistakes the 'nature of my loving sons' (I.ii.339), and the emotional error leads to dishonouring of 'a father's name' and respect for neither 'father's awe, nor kingdom's cares' (III.i.91, 94). Gorboduc foresees 'Their death and mine must 'pease the angry gods' (l.103): this is a correct view, for although he despairs Gorboduc does not become irrational. In later plays fathers lose their rational grip and, importantly, become sympathetic characters as they move away from their authoritative status. The best contrast to *Gorboduc* or to the more contemporary royal advice play, *The Misfortunes of Arthur*, is that great play, written by an 'atheistic' associate of Marlowe, *The Spanish Tragedy*. Kyd's father hero Hieronimo is a magistrate: his authority is familial, social and linguistic—he puts on shows for the king and hears petitions from suitors. When after the murder of his son he cannot obtain justice from the state in which he is a magistrate, he becomes crazy—tears up petitions, puts on shows in nonsense language. His huge speeches of grief are not listened to by the authorities, the emotional expression is an embarrassment in the father who was an authoritative legislating speaker. Hieronimo never stops being a father, but the meaning of 'father' changes. It changes because of the way the father is treated, addressed, constructed by the dominant order. The love in the father-son relationship is not, as in *Gorboduc*, mistaken, an error to be reviewed in rational hindsight; for the operation of emotion changes the subjectivity of the father himself, and the viewing position of the audience. The expression of fatherhood ceases to reinforce dominant rational values.

The father's crisis is shown in the discovery scene (II.v). Hieronimo appears in his night-shirt: not the clothes of the public role, but a state of private *un*-dress; he has answered a voice that has no apparent speaker; he sees a 'murd'rous spectacle' but learns it is not simply a spectacle in that it is related to him, his son; the bower made for pleasure now holds death. What was familiar is now alienated, and that alienation is to affect Hieronimo's self: what he sees is not just murder but 'murd'rous'; the spectacle will kill the viewer.

That he speaks of himself in the third and first persons within one line marks the problem: 'Who calls Hieronimo? Speak, here I am—'(l.4). There is no one to address him as Hieronimo; the 'I' awaits address, definition. Later in the speech it is reconstructed: 'I am thy father. Who hath slain my son?' (l.18). He is defined in that he is a father, but the father of a dead son; so the constructed 'I the father' has in it a lack, for a murdering other has entered the father-son relationship; the moment of love for the son is the moment of violence directed against the other. That other is promptly seen as inhuman, that which turns a bower into 'deathful shades'; the speech ends with a set of questions.

The specific crisis in language and identity is a logical reversal of de Mornay's definition of the Christian Trinity: 'in the Trinity we call the Son the Word or the Speech; namely the lively and perfect image and wisdom of the Father' (de Mornay, 1587, p.265). When the father loses his son, he loses his speech and the lively image of himself—that which confirms to him his own identity.

Speech gives authority to the speaker, image gives identity to what it reflects: this is the reversal of their power relations that fathers encounter. Hieronimo's later misrecognition of the Old Man as his son is a symptom of his own inner derangement; when the Old Man names his own son he then becomes the 'lively image' of Hieronimo's grief, and Hieronimo's lines become more sane. Kyd's text seems to play with the sort of division (and terminology) de Mornay makes.

Isabella's reaction to the murdered son is to look for the 'author of this endless woe', and Hieronimo says: 'To know the author were some ease of grief,/For in revenge my heart would find relief' (ll.39–41). Knowledge that the author is absent produces Isabella's emotional outpouring. Looking for the author they look for someone answerable for the text of the crime: the metaphor carries all the writing/speaking associations, constructing an image of them powerless in a text that has an absent author. Hieronimo kisses his son 'for words with tears are stay'd' (l.48) (I'm ignoring the 'additions'), but he also continues speaking and inventing new language. He will keep Horatio's bloody handkerchief as a token for revenge: that handkerchief becomes filled with meaning when it has blood on it, but the blood on it marks what is missing from Hieronimo's life—for as long as the handkerchief communicates it reminds of the lack. The private emotions make a language that cannot conceal the material loss and partakes of no general conventions of meaning. This is set up for the audience when Hieronimo tells Isabella to cease her plaints, and himself speaks a lengthy Latin dirge: for those who know no Latin it is a private expression and its condition of existence is the silenced woman. While the two claim not to speak they make a language, a contradiction the text makes noticeable by giving them frequent rhymes.

When Hieronimo next appears he claims to be woken by dreams, dogged by visions: his world is confusion, his poetry redefines its language ('Oh eyes! no eyes. . .' 'Oh life! no life. . .'); where he seems to work to a rhetorical climax he is cut off: 'See, search, show, send some man, some mean, that may—' (III.ii.23). A letter falls, a new text appears arbitrarily from nowhere: things happen to Hieronimo, a central figure who does not control the space around him, so his centrality becomes provisional, not permanent. The disorder that he speaks of coincides with his accusation that heaven cannot be termed 'just' since it deals unjustly 'with those that in your justice trust' (l.11). The experience of injustice produces large poetic speeches, a language happening in an absence—no longer the legislating utterance of the father-magistrate.

After the trial of Pedringano, Hieronimo re-enters: 'Where shall I run to breathe abroad my woes' (III.vii.1). He describes the winds conspiring with his words, his passions hovering in the air and beating at heavens' windows; but the words are frustrated. He envisages the world filled with language, yet admits the uselessness of that language. Similarly when his suit is prevented by Lorenzo he starts to dig the stage to open the earth and 'bring my son to show his deadly wounds' (III.xii.73). Again it is an attempt to fill the empty space with the expressive evidence, to satisfy the lack and receive the justice which will confirm that the world is ordered. Mad, non-authoritative as this language looks, it has its origin in the emotions of the father. Addressed as a magistrate in a society that will not hear the speech nor see the evidence of the magistrate, Hieronimo has only the sense of fatherhood, and that fatherhood is designated private, emotional, non-authoritative. The disruption of rational utterance, the incursion of hysteria into the father, is finally signalled by his plan for a vengeance shaped as a show performed in 'unknown languages' (tidied up, incidentally, by being translated by an author or printer before the play became a book). The show climaxes in the display of the dead son and the telling of the story of murder and revenge: 'now behold Hieronimo,/Author and actor in this tragedy,/ Bearing his latest fortune in his fist' (IV.iv.146–8). The moment claims to be one of fullness: he has authored his own text, owns his language which the rest of the world listens to, presents himself in the third person—the justified father become Presenter. Yet it is an illusory plenitude, for his attempt to hang himself is prevented and the king threatens tortures. Hieronimo bites out his tongue, then stabs the Duke and himself. The fullness of revenge comes when the 'I' subject puts itself outside language, only achieving identification with the lost son when the father himself loses identity.

For some audiences that revenge moment is not so much full as unfair, in that Hieronimo kills the Duke (though I rather enjoy this choice of target, being unconvinced of the innocence of aristocrats). The difficulty is important, for Kyd's text constructs Hieronimo's madness by breaking decorums of representation. The later 'additions' to the play aim to make Hieronimo into a mad character type, the speeches 'revealing' his madness. This leaves the audience watching an example of a father who may be mad, but is pitiably so, having justice on his side. Kyd's text makes the madness embarrassing and thereby questions the assumed modes of representing. As I said, Hieronimo's centrality on the stage is unsettled: when two Portingales ask him directions, he goes out one door and at once reappears from another; a similar business happens with petitioners later, but they follow him off and when he re-enters he misrecognises the Old Man as his son. The exits and entrances seem to thwart the previously agreed conventions of place; the misrecognition of the Old Man complicates representation on a stage that used doubling. Within the diegesis the expression of passion becomes comical: the Portingales laugh at his poetic talk of guilt; he throws away the rope and dagger he enters with, only to pick them up a line later; he digs at the floor with his dagger. More importantly, the speeches present problems for the audience. Apparently there is an opposition between the deceitful courtly speech of the villains (appropriately imaged in the empty box that Pedringano thinks is filled with his pardon) and the full emotional expressivity of Hieronimo. Yet his emotional speeches are highly patterned, noticeably rhetorical or remorselessly alliterative: they sound written even as they claim transparent expressivity, and that writtenness belongs with an older style of drama preceding the 'natural' blank verse. So even at the moments when the audience may look to be sharing the fullness of the unjustly treated father's emotion, as a sympathetic focal point, there is the distancing effect. Not only, then, does the text show a father who loses his authoritative status, precisely through the contradictions of his ideological position, but it makes the incursion of hysteria disrupt the pleasure itself of the representation.

Kyd's explorations of the ruptured identity of the father can be paralleled in other texts. In *Selimus*, Bajazeth complains: 'mine own sons expel me from the throne;/Ah, where shall I begin to make my moan?' (ll.1759–60). While he makes moan the man sent to kill him stands by; when Bajazeth has cursed 'my stomach dry' he drinks from the poisoned cup. The emotional expression happens in the absence of the political events that have created the need to express, but simultaneously there is no relief in cursing. Bajazeth invites Aga to share his joy when Selimus departs to kill his other son, Acomat: 'all the thoughts that troubled me/Do rest within the centre of my heart' (ll.1631–2) (rest: sleep). The moment that promises to satisfy his inner desires is the moment when his loss of real political power becomes apparent; his very centre as a subject is conditional upon the activities of his sons. The captains threaten to 'hew thy body piecemeal with our swords' (l.1657) if he does not consent to the crowning of Selimus, a threat that is appropriate since Bajazeth has no political 'wholeness': every effort to express his power limits it in a new way, every attempt to satisfy his

inner wishes encounters another denial. The apparent plenitude of the father's utterance is delimited and shaped by those
whom that utterance should correct and legislate.

Bajazeth finds Selimus pleasing because he says what
Bajazeth wants to hear. This is expanded in the love test of the
Leir story, when after discussing provision for succession,
Leir has the idea 'To try which of my daughters loves me
best:/Which till I know, I cannot be in rest' (ll.82–3). It is a
trial in which the magistrate is emotionally committed; the
father's rest, again, is constructed by those he presides over;
his inner life is subject to his subjects. Bodin made little space
for the function of emotion in paternity and kinship, but the
foregrounding of it here may have something to do with the
language of the Commons, the 'loving' messages passed to
and from the monarch. Leir asks his daughters to declare their
love 'as ye tender the safety/Of him that was the cause of
your first being' (ll.232–3). Goneril's flattering words 'revive
my dying soul' (l.255), they erase the prospect of separation;
Cordella talks instead of obligation and suppresses reference
to nature, thereby making formal the relationship of parent
and child—so Leir disclaims his paternity. At the end of the
play, after exile, he recalls his misinterpretation of her words.

The *King Leir* trial scene brings together the father, the
magistrate and the guardian of property. Leir, like Selimus,
experiences the loss of legislative authority and his consequent emotional expressivity is constructed by a lack. Less
radical in representation than *The Spanish Tragedy*'s irruption of hysteria in the discourse of the father, both plays
nevertheless work to redefine the subjectivity of the father.
The language of politics is treacherous, that of emotion has an
illusory plenitude; the father is not so much the speaker of the
Word as constructed by those who address him. This abstract
discussion may have been stimulated by the historical
evidence of the contradictions in personal rule and the
attempts of its rhetoric to naturalise its relations of power.
While presented as a mother, the queen inhibited free speech
in the Commons. In the campaign against Mary of Scots she
claimed to be moved by their concern for her safety, but was
in fact threatened by the potentially autonomous organisation
of Protestant gentry.

Before leaving fathers, it is worth looking at Marlowe's image of the influence of the father, not in 2 *Tamburlaine* (where the father teaches brutality and rule) but at the end of *Edward II*. Edward III weeps while he offers to his father's hearse the head of his father's murderer. That murderer was the boy's 'protector' and his mother's lover: he is another father. The son now has power over both the loved and hated father, but he grew up in the battles between them. He weeps and speaks of his 'innocency' in this tableau of final union with the father. But in his hand is the head of the murderous other, irremovably present in the bonding of parent and child. For that other was himself a father figure, a murdering second father. No natural original love bonding can be achieved, the 'innocency' always has the presence of the other. The male and patriarchal picture is not replete with hope for the future but is structured on love and denial, on power relations not community, which are the conditions of the 'innocency' of the male child and ruler.

(iii) The Jew of Malta

The discourses of the Turk and the father may be used to make a provisional reading of *The Jew of Malta*. The play is divided into sections by the appearances of Turks, their first arrival constituting a threat to the power of Barabas which is defined in his opening scene with its speech of distant countries and miraculous wealth, its celebration of trade and peaceful rule. The problem over the responsibility of the merchant to a city-state faced by invasion is precisely that of London in the late 1580s, where despite all the nationalist rhetoric some merchants were pro-Spanish through their commercial dealings (the Hansa merchants contributed to the Armada); in 1593 the libel on the Dutch church wall claimed 'Your Machiavellian merchant spoils the state' (Freeman, 1973, p.50). The issue of rights to private property in circumstances of national danger shaped debates on royal subsidy (the cloth-merchant Henry Jackman opposing a second royal subsidy in 1589). Above all, the relationship between mercantile interests and the rhetoric of Protestant freedom could be seen in the Netherlands: in 1590 Burghley complained of the oligarchs' 'continual furnishing of the Spaniards with all kinds of munitions' (Read, 1960, p.463), although the Spaniards were meant to be the cruel papist 'Turkish' enemy. An exploration of the power relations of the city-state (Marlowe is here not interested in landed wealth), and of the individual within that, is to be the project of the play.

Secondly, the play is concerned with the construction of the person, opposing a 'natural' explanation of human conduct—the attribution of behaviour to racial characteristics (Barabas's 'Jewish' greed, similarly 'Turkish' cruelty)—against the influence of economic structures. This concern can again be specifically historicised within the discourse of English nationalism. For example, in the subsidy debate of 1585 one speaker suggested that popish recusants pay double rates as 'strangers' did: 'Seeing they refused to live according to the laws of the realm, they were not to be accounted as subjects, but as foreigners' (Neale, 1969, II, p.56) (—the parallel may be drawn with Ferneze's treatment of Barabas). To the attack on recusants Mildmay replied, liberally: 'in coupling them with the strangers we should give them cause to think that we had wholly secluded them from our society, not accounting them as natural-born Englishmen, and thereby drive a desperation into them' (*ibid.*, p.57). The speech seems to understand that the person behaves as s/he is treated; what it doesn't question is that 'strangers' should be treated in this way. Mildmay affirms the authority of the natural-born Englishman, that worthy caught between domestic traitors and external enemies. Marlowe places Ferneze in a similar situation, which could be recognised by an English audience; at the same time Ferneze is distanced in that he is Maltese, not English, so his activities might be viewed more critically. In the world outside the play, the Maltese were the objects of English propaganda support in the ideological campaign against the Turkish 'aggressor'; but within the action of the play, as many readers note, the Christian on the central ground between domestic Jew and external Turk is the most heavily ironised politic dealer of them all. Ferneze lives up to the expectations aroused by his name (Farnese was the successful Spanish commander in the Netherlands); he is both Christian in the middle and conquering opponent, the one is the other.

'Personal' scenes are intercut with scenes of international politics. The connection between the two is made at the halfway appearance of the Turks in the text. Act III scene iv ends with Ithamore exiting with a poisoned pot, asking Barabas to pay his wages and Barabas secretly threatening to pay him 'with a vengeance'. Act III scene v opens with Ferneze, who has resolved to break with the Turks, welcoming the envoy; the envoy says he has come for gold. Both cases show treacherous hospitality, interpersonal/state aggression motivated by self-preservation, the impact of gold in human affairs. The second appearance of the Turks is sandwiched between Barabas's decision to kill his daughter and the fulfilling of that decision.

The shape of the text indicates, metaphorically, some sort of impact of Turkishness on personal life, where 'Turk' connotes both threat and cruelty. The narrative explanation of Barabas's changed relationship with his daughter is that his attempt to preserve his wealth in the new crisis takes precedence over paternal feeling for her. The wealth becomes a substitute for her: when she steals his gold for him, she remains separately placed on stage but the gold crosses the gap between them. When Barabas gets it, he hugs it, blurring his enthusiasm for gold and girl; for the two can be blurred in that Barabas, as a deprived father, is interested in the satisfaction of his desires, in the filling of the lack he experiences. His statement to Abigail: 'that I had thee here too,/Then my desires were fully satisfied' (II.i.51–2) becomes highly ironic in that he uses her to satisfy his own desire for revenge (produced by the society around him). The staging signals the exploitation: Barabas tempts Lodowick to woo his 'diamond' Abigail—the conversation is held in the slave market where the slaves have their prices written on them; at her next entry, when Abigail opens the door to Lodowick, she has to be carrying letters that deal with her father's merchandise. Like the slaves, Abigail bears the text of money; the analogy posits the father as tyrannical ruler, since the tyrant, and the Turk says Thomas Smith, rule over slaves. As a virgin, Abigail has a body yet to be penetrated by the male, but she bears texts of the father—money, letters;—always already controlled/filled by him. He does not so much protect her virginity as exploit her sexual being without allowing her sexual pleasure. Barabas becomes steadily more interested in satisfying his desire for vengeance rather than in possessing wealth; the wealth that defined his power can be seized by the state so he defines himself through the scheme of vengeance. Thus he dismisses news of a merchant defaulting on debts because in the operation of vengeance 'I have wealth enough' (II.iii.247).

Barabas decides that Abigail does not love him because she 'varies from me in belief' (III.iv.10)—for the father difference is opposition. As he is articulating this, Ithamore enters, stepping in to fill the gap experienced by the father:

> Come near, my love, come near, thy master's life,
> My trusty servant, nay, my second self!
> For I have now no hope but even in thee,
> And on that hope my happiness is built.
>
> (ll.14–17)

Barabas's paternal need to have a 'hope', a love object, is supplied by the bought slave, the captive Turk. This Turk is more typically 'Turkish' in his cruel treachery than the others in the play. His incorporation as Barabas's 'second self' halfway through the play marks what has happened to Barabas the father and stranger in a world threatened by Turkish power. From here on the revenge plans are foregrounded.

Barabas's owning of Ithamore stresses what other figures of fathers play down, namely the father's economic power (even the famous *King Leir* scene is shaped by the problematic of sincerity versus treachery in expressions of love). Abigail is Barabas's 'diamond', he is prepared to sacrifice her in his plans. His comparison of his love for her to that of Agamemnon—who sacrificed his daughter Iphigenia so that the Greek fleet could sail for Troy—writes imperialism into the paternal relations. (That 'love' works on his terms, and indeed throughout the play Abigail is an object of everyone's desires.) The replacing of Abigail by a slave in the father's love economy is facilitated by the arrival of the Christian hero, Martin del Bosco, and his ship-load of slaves.

The arrival of del Bosco shows the place of money in all human relations in the play, both domestic and national. At first Ferneze will not allow the slaves to be sold because they are Turks, and Malta has a truce with Turks in 'hope of gold'. Del Bosco encourages heroic resistance to the Turks for the honour of Christendom: he recalls the Maltese to the memory of Rhodes (ironically, since Rhodes sold out), promises Spanish funds to supply Ferneze's needs, and is then permitted to sell slaves. The scene ironises patriotic and religious rhetoric in a way that recalls Montaigne describing Guicciardini: 'of all actions how glorious soever in appearance they be of themselves, he doth ever impute the cause of them to some vicious and blameworthy occasion, or to some commodity and profit' (Montaigne, 1603, II, pp.116–17). The view is not without relevance to a London in which an aggressive foreign policy was supported by those with interests in privateering; and where a peaceful one was supported by those who wished to conserve their own profitable international trading relations. The scene ends with rhetoric against 'barbarous misbelieving Turks', but the supposedly natural barbarity of the Turks is less noticeable than that of the Christians. The economic relations structure the personal more thoroughly than religion or race; the paternity at the centre of the play has its love patterned by the lack of and desire for power.

A major drawback of my reading is that it suggests coherence of structure. Academics love tightly constructed works; the discovery of formal unity recommends an important work of art. Thus *The Jew of Malta* is often seen to be shapeless alongside *The Merchant of Venice* (1596–8 /1600), and therefore worse (although I would argue *Jew* raises questions ignored by *Merchant* and that politically *Merchant* is a naive, if not nasty, play, with its eventually OK Arianism resident in Belmont, its suggestion that there is always a Belmont above the grubby world of commerce, its silence over the links of personal and political and its sentimentalising of wealth). *Jew*'s general effect of shapelessness (though not necessarily in tightly directed performance)

is a quality that should not be argued away. It resides partly
in the juxtaposition of scenes, but more insistently in the
undercutting of 'sincere' speeches—which is more disruptive
of the audience's pleasure. Barabas speaks to his Jewish
friends 'in the trouble of my spirit' but when they leave he
points out the 'slaves' simplicity' (I.ii.208, 216). When told
his house has been seized, Barabas addresses the heavens in
despair but resolves to live on, then he announces a scheme;
there are two major ways of playing this: to rant, stop, think,
have an idea or to rant and suddenly have the idea. The first
tends to be a comically inept display of realistic thinking
(inept because too quick); the second catches an audience out
by suggesting that the rant has been conscious performance of
'sincere' emotion. It is not the narrative context that ironises
the speeches so much as the performance of them that makes
the father's emotional expressivity into something opaque,
untrustworthy.

Many people find unsettling the comedy of a play that its
(treacherous) prologue describes as 'tragedy'. That comedy
constructs the way an audience views Barabas in his society.
Setting up the governor's son Lodowick to woo Abigail,
Barabas plays on his performance in asides; talking next to an
inferior, a slave, Barabas can say to him the lines he would
have to hide from Lodowick. The stooge/funny-man roles
mimic the social power relation, as the hidden lines do with
Lodowick; but the audience is privileged to hear all the asides
and therefore does not experience the conversation with
Lodowick as an image of inferiority on Barabas's part but as a
powerful fullness of expression. By sharing the pleasure of
Barabas's performance the audience is led to misrecognise his
relations with the society which treats him as alien; the comic
pleasure is treacherous.

The discussion of Shylock, the bogeyman revealed as
victim, has little room for comedy. Shakespeare argues the
case for integrating the alien on the grounds of sympathetic
human dignity. Marlowe, who is seen as more of a racist,
takes the Vice figure, enlarges his humanity in the first two
acts, and makes him comic thereafter. Barabas is always a
nasty piece of work and he acts up the Jew role: Alleyn
played him with a false nose. When they bait Friar Jacomo,

Barabas and Ithamore play up to the racial stereotypes, the wicked Jew and Turk, though Jacomo is also morally guilty; when Barabas first 'teaches' Ithamore about himself, he tells stories of murder, especially of religious people, and Ithamore responds in kind, but the style of the speeches is handled in such a way that they could be lies. The self-presentation as racial stereotype is marked as performance: Abigail is told to behave 'like a cunning Jew'. The audience is not privileged to watch an ignorant alien unwittingly conforming to stereotype, but the fictional character looks back at them when he consciously performs a role they expect: the stereotype is thus not naturalised but acted. The false nose is easily laughed *at*, the asides are laughed *with*. The racial stereotyping is marked out as problem area, for again it encourages misrecognition of Barabas's social position. His stories of murder are extraneous to the play; he kills but he has none of the power of Ferneze. The source of real power is indicated by the Prologue: 'Hence comes it that a strong-built citadel/ Commands much more than letters can import:' (ll.22–3). Barabas lacks 'might', soldiers and munitions. A state that has 'might' and 'policy' will win, as the treacherous Ferneze does. The might is, however, difficult to see, 'letters' cannot import its full extent; particularly difficult is it to see when the letters suppress it, when an audience is invited to see, for example, 'the tragedy of a Jew' and the attendant irrelevant racial posturing. It is not so much the 'tragedy' with its focus on the individual that should be read, but the comedy, which depicts, but misreports, a set of social relations.

The tragedy occupies attention because Barabas has the largest part, and because commentaries have followed the invitation to read the tragedy of a Jew. Yet the tragedy-reading becomes untenable in the later low-life scenes. Many critics explain these scenes as Marlowe losing interest: Barabas appears as a French musician to revenge himself on Bellamira, Pilia-Borza and Ithamore, but the revenge doesn't work as quickly as might be expected; he has to listen to their abuse of himself as a Jew, and his asides for once are uncomic indignation at racism. I would like to suggest a reading that sees the sense of fruitlessness about the scene as a positive strategy of the text. Barabas's disguise foregrounds the idea of the foreigner (the great immigration 1567–80 was of *French*, not Jews) and explicitly couples it now with the entertainer. Yet the performance is dissatisfying because nothing happens; he doesn't really cap the others' wit; he does not break free of racial abuse. He has to vie with the performance of Ithamore's drunkenness (as pieces of comic acting) and becomes gradually more passive. Nobody wins in the comic power relations nor is any privileged point of view offered to the audience—they know who the French musician is, but it's not an exciting performance. The scene withholds the expressiveness of tragedy and the pleasure of comedy and consequently makes a critical distance from which to view both racial role-playing and performance itself.

Just as in *Tamburlaine*'s talk of poetry or *Faustus*'s of pleasure, Marlowe's text theorises its status as performance. The ineffectual entertainer, the buying audience that doesn't really know what is going on, the vilification of strangers by those who are blackmailers, the irrelevance of the whole scene to Ferneze's plans: it amounts to a cynical reading of the state of the Elizabethan professional stage. Previous to this the text has already played games with illusion (when we are invited to see the dead friar arranged as if he still lived, which as an actor he does) and with the author's role (when the tricked Ithamore speaks elevated love poetry to Bellamira and concludes with the famous line from a lyric associated with the real Marlowe: 'live with me, and be my love'). The interrogation of how and what the stage represents is a necessary part of a text that deconstructs the ideological positions around nation and religion in contemporary London. The irony in Ferneze's final anti-Turk defiance and Christian rhetoric is that 'Turkishness'—treachery and cruelty—have permeated all human relationships, including those of performance and audience where comedy has invited participatory laughter within cruel power relations. A critical commentary that focused only on the person of Barabas within a discourse of religion or morality, one that saw the cauldron simply as an emblem of hell, would achieve a satisfying moment of closure when Ferneze invites Calymath and the audience to 'See his end first, and fly then if thou canst' (V.v.68). My reading would be interested in how the anticipated spectacle of the first part of the sentence related to the threatened captivity of the second; how the pleasure in the punishment of the corrupt stranger or tyrannical father suppresses recognition of the treacherous power of the man who presents this morality to us.

CHAPTER 6

'Women' and Males

(i) Representing women

The politics of Elizabethan theatre must encompass its representation of gender relations as well as kingship or class. For some time feminist critics have argued the need to explore the works of Shakespeare and his contemporaries, but Elizabethan theatre presents a problem in that there are fewer 'women' in plots and they are represented in conventional ways. Marlowe in particular is difficult because of the sodomy: commentaries on Marlowe imply that nothing needs to be said because his view of sex is all too clearly obsessive, nor indeed ought anything to be said because such things are best left unspoken. Therefore, almost out of sheer bloody-mindedness and rage against queer-bashing, I want to speak of Marlowe's treatment of gender and of sodomy.

Implicit in my remarks on Elizabethan theatre was a concept of sexual political analysis that studies what happens to women characters in stories. At its worst it is concerned with what is represented rather than how it is represented, and tends to assume that texts work realistically. But where the artworks are male-authored and performed entirely by men, it seems necessary to ask how the female is identified, what devices signal womanhood. Even the most thoughtful male portrayal of a woman character can assume that certain modes of discourse or appearance are 'female'; the male writer always selects his 'woman's' language according to his own assumptions, looks at her with a male gaze. But what is male need not be masculine: it may be possible to find male texts that question the ways men in patriarchy look at women, or indeed texts that call attention to their own strategies for representing women in patriarchy; males can question the operation of masculine power. When the role of the male representer of 'woman' is not examined, when 'she'

178

is studied as a character in her own right, that which is ma
assumed to be beyond comment, normal, natural—
assumption central to masculine power. To question this
assumption, and what it supports, it is necessary to comment
on that which is male, to see how maleness is defined, to
make men in texts into case studies of the representation of
maleness. My own position as a man committed against
patriarchy leads me to think that maleness is the problem, and
I think a reading can be made of Marlowe which sees his texts
as problematising the male and masculinity (much of which
has been hidden by the 'explanation' of sodomy). So my
study here moves from the handling of women characters to
the questioning of masculinity.

There are few women characters in Marlowe's plays, the
major ones being Dido, Zenocrate and Abigail. Dido is not
much written about because the whole play is seen as minor;
Abigail, on the other hand, is seen to have real emotions
which show up the iniquity of her father; Zenocrate is not a
character but a device that helps to characterise the male hero,
'a living emblem of his gentler qualities . . . reminds us of
both his spiritual aspiration and the harshness of his ruthless
ambition' (Zucker, 1972, p.35). This sort of criticism not
only compels its readers to interpret everything from the
viewpoint of a central male, but it replaces specific stage
pictures with an abstracted model of female-male contrast. So
pervasive is this view as applied to *1 Tamburlaine* that I'll
need to centre my analysis on that text.

Zenocrate first enters as part of the loot of an ambush: the
written text insists that Tamburlaine's men carry treasure,
and his syntax balances woman and loot: 'The jewels and the
treasure we have ta'en/Shall be reserv'd, and you in better
state. . .' (I.ii.2–3). The text insists that, although silent, she
has to remain on stage for the whole scene since she is given
the last line. The staging thus marks the woman not so much
as passive and silent (which would fit with the recommenda-
tions of the dominant religious and social ideology) as
captured and silenced; treated as treasure in a world where
men fight and negotiate. The movement of the scene climaxes
in the establishment of male community, the welcoming of
Theridamas the foe into the gang, watched by the woman.

This portrayal of the 'woman's place' may, of course, be paralleled in the notorious blurring of girl and gold in the speech of Barabas the Jew after she steals his treasure for him. She is replaced by money in that she is physically separated from him, being 'above', and Barabas hugs the money-bags that she throws down. The scene encourages interrogation of the ideological values which are seemingly so emotively, so 'naturally', expressed in the dying speech of Tancred in the tragedy of *Tancred and Gismunda* when he tells fathers to use their 'jewels' more tenderly. The relations of possession assumed by such metaphors are revealed when Barabas celebrates the satisfaction of his desires without thinking of how they have been satisfied. The split staging of the scene simultaneously points up how it is the active agency of Abigail that enables Barabas's satisfaction but how it is only the inanimate money bags which cross the distance between them. To this fetishising of objects within gender relations we must return.

Another point of comparison between the Zenocrate and Abigail scenes here, and a second point about the presentation of 'woman's place', is that men control stage space. The capture of Zenocrate scene turns into the persuading of Theridamas, which she watches. The scene in which Abigail steals the gold begins with Barabas alone bemoaning his lot; Abigail's appearance above provides a new interest, fostered by her lines: 'here, behold, unseen, where I have found/The gold' (II.i.22–3). She addresses the audience and is engaged in activity; he is addressing Barabas and is sitting down: the split staging potentially invites comparison of he and she. As the gold crosses the stage space between them his mood changes and he becomes more energetic, and she is faded out of the scene. But I have to say, of both scenes, that they only *potentially* invite gender comparison, since the narrative interest in each case centres on the male project—how each central male will deal with the new crisis. So the texts could be said to work in a sexist way, marginalising the woman (except that Marlowe does not forget Zenocrate). It is possible, however, to show Marlowe's staging trying to foreground the male gaze, to show specifically the male control of stage space. This is the reading I would make of the

Agydas scene in *1 Tamburlaine*, III.ii. Agydas is a courtier captured with Zenocrate and he tries to urge her to resist and hate Tamburlaine; she, however, now speaks of her admiration for him:

> As looks the sun through Nilus' flowing stream,
> Or when the morning holds him in her arms,
> So looks my lordly love, fair Tamburlaine;
>
> (ll.47–9)

She then weeps because she considers herself unworthy of him. Unknown to her, Tamburlaine and his men are watching the conversation. Their appearance has the effect of estranging the intimacy in that the audience hears Zenocrate's words in a context different from that in which she intentionally speaks them. Her deliberately ornate picture of how Tamburlaine looks is seen not to fit with the Tamburlaine who is in fact looking at her, from whom an audience may well expect some violent response against Agydas. The personal expressivity of the woman is made into extravagant redundance when the audience watches it in awareness of the watching male. Zenocrate's emotion is not insincere, in fact the internalising of the unequal power relations is pathetic, but it is devalued on a stage overseen by the male gaze.

The other person who is looked at is Agydas, and the distancing of his words produces another sort of knowledge. For Agydas is trying to persuade Zenocrate that Tamburlaine is not the man for her since he is barbarous and fiercely martial. In addressing her, Agydas is constructing a picture of her, referring to her 'heavenly face' and her 'dainty ears' which will be offended by talk of war and blood. Although at first it may seem 'natural' to address the virginal heroine thus, the construction of the scene places Agydas's words as attempted manipulation; watched over Tamburlaine's shoulder, what Agydas is seen to be doing is plotting, and the characteristics ascribed to the woman do not so much arise from what she is as from how she may be used in a world of male politics. Such an awareness prepares an audience for the next scene in which Bajazeth and Tamburlaine match one another's brags, in a series comparing their names, their

religion, their captains' brags, then their wives: Bajazeth's
wife Zabina is praised as a mother, Zenocrate for her beauty.
Tamburlaine's speech describing her is very beautiful but it
falls into place as part of male competition: it is not so much
that Zenocrate is beautiful as that Tamburlaine's project
requires her to be seen as beautiful; masculine power
maintains itself by insisting on the difference of those who are
not masculine (Marks and de Courtivron, 1981, p.219).

As the play goes on Zenocrate is steadily more silenced. In
the two jubilant Act IV scenes she breaks the mood by asking
for pity for her father. In the first, Tamburlaine claims he has
'sworn' and can't break his word, and in the second she is not
allowed the space to plead for her father. The sorrow and
pity may be seen as traditional characteristics which mark
femaleness, but the writing of these scenes makes them
awkward disruptions. More importantly, they are ineffectual,
for Tamburlaine constructs a certain image of Zenocrate to
which he dedicates his conquests but this image is not the real
woman. Thus in the famous address to her during the siege of
Damascus he describes her weeping:

> With hair dishevelled wip'st thy watery cheeks,
> And, like to Flora in her morning's pride,
> Shaking her silver tresses in the air

(V.ii.76–8)

But the poetry suppresses the fact that it is in his power to
remove the cause of her weeping, for the poetry, initially,
arises precisely to describe her weeping—it is a condition for
his poetry that *she* weeps. She is also absent, the description
of her replacing her physical presence, much as previously his
image of her coexisted with his denial of her feelings. This
moment in the playtext shows, I think, how the ideology of
what woman should be, the preferred beauty, passivity,
goodness, originates in the man. (A comparison with *Titus
Andronicus* may demonstrate how Marlowe's text foregrounds sexism. When Marcus describes Lavinia's mutilation
in her presence (II.iv), it is his speech which makes beauty
through poetry, his speech which expresses and ornaments
the horror of the unspeaking Lavinia. The male's speech *adds*
to the fullness of the scene's emotionalism and this seems

natural, appropriate. Tamburlaine, however, clearly speaks in Zenocrate's absence: the condition of his beautiful poetry is her imposed silence, his speech is neither natural nor appropriate but repressive.)

What the text does not do is explain why the ideology takes the shape it has. Tamburlaine's first formal address to Zenocrate associates her with his ambitions of conquest:

> Thy person is more worth to Tamburlaine
> Than the possession of the Persian crown,
> Which gracious stars have promis'd at my birth.

                                                    (I.ii.90–2)

Yet he tells Techelles that this is not flattery but love (Altman, 1978, p.327, suggests that Tamburlaine indicates his sword when he explains the 'she' he really loves—which would foreground the masculinity of his project). The conventions surrounding the address to Zenocrate in Act V—the actor speaking alone—mark that moment as apparently 'real' feeling. As I shall discuss with regard to *Edward II*, Marlowe's texts show 'love' to be felt subjectively even while an audience may view it as something constructed by material determinants: really it's a basic point, that people could be said to feel what the world makes them feel, but it's not a point often connected with the famous ideology of individualism on the Elizabethan stage. Here the feeling for Zenocrate, especially the fetishising of her chastity, fits into place in the imperial project. Tamburlaine tells Theridamas that Jove has sent him this Soldan's daughter, which argues that he is destined for fame; she is a partner who may fittingly be contrasted with Bajazeth's wife; finally, the fact that her chastity has been guarded allows her father to yield to Tamburlaine and consolidate the empire—his treatment of Zenocrate works to his profit.

It might be argued that it is only natural to treat Zenocrate as chaste since, as a character, she has no desires; that the text is not showing sexist ideology, but is sexist. But here again I would argue that Marlowe makes the male way of looking and of addressing seem strange, if not contradictory, rather than natural. For example, when Tamburlaine addresses Zenocrate as 'lovelier than the love of Jove,/Brighter than is the silver Rhodope' (I.ii.87–8), the speech sees her in positions of power, being attended on by Tartars and drawn on a sled by milk-white harts, but she has to listen as a captive: the visual/verbal contrast shows that the poetry refuses to recognise the real and present power relations. This first example connects up with all the others I have looked at in that poetry is used ideologically to tell Zenocrate what she is and to conceal the conditions under which it addresses her. The stage here is doing what written poetry cannot do, in that it shows the person addressed and the conditions under which s/he is addressed. In Renaissance love poetry the responses of the addressee are only 'seen' through the poet's eyes: they cannot exist independently of the written text on the page. Indeed some women addressed were only fictional constructions and not even fictionalised real women. Often it is assumed that the 'woman' addressed is free to listen or not as she chooses, since it is part of the poet's project to communicate with her fully, using his expressive verse. The stage can open up this closed relationship in showing the context of the words, for no longer are the words alone what constructs the relationship. Thus Tamburlaine addresses a woman who is forced to listen or who is absent; and, when he brags at Bajazeth or makes deals with the Soldan, he is talking about the woman to a male audience. The context suggests that the poetry is not 'natural' expression but a means of reinforcing an unequal gender power relationship, and indeed this is how it is seen by Jane Anger in her pamphlet answer to male writers (Anger, 1589).

In *The Jew of Malta* the text makes a joke of love poetry precisely by dislocating it from context. The slave Ithamore promises the whore Bellamira: 'I'll be thy Jason, thou my golden fleece;/Where painted carpets o'er the meads are hurl'd' (IV.ii.96–7); the classical fantasy is sustained for ten lines of couplets, but as soon as Pilia-Borza enters Ithamore asks if he has the gold from Barabas. The two men discuss the Jew's reaction and Ithamore prepares another blackmail note with which Pilia-Borza leaves, remarking (ambiguously) 'You'd make a rich poet, sir.' (l.130) The two 'lovers' then return to their love-talk. Two different sorts of text are made by Ithamore, blackmail notes and love poetry, the first

he a man
she's an object.
whore, so treated like one

discussed with a man, the second with a woman. And all the time Ithamore is being tricked by the other two, so a poetry in which he is the Jason and she the fleece misrecognises the power relations. So too the emotional expressivity is seen, by the structuring, to be an illusion—Ithamore makes poetry for Bellamira as he makes blackmail notes. Marlowe may deconstruct this further by parodying his own lyric 'Come live with me and be my love', as it were declaring his own authorship behind Ithamore: and at the same time asking questions about the status of his own love lyric and its unspoken context.

The placing of the language of gender relations within financial concerns, and the questioning of sincere expressivity, are appropriate to the world of *The Jew of Malta*. I used the example to try and broaden my point, from *1 Tamburlaine*, that the language of male poetry, so natural to Elizabethan culture perhaps, is foregrounded and estranged in Marlowe's plays, which then allow exploration of its values. From here another point can be made, that instead of enjoying the description of the person addressed the focus concentrates on the speaker, so that the operation of male desire is studied. An example, from *1 Tamburlaine*, is Arabia's dying speech to Zenocrate. As her former betrothed, he makes a claim upon her and enters wounded to die in her arms; before dying he wishes that his 'deadly pangs' 'Would lend an hour's licence to my tongue,/To make discourse of some sweet accidents' (V.ii.359–60). The style of the speech, with its antithetical phrasing, its alliteration, its conceit of sweet pain, shows Arabia already to be making his discourse, and that discourse is visually shown to be an imposition on Zenocrate. She and her maid have sat among corpses in silence, with the noise of battle off-stage; Arabia appears and places his bleeding body in her arms, bringing the blood close to her, yet his speech ignores her distress. He says 'Lie down, Arabia, . . . let Zenocrate's fair eyes behold' (ll.343–4), making himself performer and she the audience. The man creates a picture, the conditions of its creation are violent; the woman speaks of herself as 'the cursed *object*'.

This double effect of male looking recurs. In *2 Tamburlaine*, Zenocrate is arranged into a patriarchal tableau: 'now

she sits in pomp and majesty,/When these, my sons, . . .
Placed by her side, look on their mother's face'—their look
creates her pomp; and written into Tamburlaine's look is the
destruction, for the sons are 'more precious *in mine
eyes*/Than all the wealthy kingdoms I subdued' (I.iv.17–20;
my italics). At the end of the great scene of her death, after all
the fantastic visions of battering the shining palace of the sun
and shivering the starry firmament, he gives orders that the
town where she has died will be burnt—and that order is real.
A scene later he enters to a dead march with her hearse and
the image of the town burning; he makes a memorial to her
and then suddenly gives his sons a lesson in warfare. The
woman is literally now an object in a male world, and the
process of memorialising her creates destruction. So too,
notoriously, in *Doctor Faustus* the hero's poetry to the Helen
apparition envisages mass destruction—'for love of thee/
Instead of Troy shall Wittenberg be sack'd' (xviii. 106–7)—
male competition and rape. In *2 Tamburlaine* an audience
sees a town burning but here it is only imagined in poetry, so
it is less noticeable (for years male scholars found this a
highpoint of poetry); but part of the strategy of *Faustus* is to
trap its audience with the pleasurable. The context for
Helen's second appearance, however, establishes how the
man uses the picture of the woman: Helen's 'sweet embraces
may extinguish clear/Those thoughts that do dissuade me
from my vow' (ll.94–5). In Faustus's gaze Helen changes
status from the magic show put on for the curious scholars,
after which Faustus says nothing, to the object of desire
which promises an end to the doubts arising in the real world;
the image remains an image but becomes desired: 'Helen',
despite the poetry, is still not Helen but a spirit. I don't know
how much the presence of a boy actor would contribute to
'Helen's' impermanence here, but I think in *1 Tamburlaine*
Marlowe uses acting conditions to point up the fetishising
within the narrative of Zenocrate. It is thought that *Tamburlaine* would have been performed with four boys in the cast
(Bevington, 1962), which means that the Zenocrate actor
would have doubled as one of the virgins who plead with
Tamburlaine (possibly, as one of the senior boys, taking one
of the speaking parts). Thus not only in the diegesis does

Zenocrate sympathise with the virgins, but (in the act of performance) in the single identity of the actor an audience sees the 'woman' (as a virgin of Damascus) denied and destroyed while it also sees the same 'woman' (as Zenocrate) praised and adored. What makes Zenocrate different from the virgin of Damascus is Tamburlaine's desire. His attitude is not a chivalric tenderness to all women but a fetishising of this one woman's beauty. The doubling seems to add to the structure of male picture-making of women and male violence that is insisted on as a characteristic of male looking at women.

Zenocrate is captured, wooed and exposed to slaughter: through it all she remains chaste. The fetishising of her chastity is not simply seen as an element of male psychology, but is given material specificity in the play in that her father can agree to her marrying Tamburlaine. Through most of the text she places her father in opposition to Tamburlaine. She was seized on the way to her father and at the end of the play he enters to her as her lover's captive, but the absent father of the text is not, on account of her, in opposition: while she is silent in the last minutes of the play, they agree on an alliance: her role is to satisfy them both. It is the patriarchal arrangement of property marriage rather than the father-lover opposition of romance that structures the final scene. More importantly, the chastity fetish can be seen to be historically specific. The propaganda of Elizabeth's rule presented her as the chaste virginal monarch. She was compared to the classical goddesses Pallas Athene and Astraea, the last being associated both with justice and with empire (see Yates, 1977). This imagery worked in immediate terms as a contrast with Mary of Scots, and by extension with all the other Catholic female rulers, including the previous English queen, who had been attacked in the works of Knox and Goodman that incidentally coincided with Elizabeth's accession. Those rulers were tyrannical, apparently, because they were controlled by their passions and desires rather than their reason, a contrast frequently projected in plays elsewhere as lustful sexual appetite against chastity. In traditional patriarchal theory the woman is more passionate, less rational than the man; Wilson (1560): 'To be born a manchild declares a courage, gravity and constancy. To be born a woman declares weakness of spirit, neshness of body and fickleness of mind' (p.13; neshness = softness). Desires have to be *mastered*: 'he deserves not other to command,/That hath no power to master his desire' (*A Knack to Know a Knave*, 1592/1594, ll.1731–2); Edward III is only ready for conquest of France after he has awakened from his 'idle dream' of adulterously desiring the Countess of Salisbury (an awakening she initiates by brandishing a dagger—the penis—to display her more than womanly resolution). Elizabeth's imagery of chastity set her apart from the temperament of other, weaker, women, although it was careful not to make 'unwomanly' claims to transcend the proper female place (this was a failing of the female tyrants). Elizabeth's speeches acknowledge the weakness of women even while she claims to have a more 'patient' temperament than most: her experiences teach her 'to bear with a better mind these treasons, than is common to my sex—yea, with a better heart perhaps than is in some men.' (Neale, 1969, II, p.118) The people are invited to trust in the fitness of their ruler rather than, perhaps, the benefits of the rule: the institution of absolutist monarchy, as Foucault notes, projects virtue as an affair of state (Foucault, 1971, p.61).

1 Tamburlaine explores the Elizabethan ideology of chaste rule by showing what the imagery suppresses. For although the Soldan (like some male critics) can accept that Tamburlaine's treatment of Zenocrate is a mark of his essential honour, the corpses still lie at his feet. Tamburlaine invites an audience to look at Zenocrate's face 'shadowing in her brows/Triumphs and trophies for my victories' (V.ii.448–9) but what the stage also shows are the corpses which Zenocrate pities. She may be 'shadowing' in two senses: looking distressed from her experiences or theatrically presenting ('shadow' was a word used of actor or acted); Tamburlaine selects only one of these meanings. The end scenes of crowning and promised marriage of the chaste woman do not conceal the bloodiness of the adventures earlier, despite Tamburlaine's speeches. The absolutist rhetoric of personal virtue is inhumane.

The propagandist contrast of modest woman and aggressive woman is likewise placed within masculine empire-building. When Bajazeth and Tamburlaine leave the stage to fight they leave their crowns with their wives, Zenocrate being invited to 'manage words with her, as we will arms' (III.iii.131). So to the sounds of off-stage battle, two women holding the symbols of male rule bitch at each other, and draw their maids into the argument. Here are women doing what the men tell them to, sustaining the violent competition. But when the men are present Zenocrate is less good at baiting Zabina: she does not succeed in taking Bajazeth's crown from Zabina to give to Tamburlaine; later when she is told to chide Zabina she gets her maid to do it. When she discovers the corpses of Zabina and Bajazeth it occasions her major outburst against what Tamburlaine does. I don't want to sentimentalise the text by suggesting a growing attachment between Zenocrate and Zabina, for it is quite possible to play Zenocrate as very snotty. But I think we have to notice a narrative that constructs Zabina into our sympathy, from her earliest opposition to Tamburlaine in his humiliation of Bajazeth to the tribute of Zenocrate's emotion. At the same time she takes pride in her rank, and after her attack on Tamburlaine's usurpation in Act IV Techelles suggests the captives must be taught to 'rein their lavish tongues' (IV.ii.67). The pride in rank and the outspokenness are marks of the passionate queen, seemingly confirmed in her nature when she suddenly goes mad with grief rather than patiently bearing it. Yet she opposes Tamburlaine as a lone voice and is mourned by Zenocrate. Tamburlaine singles out Zabina for particular humiliation, specifically insisting that other women mistreat her, just as he singles out Zenocrate for particular veneration. The ideological opposition of passionate/chaste woman is inflected by the male conqueror (as images of the virgin queen were employed in Leicester's processions in the Netherlands), but is broken down by the playtext's construction of sympathies. The preference of Zenocrate's passivity to Zabina's cursing is an attempt to silence what those curses say and to present as chivalrous and honourable the conqueror who causes bloodshed. Situated historically, this element of *1 Tamburlaine* (which Marlowe largely adds to what he got from his source material) deconstructs an imagery which both legitimated Elizabeth's personal rule and structured Elizabethan thinking about sexual relations.

(ii) Gendered language

One contemporary theory in feminism suggests that the differences between masculine and feminine are structured by the acquisition of language. While this may be debated in our society (Lovell, 1983), in the Renaissance women were excluded generally from the education offered by academic institutions (Ong, 1982), which meant an exclusion from Latin and from rhetoric. Men learn to work with language, women merely speak. Citing the French Renaissance theorists, Vigenère and Duret, Foucault says: speaking 'is merely the female part of language . . . just as its intellect is passive; Writing, on the other hand, is the active intellect, the "male principle" of language. It alone harbours the truth.' (Foucault, 1974, p.39) Against *Matron* Eloquence or *Dame* Rhetoric the plain style movement asserted a language that expressed *the* truth and rationality. Such language is not just male but *public*:

> Public society and commerce of men
>   Require another grace, another port:
>   This eloquence, these rhymes, these phrases then
>   Begot in shades, do serve us in no sort;
>   Th' unmaterial swellings of your pen
>   Touch not the spirit that action doth import.
> A manly style fitted to manly ears
>   Best 'grees with wit, not that which goes so gay,
>   (Daniel, 1599, 'Musophilus', ll.500–7)

Ornamental or private languages are not manly. This notion of the gendering of language may be illustrated, I think, in *Edward II* where Isabella's early speech of grief contrasts with the stripped-down language of the other characters. It seems overblown: 'Like frantic Juno will I fill the earth/With ghastly murmur of my sighs and cries' (I.iv.179–80). There are several markings of the redundancy of the speech—the mythological reference in a play that knows no supernatural, assonances and rhymes that are musical but address no one, fictional role-playing that does not claim an office in the real world. Isabella cannot 'fill' the earth because it is already filled with a different sort of speech, and her language is both private and non-functional. Although she can talk articulately, just as Zenocrate does when presenting the corpses of Bajazeth and Zabina to the audience, when all the men re-enter she is silent. The silence is shown by her talking in dumb-show to Mortimer, a political intervention that cannot be heard. During the play Mortimer specifically curtails her emotional utterances: 'Cease to lament, and tell us where's the king?' (II.iv.31) 'Nay, madam, if you be a warrior,/You must not grow so passionate in speeches' (IV.iv.15–16). Isabella learns to be a proper warrior for as her relationship with Mortimer develops so her speech uses stylistic devices that make it sound more 'rational', less passionate. Through her language she becomes masculinised, less emotional.

Isabella is more sympathetic when she is emotional than when she is rational. Although this can be taken to be part of the play's attack on the discourse of masculinity, the association of emotion and its language with woman is nevertheless derived from dominant ideology. As we have seen, the woman was supposedly more inclined to be governed by passion or hysteria. My argument is that Marlowe's texts encourage exploration both of the portrayal of that emotion and of its value. In Renaissance plays women characters often move from distress to passion, if not to hysteria and madness: in *The Spanish Tragedy*, for example, Isabella's mad talk, like Zabina's, is produced by the repressive decorum of the Spanish court. The emotional trajectory is, however, re-plotted in Zenocrate who, at the precise moment that emotional collapse might be expected— the discovery of the corpses, which Marlowe holds back for a while—instead delivers a most formally patterned oration. With the repeated line 'Behold the Turk and his great emperess' she presents the corpses, noting at the end of her speech that she had been insufficiently emotional: 'pardon me that was not moved with ruth/To see them live so long in misery' (V.ii.305–6). Far from collapsing into 'female' hysteria, Zenocrate takes on the role of Presenter, a role that was traditionally the male narrative voice of truth against the

mimesis of emotion. From addressing herself as the grieving
woman Zenocrate turns, in one of the play's breaches of
'realistic' continuity, to present to the audience. In a similar
way the text of *Dido* changes its source at the farewell of Dido
and Aeneas. Virgil's account has her break down with
emotion, verbally defeated, and the poetry then describes
Aeneas's emotion. In the play it is Dido who has the fullness
of speech, the male is silent and he leaves silently; she only
cries after he has gone. As speaker she is the central emotional
focus.

One of the implications of female passion is that a woman's
inner emotions will always be revealed. When Zenocrate does
not collapse, the moment of expected transparency becomes
opaque, the privileged insight is not offered. This complica-
tion of the viewing relationship is clearer with Isabella in
Edward II, for her language of private grievance feels almost
embarrassingly overwritten in the context of the rest of the
play; there is nearly impropriety in its attempted fullness,
which unsettles theatrical pleasure. The emotion hence is
made difficult to respond to, stylistically opaque rather than
transparently expressive. (It is possible that there are similar
problems of 'tone' with Abigail who is initially presented as
articulate and capable but is more sexually innocent than the
world around her, so the sincerity of her death confession is
capped by the friar's disappointment that she dies a virgin;
her attempt to explain her new knowledge, her seeing the
'difference of things', is undercut by a phallic pun on
'things'—the masculine connotation cancels the dignity of
female knowledge.)

Woman's emotionalism was commonly seen as a bad thing,
that which debilitated her from governing. Yet Zenocrate's
distress at slaughter is preferable to Tamburlaine's tableaux;
nevertheless Isabella loses sympathy as she becomes less
emotional. The problems of value are highlighted in *Dido,
Queen of Carthage*, for Dido was supposedly a woman
whose desires tried to obstruct the project of empire by
delaying Aeneas on his way from Troy to Italy. The relevance
of this story to an English audience derives from the myth of
London as the new Troy, so Dido takes her place as yet
another type of the passionate woman, the antithesis to

virginal rule. In the play Venus compels Dido to love Aeneas
so that she will provide him with the materials necessary to
refurbish his expedition. In the centre of the play Venus
argues with Juno about her hostility to Aeneas and they
discuss the possibility of marrying him to Dido, though it
looks unlikely in view of his imperial plans. The scene is
placed to locate the 'love' within the project of empire. The
end of the play focuses on the loser Dido, alone with the
relics of her relationship with Aeneas which she burns before
immolating herself. The image of the abandoned woman is
intensified by giving the last speech of the play to Dido's
sister Anna, who throughout the play has desired Iarbas, who
in turn desired Dido. The imagery of the flames and
self-destruction is a traditional moral labelling of desire, but
nevertheless it is the passion not the empire-builder which
occupies the dramatic focus.

My analysis of *Dido* will need to be fuller to show properly
how it contributes to the revaluing of passion; it will include
further discussion of the markers of feminine and masculine
difference. I have kept this play separate because its performance conditions were different, being a play for boy actors.
Neither fully-grown man nor woman, the boy takes both sex
roles; several plays exploit the interchangeability to create
scenes of mistaken wooing, leading to the comic frustration
of *Gallathea* (1584/1592) or the delineation of proper
masculinity, as when in *The Wars of Cyrus* the disguised page
Libanio stabs the man who has been wooing him: 'Remember
that thou art Libanio—/No woman, but a bondman! Strike
and fly!' (ll.956–7; the stage direction says 'She kills him').
With voices and bodies sounding and looking alike, other
means have to be used to signify gender, and *Dido* uses props.
In a pattern of scenes the relationship is articulated through
fetishised objects (see also the analysis by Powell, 1964). In
Act III Dido and Aeneas swear love and fidelity, which Dido
celebrates by dressing Aeneas in her jewels: 'These golden
bracelets, and this wedding-ring,/Wherewith my husband
woo'd me yet a maid' (III.iv.61–2). She takes the 'male' part
of wooer, the powerful woman dressing a man as she wants to
see him, choosing to transfer her tokens of allegiance from
one man to another. But the sexual articulation of the gesture

is given different meaning by the narrative context, that the gods have landed Aeneas here so that Dido's wealth can be used to mend his fleet. The jewels as they move express two different commitments. They also mark perpetual separation, for two people cannot wear the same jewel at one time: Dido's power is delimited by Aeneas's.

In Act IV Dido tries to prevent Aeneas's departure by giving him coronation jewels, but he rejects the crown and sceptre that he holds: 'A burgonet of steel and not a crown,/A sword and not a sceptre fits Aeneas' (IV.iv.42–3). Nevertheless she convinces him to stay and he exits wearing the jewels, which in one sense do fit him in that they are riches. By contrast the scene ends with Dido talking to the tackling, oars and sails that she has ordered removed from the ships to prevent departure. The pomp of Aeneas's exit to play the role of Dido's husband is matched by her private speech addressed to inanimate objects. For Aeneas she creates a public role and finery, for herself she ties knots in rope. The mythological fantasy for Aeneas is balanced by a rejection of myth: she tells the oars:

> The water which our poets term a nymph,
> Why did it suffer thee to touch her breast
> And shrunk not back, knowing my love was there?
> The water is an element, no nymph.
>
> (ll.144–7)

The props only function in the man's world, the jewels creating a role for Aeneas to play, the tackling useless off the ship. The narrative of the scene apparently tells of Dido's power, but the contrasts of public/private, meaningful/useless objects, poetry/failed poetry build a distinction between 'masculine' and 'feminine'.

In her final scene Dido lays out more objects: the sword Aeneas swore love by, the garment she first dressed him in, the 'letters, lines, and perjur'd papers' (V.i.300). The woman is again surrounded by redundant objects—a tableau to be used again with Zenocrate and the corpses, and Olympia and the funeral pyre. This time the objects have been made redundant for her by the man: she is visually defined as static recipient, no longer handling jewels but treacherous texts. When she was first divinely caused to love Aeneas the love was shaped by her position of wealth and power as a ruler:

> His glistering eyes shall be my looking-glass,. . .
> His looks shall be my only library;
> And thou, Aeneas, Dido's treasury
>
> (III.i.85, 89–90)

Like the property, he will reflect and confirm her power. From this unequal relationship the play moves to another version of it as Aeneas takes the wealth and continues on his journey. The departure of her 'looking-glass' makes Dido lose her grip on reality, to have 'thoughts of lunacy'. Her sister urges: 'remember who you are' (V.i.263), but what constitutes 'Dido' is now a problem. She burns herself alongside his relics. She learnt to define herself by the male world and becomes its leavings. It takes away her power and produces her lunacy. Thus her 'passionate' end is an indictment of masculine action. Gender is articulated through objects that have private and public meanings; personal feeling expressed through objects is not separable from control and competition. The definition of gender is shaped by the project of empire. The play invites sympathy with the redundant woman and her fantasies, lunacy and false texts. When she asks for an avenger to rise up and plough Aeneas's countries with the sword, Dido repeats an English hostility to Italy; but so too the passionate woman urges destruction of the lands of the descendants of Troy, which has another meaning in Tudor myth (where London is new Troy).

As a representation of woman the picture of Dido is that of defeat and powerlessness. The relics of Aeneas suggest what has made that picture, but the stage image does not challenge the pathos of the woman victim. The force of the play may perhaps depend on its conditions of production and its intertextuality. As a boys' play it was probably performed in some richly decorated hall: the wealthy furnishings and dress of the audience are themselves ironised (if not pressed . . .) by a narrative in which property treacherously constructs and exploits human relations. By ending the play with Dido's death, the passionate woman is given major emphasis—not only against Aeneas who, as Gibbons suggests (Morris, 1968, p.41), is already a contradictory figure, but against the usual emphasising of properly chaste women in boys' plays (as in *The Wars of Cyrus*).

This section can be concluded by looking at a similar picture in *2 Tamburlaine* where the masculine language is written into the scene and thus complicates theatrical pleasure. It should be said that, as Marlowe's text, the scene is all male language; nevertheless it works to present and evaluate the *masculine* as gender power. Olympia is burning the bodies of her husband and son, and about to kill herself when Theridamas and Techelles enter. The scene is split in two, the heroics of victims/the triumphing conquerors, but presumably what remains visually constant, apart from Olympia, are the flames and/or the corpses. Theridamas invites Olympia to go to Tamburlaine, whose power he describes at rhetorical length: using a familiar method, the verbal praise is juxtaposed with the apparatus of death and weeping woman. The fullness of the speech is repressive; the woman is a picture of emotion. What complicates the scene usefully, I think, is that the two men also respond to that picture: 'Madam, sooner shall fire consume us both/Than scorch a face so beautiful as this' (III.iv.73–4); Theridamas adds that he is in love with her and she must go with them. Up to this point the lessons are easy: the verbal description of the absent man denies the real experience of the present woman, masculine language oppresses. But even while this point is made it is possible to derive specular pleasure from the victim, and it is the nature of this pleasure that is questioned by the men's lines. The language of the male-authored scene has itself produced an image which encourages masculine pleasure; that pleasure is associated within the scene with repression.

Marlowe's texts, then, could be said to explore the construction of gender difference in representation and to problematise it. Expectations about 'feminine' speech and emotionalism are questioned, assumed values rejected. At moments the privileged male gaze, which oversees the differentiation of gender, has its power and pleasure unsettled.

(iii) Manliness and sodomy

Assumed values of sex roles derived from the ideology of manliness, which Elizabethan plays persistently affirm. From a few texts I shall try to display some of what the repeated word 'manly' signifies.

The Saxons who resist Danish overlords in *Edmund Ironside* have a 'stubborn nature'; they 'Assault us manly' (ll.120, 122). The resistance to foreign power and defence of traditional rights are sympathetically seen, for the Saxons have qualities attributed to the English, who had a reputation, as Hatton said, for 'valour and manhood'. The virtue of 'manly' assault is clarified when Bajazeth, in *Selimus*, forgives his son's attack: 'For thou didst set upon me manfully,/And moved by an occasion, though unjust' (ll.1282–3). Contrasted with the 'unnatural' cruelties of his brother Acomat, Selimus's action is overt and acknowledges rules of combat. He acts because he is 'moved'; manliness does not exclude emotion: Porrex's heart is 'Melting in tears within a manly breast' (*Gorboduc*, IV.ii.41). It is possible to uphold a 'wrong' position and be manly, for the virtue of manliness lies in a mode of acting, particularly in the relationship between the inner person and public action. When vexed by cowardly men, Ragan wishes she 'had been but made a man;/Or that my strength were equal with my will.' (*King Leir*, ll.2371–2) The manly Saxons are said, like the English, to scorn being compelled 'against their wills': manliness acts out its inner feeling. Thus Mustaffa distinguishes unmanly from manly action: 'Let women weep, let children pour forth tears,/And cowards spend the time in bootless moan' (*Selimus*, ll.1505–6); instead the weeping Bajazeth is urged to 'stir up thy manly heart,/And send forth all thy warlike Janizaries/To chastise that rebellious Acomat' (ll.1518–20). A biological male can weep, but a manly man expresses his emotion in social intervention. The end may not be good, but the manly mode of behaviour is still virtuous. Within the emotional economy, manliness gets returns for itself: its sorrows are not 'bootless'. The ideology of manliness, or masculinity, inscribes the individual within interpersonal competition and denigrates emotion without action.

In the light of this formulation, *Edward II* could be interpreted to show, unsympathetically, such masculinity. The barons frequently draw swords, scenes of quarrelling rapidly become physically violent; Spenser advises Edward to 'refer your vengeance to the sword' (III.ii.126). The sword supplies many phallic puns on the Renaissance stage and its frequent usage in *Edward II* marks both the masculinity and the violence of interpersonal communication: 'henceforth parley with our naked swords'; 'We never beg, but use such prayers as these'—*seizing sword* (I.i.126; II.ii.153). Other chivalric weaponry is also foregrounded, with much talk of advancing standards to the battlefield and Elder Spenser directed to carry his 'truncheon' when he brings troops to express his 'love' for the king. Love in the play is structured by competition, Mortimer advising Isabella not to lament the loss of Edward's love but 'Cry quittance, madam, then, and love not him' (I.iv.197).

The association between masculinity and violence is regarded by most commentators not as a critique but as a personal kink of Marlowe's deriving from his homosexuality. Steane suggests that he was 'attracted perhaps' to the reign of Edward by 'sex and sadism' (Steane, 1964, p.234); Henderson explains that in the play he 'gives full reign [sic – Marlowe, of course, being a queen] to that taste for cruelty that is so often found in the sexually abnormal' (Henderson, 1937, p.290); Bakeless bemoans his 'unhealthy interest in unnatural vice' (Bakeless, 1942, I, p.112); Sanders wonders earnestly if Marlowe uses 'the homosexual motif, or does it use him? Does it simply gush up from . . . the Unconscious?'—it is refreshing and unusual, adds Sanders, to find the character Pembroke wanting to visit his wife, thus placing the action 'in a context of everyday reality' (hidden word = heterosexual) (Sanders, 1968, pp.125, 126). These quotations exemplify a viewpoint which, based on wonky ideas about homosexuality, suppresses Marlowe as sexual political thinker beneath

Marlowe the compulsive. Thus the attack on masculinity is seen only as a symptom of a sick condition. There is no space to engage with the ideological ramifications of such remarks, but they do indicate how criticism constructs its subject (you can see how Sanders is firmly trapped within 1960s thinking about homosexuality). More important, perhaps, is to look at the 'homosexual' scenes.

First, however, the word 'homosexual' has to be erased, since Elizabethan culture had no conception of 'homosexuality' as a positive form of sexuality in its own right (the word itself is a nineteenth-century invention). When the Elizabethans spoke of sodomy or buggery they tended to speak of debauchery (more broad than homosexual activity) and the words were loaded with overtones of disorder and unnaturalness; yet homosexual acts took place, and despite the fuss prosecution was rare. (For all of this, see the fascinating book by Bray, 1982.) Marlowe's texts can be seen to make definitions of their own and maybe even to question the values in sodomy: not so much 'compulsion' as interrogation.

The most normative representations are the sodomite behaviours of Henry III and (possibly) Mycetes. Both are bad kings: Henry III's obsession with his 'minions' leads him to ignore public responsibility and the Guise bid for power. He only wants to 'delight himself', and the choice of male minions marks the disorder. Mycetes is an incapable king who uses counsellors to speak and fight for him. He refers to Meander whom 'I may term a Damon for thy love' (*1 Tamburlaine*, I.i.50); he invites Theridamas to bring back corpses: 'Go frowning forth; but come thou smiling home,/ As did Sir Paris with the Grecian dame' (ll.65–6). Mycetes illustrates the problem about identifying homosexuality: there is no talk of minions, but there is a self-indulgent incapability marked by inappropriate sexual references (in male company). Both kings are more given to personal (sexual) appetite than public order, a reverse of what constitutes manliness.

Sodomy here may be made sense of as political labelling. More notorious is the opening to *Dido*—'minor and quickly forgotten', gulps one editor; unnecessary and therefore obsessional, think others. (Why is it that homosexuals are

obsessional and heterosexuals are not?—are their sexual lives
so boring?) 'Jupiter dandling Ganymede upon his knee' is
discovered: Jupiter offers Ganymede love and protection
from his wife Juno, and gives him some of her wedding
jewels; Ganymede promises embraces in return for a jewel for
his ear and a brooch for his hat. The giving of jewels between
'lovers' will be echoed later in the play, as will the gestures,
for example when Dido sits Cupid on her lap (thinking him
Ascanius) and he asks: 'What will you give me? Now I'll have
this fan' (III.i.32). And again, when the Nurse carries
'Ascanius' (as he asks her to) and talks of her desire for 'love'
although she is old. Comparison of the three similar scenes
(older figures carrying boys) sees the Nurse mocked for her
sexual desire and Dido commencing on a tragic infatuation:
only Jupiter is successful. The Nurse and Dido are both
tricked by Cupid disguised as Ascanius (who could be
performed by the Ganymede actor), and they and Anna are
abandoned by mortal men. This treatment of women's
emotion is initiated by Jupiter's threats against Juno, just as a
'love' expressed through jewel giving is likewise going to
mark sexual relations.

On the model of a play such as *The Rare Triumphs of Love
and Fortune* the gods could be expected to provide a frame of
commentary which highlights the moral mistakes of mortals,
even while it influences action. The authority of this frame is
immediately undercut in *Dido* by the sodomy, so that there is
no rational overview beyond the chaos of passions. More
importantly, the assumption that rationality is male and
passion female is challenged, and male desire is foregrounded
at the start of a play about a woman who classically
exemplifies destructive desire. That male desire is associated
with power over others, particularly humiliation of women,
and commercialised 'love'. Thus the first scene relates to, but
radically shifts evaluation of, Dido's collapse from 'female'
passion. Instead of ideological affirmation that women by
nature have fatally ungovernable desires, these desires are
seen to be produced, shaped and exploited by a power
structure dominated by men. Jupiter takes from others to
give to Ganymede, Aeneas just takes; Dido gives all. Jupiter
can choose the sex object he prefers, Aeneas can leave; Dido,

Anna, the Nurse either cannot choose their sexual objects or cannot fulfil their desires.

The sodomy scene questions definitions of maleness in that it shows successful non-chivalric male desire. In *The Wars of Cyrus* (which Marlowe 'answers' in *Tamburlaine*, rather than vice-versa—see Brawner edn.) the hero is proof against love, his judgement controls his eyes; his officer, Araspas, who succumbs to passion is a social failure. The absence of desire in the hero leads him to use his power fairly. *Dido* questions what is suppressed, namely how power facilitates desire: it refuses the mystification of male innocence in a world dominated by men. It also refuses the sexual tease, the cross-gender scenes, which boys' plays are capable of, for the dramatic thrill of the same-sex seduction aids in the policing of desire: the near-sodomy is produced by disorder in the plot and will be avoided when all comes right or 'truth' is revealed. *Dido* begins with the fact of Jupiter's sodomy and shows it to be truer to male sexual contact—with women—than moralist writings allowed.

Marlowe's 'compulsion' could still be argued to be present at a different level of the representation, since the play makes male sex objects, in particular Aeneas: the text has the boy actor lovingly dressed on stage. At the same time the scenic construction works powerfully to draw Aeneas alongside Ganymede and Cupid, all alike as sex objects who get what they want. The failures are the 'female' sex objects. The text homosexualises male success, the empire-builder is also sex object; this staging contradicts an ideology that sees the man as the lover and the author of love discourse directed at another, for he in turn may be desired; it unsettles a belief that men represent a *quality*, whereas women can be reduced to their physicality (Marks and de Courtivron, 1981, p.228). These possibilities question representation of male power in that there may be something beyond the controlling male look. For example, Cyrus's judgement controlled his eyes and thus avoided a possible crisis had he fallen for Panthea; the narrative is solved by his correct seeing, and the audience is invited to see as the hero sees. Cyrus himself is not looked at with desire and thereby trapped into a structure not controllable by the operation of his own judgement. I suspect

this uncertainty about the way male figures are being looked
at contributes to the anxiety about Marlowe's 'obsession'.

The sexualising of the male becomes more unsettling in
texts for adult actors, since the gender divisions may be more
clearly marked with boys only as women. The best example
of this is the temptation of Theridamas in *1 Tamburlaine*. The
scene looks like simple bribery, with the loot laid out and
Tamburlaine's talk of money and power. Yet Techelles notes
that Theridamas's 'deep affections make him passionate'
(I.ii.164), writing passion into the scene's expectations; and
Tamburlaine notes the majesty of his looks. Theridamas feels
enticed by 'strong enchantments' and admits he is 'Won with
thy words and conquered with thy looks' (l.228). Rhetorical
words are designed to 'win', but the 'looks' raise a problem.
Tamburlaine may still be wearing rich armour but he says
'Jove sometime masked in a shepherd's weed' (l.199) as if to
explain himself. Zenocrate had earlier been impressed with
his appearance. The 'looks' may not be just a promise of
wealth; and indeed wealth is marginalised by the terms of the
final allegiance gesture:

> Thus shall my heart be still combined with thine,
> Until our bodies turn to elements,
> And both our souls aspire celestial thrones.
>
> (ll.235–7)

The men holding hands suggests fealty-swearing, a common
scene (see Fleischer, 1974), yet the language also implies
betrothal (Greenblatt also notes this is a 'passionate' love
scene (in Kernan, 1977, p.56)).

The looks of Tamburlaine twice work on apparent
enemies; during the scene he dresses himself (at least once).
While he puts on captured armour he talks to Zenocrate,
transforming himself while he talks. This has the effect of
drawing attention to the speaker rather than the spoken to,
visually centring him: he is both powerful speaking presence
and object to be looked at, yet what he wears is illegal, is
dressing up, non-authoritative. Tamburlaine as much as
Aeneas, I would suggest, is fetishistically dressed. When this
happens the text locks the viewer into a contradiction

between (narcissistic) identification with Tamburlaine (the
star actor, the successful leader unlike Mycetes) and specular
pleasure in Tamburlaine as erotic object to be looked at (see
the terms used by Flitterman, 1981, p.247). This difficulty
experienced in theatrical viewing foregrounds a problem
about maleness. The scene is not just a tactical tempting of an
enemy, but is structured so that what happens to Zenocrate
balances Theridamas (see Hattaway, 1982, p.58). Zenocrate is
represented as the silenced woman on the margin of a formed
male-male relationship. Zenocrate with the treasure has
object status, Theridamas promises social power. The male
group forms around Theridamas; the women, prisoners,
money are piled up elsewhere. Again masculinity is associated
with wealth and power, a power consolidated by male mutual
appreciation to the exclusion of women.

It could be argued that Marlowe explores a contradiction
within thinking about sodomy, for sodomy between clowns
and commoners passes without note, as in the unremarked
exit of Antic and Smith in *The Old Wives Tale*: 'Come on my
lad, thou shalt take thy unnatural rest with me' (ll.102–3). In
rulers sodomy matters because it apparently marks an
improper excess of desire, as in Mycetes or Henry III: thus
the Moorish villain Eleazar spends money on 'smooth boys'
(l.127) while he also has a sexual liaison with the queen (*Lust's
Dominion*, ?1599/1657), and Philarchus is attacked because
he was 'once bedfellow to the king' (*A Knack to Know a
Knave*, l.549). Dominant ideology suggests that the male
ruler's sexual interest in other men is a deviation from true
rule; but Tamburlaine's interest in Theridamas is a consolidation of his power. Within patriarchy men maintain an
exclusive power, so the real object of their desire is in fact
male achievement: this is misrepresented, or deflected, by
attacks on sodomy, which aim to affirm masculine power by
seeing the proper man as rational against disordering female
desire. Secondly, dominant ideology tells Philarchus he has
'disobeyed the laws both of God and nature' (*A Knack*, l.527)
in loving the king and defying his father; but in the Marlowe
plays the relationships of Jupiter and Ganymede or Tamburlaine and Theridamas are seen to be based on economic and
military gain—the relationships are shaped by the interests of

masculine social power. It is the economics of gender power
rather than an ascribed nature of gender which shapes social
relations.

Edward II centres the issue of sodomy. The choice of
emphasis is largely Marlowe's: Bray notes how Taylor's
account of the reign sees Edward's love as 'immoderate'
(Bray, 1982, p.26), and Wentworth said Edward was ruled by
'ill counsellors' and wasted the nation's money (Wentworth,
1598, p.79). The unnamed homoeroticism of Tamburlaine is
named in *Edward*, but at the same time the play challenges its
value. Edward's language is gendered female when it talks of
mythology and role-play, Lancaster and others describe it as
'passions'. The prison-cell agonising about kingship is said to
be a waste of time, embarrassing in front of the silent
messengers; the attempt to move Lightborn is redundant.
Against this Edward can speak the language of the sword. He
is inconsistently masculine. Thus when Elder Mortimer lists
the 'mightiest kings' who 'have had their minions'—'Great
Alexander', 'conquering Hercules', 'stern Achilles'—the
adjectives are important as a contrast with Edward (I.iv.393–
6). The two Mortimers are used to discuss the terms on which
manliness accepts sodomy. Elder Mortimer argues Edward
should 'freely enjoy' Gaveston because he 'promiseth as
much as we can wish' (ll.401–2)—the terms of 'personal'
freedom are measured, the ideology of the 'free' individual
questioned. Younger Mortimer cannot forgive Gaveston's
base birth nor the spending of national wealth, but is
unoffended by the 'wanton humour'. The allowed sodomy
conforms to the established structures of wealth and
class. . .plus ça change.

The 'humour' is seen as a passing phase, a 'toy', the
dismissable personal disorder. But Edward replaces Gaveston
with Spenser and he desires more fiercely the more he is
opposed. Moralistic history notes only the fatal effects of
personal desire in a 'wilful' or 'humorous' monarch, but it
does not ask what produces the 'humour' nor what shapes it.
Marlowe's text explores the connections of personal and
social, and the shaping of disorder by 'order' (rather than vice
versa). 'Love' is structured within reward and patronage in
the play: Gaveston and Isabella both feel themselves *robbed*

personal use of that word calling human being 'my'.

of Edward. It is spoken by discourses of 'public' diplomacy and 'private' emotion, leading to the contradiction of barons whose 'loving' is ironised early on and overtly violent later. Competitive discrimination is, contradictorily, inscribed into the expression of 'love': 'I love him more' says Isabella 'Than he can Gaveston' (I.iv.304–5); Edward will love Isabella *if* she loves Gaveston. Thus Edward's defiance: 'They love me not that hate my Gaveston' (II.ii.37)—his identification with his lover is established and strengthened by opposition.

Interpersonal relations are constructed as competition by masculinity, and Edward's 'humour' is itself thus shaped and strengthened by denial. Not so much a 'toy', the desire is more permanent than its object. The personal disorder of moral biography is here shown to be shaped by the accepted order; the sodomy is not so much an individual case-study of an anomaly but part of a debased form of human relations. The privileged viewpoint of the spectator of moral biography is unsettled, since for most of the play it is difficult to find either an overview or identification point, as the language has no emotional plenitude with its brutal plainness, its devalued 'love', its embarrassing expressiveness. It is a very male play though not an enjoyably male-centred one (Steane calls it 'nasty'). Masculinity is not privileged over sodomy: there is little pleasurable or reassuring differentiation between order and disorder, personal and social.

One of the play's most expressive images comes, crucially, at the end. The figure of Edward III is used to close the play, and consequently, I think, is less inspected. His attachment to his father is only explicable as 'natural' feeling, where little else in the play has this status. Yet memory of his father causes him to weep (for the last 70 lines) for which he demands space:

> Forbid me not to weep; he was my father,
> And had you lov'd him half so well as I,
> You could not bear his death thus patiently
>
> (V.vi.34–6)

The measuring of love repeats an idea; but the tearful memory of a father contrasts with Edward II's memory of his own father, which hardens him. The manliness of Edward III here is a problem: the emotionally expressive, embarrassing tears are not manly; the orders to punish the murderers, while he weeps, are. Edward claims 'in me my loving father speaks' (l.41), yet 'loving' is a perfunctory word now. The tears, on the other hand, are not shown to be a trick.

The final tableau has Edward putting on mourning robes and offering Mortimer's head to the hearse of his father, asking that his tears 'Be witness of my grief and innocency' (l.102). The image feels full, but the last word is a problem: how is Edward innocent? He and the country are free of the oppressive protector and the incapable father, and he combines the toughness of the one with the emotionalism of the other. It could be a picture of the proper ruler. At the same time, it is a completely male picture, it suppresses the figure of Isabella with her very different earlier status, it is emotional and brutal. Edward has given the order for death and he is shown to construct the scene, so in this sense he is not innocent. On the one hand the tableau is satisfyingly balanced, but on the other it questions whether any manly male is innocent, whether the blend of emotion and brutality is ever avoidable.

I have let the discussion of sodomy return to manliness in following the narrative of *Edward II*. What that discussion has avoided is any question of the naturalness of being manly, an evasion facilitated by thinking in terms of sodomitic disorder versus manly order. Yet the doubts about constructed manliness at *Edward*'s end are given force by the earlier project of *2 Tamburlaine*, with which I shall finish. For the follow-up to the conquest play concerns consolidation, the wooing is followed by training sons. Tamburlaine warns that his sons will not inherit 'unless thou bear/A mind courageous and invincible' *(2 Tamburlaine*, I.iv.72–3), and he sets about building this. The historical specificity of this idea is late Elizabethan concern over royal succession and factional squabble over candidates for rule. Most succession plays press the urgency of the problem by showing a sick father, but Marlowe's text shows how personal rule reproduces itself through an unquestioned ideology of leadership.

The play, however, does question by setting up debate:

Zenocrate suggests that Tamburlaine's description of brutality 'Dismays their minds before they come to prove/The
wounding troubles angry war affords', but her son Celebinus
says 'these are speeches fit for us' (Il.86–8). The woman
speaks of 'proving', experiencing; the young man of 'fitness',
observation of rules. Talking of proving, Zenocrate is like
Abigail who learns from 'experience', even like Dido who is
emotionally distressed by Aeneas's brutal description of the
destruction of Troy. This is not 'female' emotion against
'male' reason, but experience—one form of knowledge—against inherited rules—another. So the grimness in
Tamburlaine's final lesson in manliness, the killing of the
cowardly Calyphas, comes in the emphasis on rule. To those
who plead for Calyphas he says: 'Know ye not yet the
argument of arms?' and goes on to speak of himself as a
conqueror: 'I must apply myself to fit those terms' (IV.i.98,
153). Manliness is an argument, a rhetorical construction, to
be learnt. The 'terms' precede the person and shape him.
Constructed according to rules, the manly man still practises
real violence. In the centre of the play, father and sons
construct a memorial to their dead mother, fixing her in art
and writing. Then they break off and Tamburlaine talks at
great length about military matters, ending by cutting his arm
to teach them fit courage. While he speaks and while he
privileges the image of himself, a destroyed town burns and
Zenocrate's hearse is on stage. The manliness is experienced
by the audience as a tiresome speech and a flash piece of
theatre, suppressing mention of the contradictions in the
deaths it mourns and makes.

In these ways the order that is manliness is alienated. Its
claim to express the inner person in social action is shown as a
repression of experience and a construction of an inner
person, not so much expressed as trained. In particular,
manliness invents pictures of women and denies them
feelings. These sorts of ideas seem to me altogether more
complex than homosexual 'compulsion' would describe.

An Ending

There is no formal conclusion to this book, says he setting out on what looks remarkably like one.

Too many issues remain insufficiently theorised, insufficiently researched, to be concluded. There are problems over the relationship between doubling and narrative, the gender status of boy performers, the discourse of star actors within the meaning of plays. There are problems over the definition and self-definition of the writer within and outside the players' company, the relationship between printing and performing, the selection of an 'authoritative' text for study. Closer work needs to be done on the connections between theatres and MPs, aldermen and courtiers, and on the uses puritans made of theatre and drama. Closer work needs to be done on reference to and borrowing from non-fictional, especially political, literature. Above all, and I think this is the most pressing issue, work has to be done on how Elizabethan drama is studied: to look at how it is defined and presented at A level and degree level, to look at how Shakespeare is privileged within teaching, how the author is deferred to as a controlling authority, to look at how editing constructs meaning in texts, what values and assumptions underlie the presentation of a text, to look at how the figure of the Elizabethan theatre scholar is constructed within the apparatuses of the academy and what power s/he wields. Then the plays need to be performed. And published.

My task here is to answer the problem with which I set out and to talk of Marlowe's relationship with the politics of Elizabethan theatre. My first point is that his texts not only question some of the values within conservative nationalist Protestantism, but question the way the theatre affirmed these values. And secondly, that this questioning is set up by problematising theatrical pleasure. Thus at a time of national crisis, with vigilante talk of traitors within the realm and the status of aliens and strangers in London, Barabas is brought on stage as a Morality Vice, costumed as a racial type to be laughed at. Yet the easy availability of Morality characterisation to support racist politics begins to stick in the problems of laughing at or with Barabas and the suggestion that 'policy' infects all areas of the play world and that Barabas is only a product of that world: the privileged position offered the audience by Morality figures, the supreme pleasurable knowledgeability, is unsettled, as is the racism. At a time of increased propaganda against religious deviations, and of painful argument about the status of religious truth, Faustus is presented as a type of ambitious enquirer and his story is framed by Morality figures from hell and heaven. But the Morality framework which should be so reassuring and clarifying ceases to communicate a trustworthy message. Its figures and debates come into tension with scopic pleasure in theatrical spectacle, the source of its authority can be debated, the audience is not neutrally observing but is part of 'hell', and hell itself is redefined. The terms of contemporary debate, the very relationship between individual life and moral absolutes, are interrogated. In the years of crisis with Spain, when many people desired a strong leader and an active military force, Tamburlaine is invented on stage. He intermittently acts like a Presenter and he is characterised with the conventional markers of heroism. The character and narrative invite an enjoyment of his capability against other weaker rulers and a scopic pleasure in the attractions of his person. But the apparent fullness of his presence and poetry repress and conceal, they make problematic the imagery of the hero within the Elizabethan theatre and state, they ask questions about the desire for strong rule and the rationale of calling someone a scourge of God (a specific example of the misrecognition created by the discourse of heroism might be the ousting of Leicester's power from the Privy Council behind the scenes while his 'crusade' in the Netherlands against the Spanish occupied the limelight). When dramatists were writing about the succession issue which was a major problem of domestic politics, and when the queen and her ministers spoke of a personal rule authorised by God,

Marlowe presented the famous story of a deposed monarch. The narrative might have been expected to offer lessons about rule and to construct the pathos of a victim king, offering an emotional fullness. But the fully expressed passions are illegitimately sodomitical, Edward is no more likeable than his barons, there is very little notion of an organic 'England' that is being squabbled over and very little notion that there is a God which will make final sense of history. It is a history play which refuses the eternal values of Elizabethan history writing, the idea of the book written by God about a continuity which is England. In *Edward II* as in the other plays there are no 'truths' of history beyond a shifting set of power relations. The Marlowe texts could be said to take a number of the ideological truths of the Elizabethan theatre and reveal them to be discourses, and to show those discourses spoken within power relations. Unfortunately it was the very operation of the power relations in society that put an end to the texts that analysed them in the theatre.

Bibliography

Abbreviations

ELH: English Literary History
ELR: English Literary Renaissance
ES: English Studies
HLQ: Huntington Library Quarterly
JEGP: Journal of English and Germanic Philology
JHI: Journal of the History of Ideas
JWCI: Journal of the Warburg and Courtauld Institutes
MLN: Modern Language Notes
MLR: Modern Language Review
MP: Modern Philology
N&Q: Notes and Queries
PMLA: Proceedings of the Modern Language Association of
    America
PQ: Philological Quarterly
Ren. Drama: Renaissance Drama
Ren. Q: Renaissance Quarterly
RES: Review of English Studies
RORD: Research Opportunities in Renaissance Drama
SEL: Studies in English Literature
Sh.Q: Shakespeare Quarterly
SP: Studies in Philology
SS: Shakespeare Survey
TDR: Tulane Drama Review
U.P.: University Press

Notes: The double dates which accompany play titles denote approximate date of performance (always difficult to settle) and date of first printing; I have used the conjectures of individual editors where possible.

Place of Publication: The rule I have adopted is to give publishers' names for post-1900 publications and place of publication for pre-1900 works. If no place is given, this is because it is not known.

Adams, B.B. 'The Audiences of *The Spanish Tragedy*', *JEGP* 68 (1969).

Allen, J.W. *A History of Political Thought in the Sixteenth Century*, (Methuen, 1928/1960).

Alphonsus King of Arragon, see Greene, R.

Altman, J.B. *The Tudor Play of Mind*, (California U.P., 1978).

Anderson, P. *Lineages of the Absolutist State*, (Verso, 1979).

Anderson, R.L. *Elizabethan Psychology and Shakespeare's Plays*, (Univ. Iowa Humanistic Studies, 3.4, 1927).

Andrews, K.R. (ed.) *English Privateering Voyages to the West Indies 1588–95*, (Hakluyt Society, 1959).

Anger, J. *Her Protection for Women*, (London, 1589).

Arden of Faversham, The Tragedy of (1588–91/1592), ed. M.L. Wine (Methuen, 1973).

Armstrong, W.A. '*Damon and Pithias* and Renaissance Theories of Tragedy', *ES* 39 (1958).

Armstrong, W.A. *Marlowe's Tamburlaine – The Image and the Stage*, (Hull U.P., 1966).

Armstrong, W.A. 'The Elizabethan Conception of the Tyrant', *RES* 22 (1946).

Armstrong, W.A. 'Shakespeare and the Acting of Edward Alleyn', *SS* 7 (1954).

Armstrong, W.A. 'The Topicality of *The Misfortunes of Arthur*', *N&Q* 200 (1955).

Armstrong, W.A. '*Tamburlaine* and *The Wounds of Civil War*', *N&Q* 203 (1958).

Ascham, R. *The Schoolmaster* (1570), ed. L.V. Ryan (Cornell U.P., 1967).

Ashton, P. (trs.) *A Short Treatise upon the Turks Chronicles*, (1546).

Atkins, J.W.H. *English Literary Criticism: The Renascence*, (Methuen, 1947).

Axton, M. *The Queen's Two Bodies*, (Royal Historical Society, 1977).

Babb, H.S. '*Policy* in Marlowe's *The Jew of Malta*', *ELH* 24 (1957).

Bacon, F. *Essays*, (1625; Dent, 1906/1968).

Bakeless, J. *The Tragical History of Christopher Marlowe*, (Harvard U.P., 1942), 2 vols.

Baldwin, T.W. *Shakespeare's Five-Act Structure*, (Illinois U.P., 1947).

Baldwin, T.W. *William Shakespeare's Small Latine and Lesse Greeke*, (Illinois U.P., 1944), 2 vols.

Barroll, J.L. *Artificial Persons*, (South Carolina U.P., 1974).

Barroll, J.L. *et al.* (eds.) *The Revels History of Drama in English, 1576–1613*, (Methuen, 1975).

Battenhouse, R.W. *Marlowe's Tamburlaine*, (Vanderbilt U.P., 1941).

Battenhouse, R.W. 'Tamburlaine, the "Scourge of God"', *PMLA* 56 (1941).

Battenhouse, R.W. 'Protestant Apologetics and the Subplot of *2 Tamburlaine*', *ELR* 3 (1973).

Battle of Alcazar, The, ed. J. Yoklavich, see Peele, G.

Baumer, F.L.V. *The Early Tudor Theory of Kingship*, (Yale Historical Publications, 1940).

Bawcutt, N.W. 'Some Elizabethan Allusions to Machiavelli', *English Miscellany* 20 (1969).

Bawcutt, N.W. 'Machiavelli and Marlowe's *The Jew of Malta*', *Ren. Drama* n.s.3 (1970).

Bent, J.T. (ed.) *Early Voyages and Travels to the Levant*, (London, 1896).

Bergeron, D.M. 'Venetian State Papers and English Civic Pageantry, 1558–1642', *Ren. Q* 23 (1970).

Bergeron, D.M. *English Civic Pageantry 1558–1642* (Arnold, 1971).

Bethell, S.L. *Shakespeare and the Popular Dramatic Tradition*, (King and Staples, 1944).

Bevington, D.M. *From 'Mankind' to Marlowe*, (Harvard U.P., 1962).

Bevington, D.M. *Tudor Drama and Politics*, (Harvard U.P., 1968).

Bindoff, S.T. (ed.) *Elizabethan Government and Society*, (Athlone Press, 1961).

Bland, D.S. 'Arthur Broke, Gerard Legh and the Inner Temple' *N&Q* 214 (1969).

Bluestone, M. '*Libido Speculandi* – Doctrine and Dramaturgy in Contemporary Interpretations of Marlowe's *Doctor Faustus*' in *Reinterpretations of Elizabethan Drama*, ed. N. Rabkin (Columbia U.P., 1969).

Bodin, J. *Method for the Easy Comprehension of History* (1566), trs. B. Reynolds (Octagon, 1966).

Boyle, H.H. 'Elizabeth's Entertainment at Elvetham – War Policy in Pageantry', *SP* 68 (1971).

Bradbrook, M.C. *The School of Night*, (Cambridge U.P., 1936).

Bradbrook, M.C. *The Rise of the Common Player*, (Chatto, 1962).

Bradner, L. 'Poems on the Defeat of the Spanish Armada', *JEGP* 43 (1944).

Bray, A. *Homosexuality in Renaissance England*, (Gay Men's Press, 1982).

Brooke, N. 'The Moral Tragedy of *Doctor Faustus*', *Cambridge Journal* 5 (1952).

Brooke, N. 'Marlowe the Dramatist' in *Elizabethan Theatre*, ed. J.R. Brown and B. Harris (Arnold, 1966).

Brooks, C. '*Tamburlaine* and Attitudes Toward Women', *ELH* 24 (1957).

Brooks, E.S. *Sir Christopher Hatton*, (Cape, 1946).

Brown, J.R. (ed.) *Marlowe – Tamburlaine the Great, Edward the Second and The Jew of Malta*, (Macmillan, 1982).

Bullough, G. (ed.) *Narrative and Dramatic Sources of Shakespeare*, (Routledge & Kegan Paul, 1962), vols. 3 and 4.

Byshop, J. *Beautiful Blossoms*, (London, 1577).

Cambini, A. *Two very Notable Commentaries*, trs. J. Shute (London, 1562).

Campbell, L.B. *Shakespeare's 'Histories'*, (Huntington Library, 1947).

Campbell, L.B. '*Doctor Faustus*: A Case of Conscience', *PMLA* 67 (1952).

Campion, T. *Observations in the Art of English Poesy*, (1602; John Lane, 1925).

Caughie, J. (ed.) *Theories of Authorship*, (Routledge & Kegan Paul, 1981).

Chambers, E.K. *The Elizabethan Stage*, (Clarendon, 1923), 4 vols.

Charlton, H.B. *Castelvetro's Theory of Poetry*, (Manchester U.P., 1913).

Chew, S.C. *The Crescent and the Rose*, (Oxford U.P., 1937).

Clark, B.H. *European Theories of the Drama*, (Crown Publications, 1947).

Clark, D.L. *Rhetoric and Poetry in the Renaissance*, (Columbia U.P., 1963).

Clark, E.G. *Ralegh and Marlowe*, (Russell, 1965).

Clemen, W. *English Tragedy Before Shakespeare*, (Methuen, 1961).

Clough, W.O. 'The Broken English of Foreign Characters of the Elizabethan Stage', *PQ* 12 (1933).

Cobbler's Prophecy, The, see Wilson, R.

Cole, D. *Suffering and Evil in the Plays of Christopher Marlowe*, (Princeton U.P., 1962).

Collinson, P. 'John Field and Elizabethan Puritanism', in Bindoff (1961).

Collinson, P. *The Elizabethan Puritan Movement*, (Cape, 1967).

Crane, W.G. *Wit and Rhetoric in the Renaissance*, (Columbia U.P., 1937).

Cross, C. *The Puritan Earl*, (Macmillan, 1966).

Cunliffe, J.W. *The Influence of Seneca on Elizabethan Tragedy*, (London, 1893).

Daniel, S. 'Musophilus' (1599) see *Poems and a Defence of Rhyme*.

Daniel, S. *Poems and A Defence of Rhyme*, ed. A.C. Sprague, (Routledge & Kegan Paul, 1950).

Debray, R. *Teachers, Writers, Celebrities*, trs. D. Macey (Verso, 1981).

della Volpe, G. *A Critique of Taste*, trs. M. Caesar (New Left Books, 1978).

de Mornay, P. *The Trueness of Christian Religion*, trs. P. Sidney (1587), [the first 6 chapters] in *Prose Works of Sidney*, ed. A. Feuillerat (Cambridge U.P., 1963), vol.3.

Dessen, A.C. *Elizabethan Drama and The Viewer's Eye*, (N. Carolina U.P., 1977).

Diehl, H. 'The Iconography of Violence in English Renaissance Tragedy', *Ren. Drama* n.s.11 (1980).

Doctor Faustus, see Marlowe, C.

Dodd, A.H. 'Mr Myddleton the Merchant of Tower Street', in Bindoff (1961).

Dollimore, J. *Radical Tragedy*, (Harvester, 1984).

Doran, M. *Endeavours of Art*, (Wisconsin U.P., 1954).

Damon and Pithias, see Edwards, R.

Duthie, G.I. 'The Dramatic Structure of Marlowe's *Tamburlaine the Great*, Parts I and II', *Essays and Studies* n.s.1 (1948).

Edmund Ironside (?1590s) in *Six Early Plays*, ed. E.B. Everitt (Rosenkilde & Bagger, 1965).

Edward I, ed. F.S. Hook, see Peele, G.

Edward III (?1590/1596) in *Six Early Plays*, ed. R.L. Armstrong (Rosenkilde & Bagger, 1965).

Edwards, P. *Threshold of a Nation*, (Cambridge U.P., 1979).

Edwards, R. *Damon and Pithias* (1565/1571) in *Old English Plays*, ed. W.C. Hazlitt (London, 1874), vol.4.

Eisenstein, S. *The Film Sense*, trs. J. Leyda (Faber, 1968).

Elam, K. *The Semiotics of Theatre and Drama*, (Methuen, 1980).

Famous Victories of Henry V, The (>1588/1598) in Bullough (1962), vol.4.

Farnham, W. 'The Progeny of *A Mirror for Magistrates*, *MP* 29 (1932).

Farnham, W. *The Medieval Heritage of Elizabethan Tragedy*, (Oxford U.P., 1936/70).

Field, J. *An Admonition to the Parliament*, (1572).

Field, J. *A Godly Exhortation*, (London, 1583).

Fieler, F.B. *Tamburlaine, Part I and its Audience*, (Florida U.P., 1961).

Fleay, F.G. *A Chronicle History of the London Stage, 1559–1642*, (London, 1890).

Fleischer, M.H. *The Iconography of the English History Play*, (Salzburg Studies, 1974).

Fletcher, A. *Tudor Rebellions*, (Longman, 1968/83).

Flitterman, S. 'Woman, Desire and the Look: Feminism and the Enunciative Apparatus in Cinema', in Caughie (1981).

Forest, L.C.T. 'A Caveat for Critics Against Invoking Elizabethan Psychology', *PMLA* 61 (1946).

Foster, F.F. *The Politics of Stability*, (Royal Historical Society, 1977).

Foucault, M. *Madness and Civilisation*, trs. R. Howard (Tavistock, 1971).

Foucault, M. *The Order of Things*, (Tavistock, 1974).

Foucault, M. *Power/Knowledge*, ed. C. Gordon (Harvester, 1980).

Foxe, J. *A Sermon, of Christ Crucified*, (London, 1575).

Freeman, A. *Thomas Kyd – Facts and Problems*, (Clarendon Press, 1967).

Freeman, A. 'Marlowe, Kyd, and the Dutch Church Libel', *ELR* 3 (1973).

Friar Bacon and Friar Bungay, see Greene, R.

Gallathea, see Lyly, J.

Gascoigne, G. *Certain Notes of Instruction in English Verse* (1575), ed. E. Arber (London, 1868).

Gascoigne, G. and Kinwelmersh, F. *Jocasta* (1566/1573) in *Early English Classical Tragedies*, ed. J.W. Cunliffe, (Oxford U.P., 1912).

Gerber, A. 'All of the Five Fictitious Italian Editions of Writings of Machiavelli', *MLN* 22 (1907).

Gilbert, A.H. *Literary Criticism – Plato to Dryden*, (American Book Co., 1940).

Gildersleeve, V.C. *Government Regulation of the Elizabethan Drama*, (Columbia U.P., 1908/61).

Goodman, C. *How Superior Powers Ought to be Obeyed*, (Geneva, 1558).

Gorboduc, see Norton, T. and Sackville, T.

Gosson, S. *Plays Confuted in Five Actions*, (London, ?1590).

Gosson, S. *The School of Abuse* (1579), ed. E. Arber (Constable, 1906).

Greenblatt, S. *Renaissance Self-Fashioning*, (Chicago U.P., 1980).

Greene, R. *The Scottish History of James IV* (1591/1598), ed. J.A. Lavin (Benn, 1967).

Greene, R. *Friar Bacon and Friar Bungay* (c.1589/1594), ed. J.A.

Lavin (Benn, 1969).

Greene, R. *The Scottish History of James IV* (1591/1598), ed. N. Sanders (Methuen, 1970).

Greene, R. *Alphonsus King of Arragon* (1591/1599) in *Plays and Poems*, ed. J.C. Collins (Books for Libraries, 1970).

Greene, R. and Lodge, T. *A Looking Glass for* London and England (c.1590/1594) in *Plays and Poems*, ed. J.C. Collins (Books for Libraries, 1970).

Greg, W.W. *Dramatic Documents from the Elizabethan Playhouses*, (Oxford U.P., 1931).

Greville, F. *A Treatie of Wars* (1633) in *Works*, ed. A. B. Grosart (London, 1870), vol.2.

Gurr, A.J. 'Who Strutted and Bellowed?', *SS* 16 (1963).

Haaker, A. '*Non sine causa* – The Use of Emblematic Method and Iconology in the Thematic Structure of *Titus Andronicus*', *RORD* 13/14 (1970/71).

Hakluyt, R. *The Principal Navigations, Voyages, Traffics and Discoveries of the English Nation*, (1598–1600; James MacLehose, 1903–5), 12 vols.

Hale, D.G. *The Body Politic*, (Mouton, 1971).

Harbage, A. 'Innocent Barabas', *TDR* 8 (1964).

Harington, J. 'A Brief Apology of Poetry': Preface to *Orlando Furioso*, (1591; Clarendon Press, 1972).

Harvey, G. *Works*, ed. A.B. Grosart, (London, 1884), 3 vols.

Hattaway, M. 'The Theology of Marlowe's *Doctor Faustus*', *Ren. Drama* n.s.3 (1970).

Hattaway, M. *Elizabethan Popular Theatre*, (Routledge & Kegan Paul, 1982).

Hawkes, T. *Shakespeare's Talking Animals*, (Arnold, 1973).

Haydn, H. *The Counter-Renaissance*, (Grove Press, 1950).

Hearnshaw, F.J.C.(ed.) *The Social and Political Ideas of Some Great Thinkers of the 16th and 17th Centuries*, (Harrap, 1926).

Henderson, P. *And Morning in his Eyes*, (Boriswood, 1937).

1 Hieronimo, see Kyd, T.

Hill, C. *Intellectual Origins of the English Revolution*, (Oxford U.P., 1965).

Hill, C. *Society and Puritanism in Pre-Revolutionary England*, (Mercury, 1966).

Holinshed, R. *Chronicles of England, Scotland and Ireland*, (1587; London, 1807–8), 6 vols.

Holland, P. *The Ornament of Action*, (Cambridge U.P., 1979).

Hooker, R. *Of the Laws of Ecclesiastical Polity* (1593–7), intro. C. Morris (Dent, 1907/58), 2 vols.

Hotman, F. *Francogallia* (1573), trs. J.H.M. Salmon (Cambridge U.P., 1972).

Hughes, T. *The Misfortunes of Arthur* (1588) in *Early English Classical Tragedies*, ed. J.W. Cunliffe (Clarendon Press, 1912).

Hunter, G.K. 'The Theology of Marlowe's *The Jew of Malta*', *JWCI* 27 (1964).

Izard, T.C. 'The Principal Source for Marlowe's *Tamburlaine*', *MLN* 58 (1943).

Jack Straw, The Life and Death of (?1591/1594; Malone Society, 1957).

Jocasta, see Gascoigne, G. and Kinwelmersh, F.

Jones, R.F. *The Triumph of the English Language*, (Oxford U.P., 1953).

Kearney, H. *Scholars and Gentlemen*, (Faber, 1970).

Kennedy, M.B. *The Oration in Shakespeare*, (Chapel Hill, 1942).

Kernan, A. (ed.) *Two Renaissance Mythmakers*, (Johns Hopkins U.P., 1977).

Kernodle, G.R. *From Art to Theatre*, (Chicago U.P., 1944).

King Leir, The True Chronicle History of (revived 1594/1605) in *Six Early Plays*, ed. E.B. Everitt (Rosenkilde & Bagger, 1965).

Knack to Know a Knave, A (1592/1594; Malone Society, 1963).

Kocher, P.H. 'Francois Hotman and Marlowe's *The Massacre at Paris*', *PMLA* 56 (1941).

Kocher, P.H. *Christopher Marlowe*, (Russell, 1962).

Kocher, P.H. 'English Legal History in Marlowe's *Jew of Malta*', *HLQ* 26 (1963).

Kyd, T. *Soliman and Perseda* (1587/1592) in *Works*, ed. F.S. Boas (Oxford U.P., 1901/1962).

Kyd, T. *The First Part of Hieronimo* (?1585–7/1605) and *The Spanish Tragedy* (1585–7/1592), ed. A.S. Cairncross (Arnold, 1967).

Laird, D. 'Hieronimo's Dilemma', *SP* 62 (1965).

Lamont, W. (ed.) *The Tudors and Stuarts*, (Sussex Books, 1976).

Lathrop, H.B. *Translations from the Classics into English from Caxton to Chapman 1477–1620*, (Octagon, 1967).

Lehmberg, S.E. *Sir Walter Mildmay and Tudor Government*, (Texas U.P., 1964).

Leslie, N.T. '*Tamburlaine* in the Theatre', *Ren. Drama* n.s.4 (1971).

Levin, H. *Christopher Marlowe – The Overreacher*, (Faber, 1967).

Locrine, The Lamentable Tragedy of, (1591/1595; Malone Society, 1908).

Lodge, T. *The Wounds of Civil War* (1586–9/1594), ed. J.W. Houppert (Arnold, 1970).

Looking Glass for London and England, A, see Greene, R. and Lodge, T.

Lovell, T. 'Writing Like A Woman – A Question of Politics' in *The Politics of Theory*, ed. F. Barker *et al.* (Essex U.P., 1983).

Lowers, J.K. *Mirrors for Rebels*, (California U.P., 1953).

Lust's Dominion or The Lascivious Queen (?1595/1657), ed. J. Le Gay Brereton (Librairie Universitaire, 1931).

Lyly, J. *Gallathea* (1584/1592), ed. A.B. Lancashire (Arnold, 1970).

MacCaffery, W.T. 'Place and Patronage in Elizabethan Politics', in Bindoff (1961).

McGrath, P. *Papists and Puritans under Elizabeth I*, (Blandford, 1967).

Machiavelli, N. *The Prince* (1532), trs. G. Bull (Penguin, 1961).

Machiavelli, N. *The Discourses* (1531), trs. L. J. Walker (Routledge & Kegan Paul, 1975), 2 vols.

Mahood, M.M. *Poetry and Humanism*, (Cape, 1950).

Maitra, S. *Psychological Realism and Archetypes*, (Bookland, 1967).

Manheim, M. 'The Weak King History Play of the Early 1590s', *Ren. Drama* n.s.2 (1969).

Marks, E. and de Courtivron, I. *New French Feminisms*, (Harvester, 1981).

Marlowe, C. *Collected Plays*, ed. J.B. Steane (Penguin, 1969).

Marlowe, C. *Collected Plays*, ed. F. Bowers (Cambridge U.P., 1973), 2 vols.

Marlowe, C. *Doctor Faustus* (c.1592/1604), ed. J.D. Jump (Manchester U.P., 1982).

Marlowe, C. *Dido, Queen of Carthage* (>1593/1594) and *The Massacre at Paris* (1593/?1602), ed. H.J. Oliver (Methuen, 1968).

Marlowe, C. *Tamburlaine the Great, Parts I and II* (1587–8/1590), ed. J.W. Harper (Benn, 1971).

Marlowe, C. *The Jew of Malta* (1589/1633), ed. N.W. Bawcutt (Manchester U.P., 1978).

Marprelate Tracts, The (1588–9), ed. W. Pierce (Clarke and Co., 1911).

Matalene, H.W. 'Marlowe's *Faustus* and the Comforts of Academicism', *ELH* 39 (1972).

Mattingly, G. *The Defeat of the Spanish Armada*, (Penguin, 1962).

Maxwell, J.C. 'How Bad is the Text of *The Jew of Malta*?', *MLR* 48 (1953).

Mehl, D. *The Elizabethan Dumb Show*, (Methuen, 1965).

Merbury, C. *A Brief Discourse of Royal Monarchy*, (London, 1581).

Metz, C. 'History/discourse – a note on two voyeurisms', in Caughie (1981).

Meyer, E. *Machiavelli and the Elizabethan Drama*, (Weimar, 1897).

Mills, L.J. 'The Meaning of *Edward II*', *MP* 32 (1935).

Minshull, C. 'Marlowe's "Sound Machevill"', *Ren. Drama* n.s.13 (1982).

Mirror for Magistrates, The (1559–87), ed. L.B. Campbell (Cambridge U.P., 1938).

Misfortunes of Arthur, The, see Hughes, T.

Moi, T. 'Sexual/Textual Politics' in *The Politics of Theory*, ed. F. Barker *et al.* (Essex U.P., 1983).

Montaigne, M. *Essays*, trs. J. Florio (1603; Oxford U.P., 1904–6), 3 vols.

Morris, B. (ed.) *Christopher Marlowe*, (Benn, 1968).

Nagler, A.M. (ed.) *A Source Book in Theatrical History*, (Dover, 1959).

Nashe, T. Preface to Greene's *Menaphon* (1589), ed. E. Arber (Westminster, 1895).

Nashe, T. *Pierce Penniless* (1592) in *The Unfortunate Traveller & Other Works*, ed. J.B. Steane (Penguin, 1972).

Neale, J.E. *Elizabeth I and her Parliaments 1559–1601*, (Cape, 1969), 2 vols.

Newton, T. (trs.) *A Notable History of the Saracens*, (1575).

Nichols, J. *The Progresses and Public Processions of Queen Elizabeth*, (London, 1823), 3 vols.

Norbrook, D. *Poetry and Politics in the English Renaissance*, (Routledge & Kegan Paul, 1984).

Norgaard, H. 'Never Wrong but with just Cause', *ES* 45 (1964).

North, T. (trs.) *The Lives of the Noble Grecians and Romans*, (1579; Blackwell, 1928), vol.1.

Norton, T. and Sackville, T. *Gorboduc* (1561–2/1565) in *Five Elizabethan Tragedies*, ed. A.K. McIlwraith (Oxford U.P., 1976).

Nowell, A. *A Catechism*, trs. T. Norton (1570), ed. G. E. Corrie (Cambridge, 1853).

Old Wives Tale, The, ed. F. S. Hook, see Peele, G.

Ong, W. J. *Ramus, Method and the Decay of Dialogue*, (Harvard U.P., 1958).

Ong, W. J. *Orality and Literacy*, (Methuen, 1982).

Part of a Register, A, (Middelburg, 1593).

Peddlar's Prophecy, The, (>1594/1595; Malone Society, 1914).

Peele, G. *Life and Works*, ed. C.T. Prouty *et al.* (Yale U.P., 1952–70).

Peet, D. 'The Rhetoric of *Tamburlaine*', *ELH* 26 (1959).

Ponet, J. *A Short Treatise of Politic Power*, ([Strasbourg], 1556).

Powell, J. 'Marlowe's Spectacle', *TDR* 8 (1964).

Puttenham, G. *The Art of English Poesy* (1589), ed. G.D. Willcock and A. Walker (Cambridge U.P., 1936).

Raab, F. *The English Face of Machiavelli*, (Routledge & Kegan Paul, 1964).

Ramel, J. 'Biographical Notices on the Authors of *The Misfortunes of Arthur* (1588)', *N&Q* 212 (1967).

Ramus, P. *The Logike*, (London, 1574).

Rare Triumphs of Love and Fortune, The (?1582/1589) in *Old English Plays*, ed W.C. Hazlitt (London, 1874), vol.6.

Ratliff, J.D. 'Hieronimo Explains Himself', *SP* 54 (1957).

Read, C. *Mr Secretary Walsingham and the Policy of Queen Elizabeth*, (Oxford U.P., 1925), vol.3.

Read, C. *Lord Burghley and Queen Elizabeth*, (Cape, 1960).

Read, C. 'William Cecil and Elizabethan Public Relations', in Bindoff (1961).

Ribner, I. 'The Idea of History in Marlowe's *Tamburlaine*', *ELH* 20 (1953).

Ribner, I. 'Marlowe and Machiavelli', *Comparative Literature* 6 (1954).

Ribner, I. '*Tamburlaine* and *The Wars of Cyrus*', *JEGP* 53 (1954).

Ribner, I. *The English History Play in the Age of Shakespeare*, (Methuen, 1957).

Ribner, I. 'Marlowe and Shakespeare', *Sh. Q* 15 (1964).

Righter, A. *Shakespeare and the Idea of the Play*, (Chatto, 1964).

Rosenberg, E. *Leicester – Patron of Letters*, (Columbia U.P., 1955).

Rosenberg, M. 'Elizabethan Actors – Men or Marionettes?' *PMLA* 69 (1954).

Russell, C. *The Crisis of Parliaments*, (Oxford U.P., 1971/1982).

Sanders, W. *The Dramatist and the Received Idea*, (Cambridge U.P., 1968).

222   *Marlowe*

Schelling, F.E. *The English Chronicle Play*, (Haskell House, 1964).
Scottish History of James IV, The, see Greene, R.
Selimus, The first part of the tragical reign of, (?1591/1594; Malone Society, 1908).
Shakespeare, W. *Richard III* (1593/1597), ed. M. Eccles (New American Library, 1964).
Shakespeare, W. *1 Henry VI* (1590/1623), ed. L.V. Ryan (New American Library, 1967).
Shakespeare, W. *2 Henry VI* (c.1590/1623) and *3 Henry VI*(c.1590/1623), ed. N. Sanders (Penguin, 1981).
Shakespeare, W. *Titus Andronicus* (c.1593/1594), ed. E.M. Waith (Oxford U.P., 1984).
Shirley, J.W. (ed.) *Thomas Harriot – Renaissance Scientist*, (Oxford U.P., 1974).
Sidney, P. *A Defence of Poetry* (1595), ed. J.A. van Dorsten (Oxford U.P., 1966/75).
Simmons, J.C. 'Elizabethan Stage Practice and Marlowe's *The Jew of Malta*,' *Ren. Drama* n.s.4 (1971).
Sinfield, A. *Literature in Protestant England 1560–1660*, (Croom Helm, 1983).
Smith, T. *De Republica Anglorum*, ed. L. Alston (1583; Cambridge U.P., 1906).
Smith, W. 'Anti-Catholic Propaganda in Elizabethan London', *MP* 28 (1930).
Soliman and Perseda, see Kyd, T.
Spanish Tragedy, The, see Kyd, T.
Spedding, J. *An Account of the Life and Times of Francis Bacon*, (London, 1878), 2 vols.
Spingarn, J.E. *A History of Literary Criticism in the Renaissance*, (Columbia U.P., 1930).
Spivack, B. *Shakespeare and the Allegory of Evil*, (Columbia U.P., 1958).
Stapleton, L. 'Halifax and Raleigh', *JHI* 2.2 (1941).
Steadman, J.M. 'Iconography and Renaissance Drama', *RORD* 13/14 (1970–71).
Steane, J.B. *Marlowe – A Critical Study*, (Cambridge U.P., 1964).
Stocker, T. (trs.) *A Tragical History of the Troubles and Civil Wars of the Low Countries*, (1583).
Stone, L. *The Crisis of the Aristocracy 1558–1641*, (Oxford U.P., 1967).
Strong, R.C. and van Dorsten, J.A. *Leicester's Triumph*, (Leiden U.P., 1964).
Sunesen, B. 'Marlowe and the Dumb Show', *ES* 35 (1954).
Sweeting, E.J. *Early Tudor Criticism*, (Blackwell, 1940).

Talbert, E.W. 'The Interpretation of Jonson's Courtly Spectacles', *PMLA* 61 (1946).

Talbert, E.W. *The Problem of Order*, (North Carolina U.P., 1962).

Talbert, E.W. *Elizabethan Drama and Shakespeare's Early Plays*, (North Carolina U.P., 1963).

Tamburlaine the Great, Parts I and II, see Marlowe, C.

Tancred and Gismunda, see Wilmot, R.

Taylor, R. *The Political Prophecy in England*, (Columbia U.P., 1911).

Thaler, A. *Shakespeare's Silences*, (Harvard U.P., 1929).

Therborn, G. *The Ideology of Power and the Power of Ideology*, (Verso, 1980).

Thomas of Woodstock (c.1592), ed. G. Parfitt and S. Shepherd (Nottingham Drama Texts, 1977).

Thomas, K.V. *Religion and the Decline of Magic*, (Penguin, 1973/1978).

Three Ladies of London, The, see Wilson, R.

Three Lords and Three Ladies of London, The, see Wilson, R.

Troublesome Reign of John King of England, The (1587–91/1591) in *Six Early Plays*, ed. E.B. Everitt (Rosenkilde & Bagger, 1965).

Troublesome Reign of John King of England, The (1587–91/1591), ed. J.W. Sider (Garland, 1979).

True Tragedy of Richard III, The, (1590/1594; Malone Society, 1929).

Tweedie, E.M. '"Action is Eloquence" – The Staging of Thomas Kyd's *Spanish Tragedy*', *SEL* 16 (1976).

Venezky, A.S. *Pageantry on the Shakespearean Stage*, (Twayne, 1951).

Waith, E.M. 'The Metamorphosis of Violence in *Titus Andronicus*', *SS* 10 (1957).

Waller, E.H. 'A Possible Interpretation of *The Misfortunes of Arthur*', *JEGP* 24 (1925).

Ward, B.M. '*The Famous Victories of Henry V* – Its Place in Elizabethan Dramatic Literature', *RES* 4 (1928).

Warning for Fair Women, A (?/1599) in *The School of Shakespeare*, ed. R. Simpson (New York, 1878), vol.2.

Wars of Cyrus, The (1576–7/1594), ed. J.P. Brawner (Illinois U.P., 1942).

Watson, S.R. '*Gorboduc* and the Theory of Tyrannicide', *MLR* 34 (1939).

Webbe, W. *A Discourse of English Poetry* (1586), ed. E. Arber (Westminster, 1895).

Weil, J. *Christopher Marlowe – Merlin's Prophet*, (Cambridge U.P., 1977).

Wentworth, P. *A Pithy Exhortation to Her Majesty*, (1598).

Wernham, R.B. 'Elizabethan War Aims and Strategy', in Bindoff (1961).

Whetstone, G. *The English Mirror*, (London, 1586).

Williams, R. *Culture*, (Fontana, 1981).

Williams, R. 'On Dramatic Dialogue and Monologue' in *Writing in Society*, (Verso, 1983).

Willson, D.H. *King James VI and I*, (Cape, 1956/1962).

Wilmot, R. *Tancred and Gismunda* (?1566/1591) in *Old English Plays*, ed. W.C. Hazlitt (London, 1874), vol.7.

Wilson, F.P. *Marlowe and the Early Shakespeare*, (Clarendon Press, 1953).

Wilson, J. (ed.) *Entertainments for Elizabeth I*, (Brewer, 1980).

Wilson, R. *The Three Ladies of London* (1581/1584) and *The Three Lords and Three Ladies of London* (c1589/1590) in *Old English Plays*, ed. W. C. Hazlitt (London, 1874), vol. 6.

Wilson, R. *The Cobbler's Prophecy*, (1594; Malone Society, 1914).

Wilson, T. *The Art of Rhetoric*, (1560; Clarendon Press, 1909).

Withington, R. *English Pageantry*, (Benjamin Blom, 1918/63), 2 vols.

Wounds of Civil War, The, see Lodge, T.

Wright, L. B. 'Social Aspects of some Belated Moralities', *Anglia* 54 (1930).

Yates, F. A. *Astraea*, (Penguin, 1977).

Zucker, D. H. *Stage and Image in the Plays of Christopher Marlowe*, (Salzburg Studies, 1972).

Index

KING ALFRED'S COLLEGE
LIBRARY